For the Love of a Girl

William Hiles

ISBN: 978-1-4120-3158-5 (sc)

Trafford rev. 08/31/2020

www.trafford.com

North America & international
toll-free: 844-688-6899 (USA & Canada)
fax: 812 355 4082

Contents

For Bonnie and our two wonderful children.
For Mom and Dad.
And for all who never made it back
And for their Brothers in Arms.

Americanism

Some call me "Old Glory", others call me "The Star spangled Banner." Whatever they call me, I am your flag, the Flag of the United States of America.

I remember some time ago, people lined up on both sides of the street to watch the parade I was leading. I was proudly waving in the breeze. When your daddy saw me coming, he removed his hat and placed it on his left shoulder so his right hand was directly over his heart. Do you remember?

I remember you too, standing there straight as a soldier. You didn't have a hat but were giving the right salute with your hand over your heart.

Remember little sister? Not to be outdone, she was saluting the same as you.

What happened? I'm still the same old flag – perhaps with a few more stars since you were a boy. But now I don't feel as proud as I used to. When I come down the street many just stand there with their hands in their pockets. Children run around and shout, paying no attention – they don't seem to know who I am.

Now, I may be a little conceited. Well, I am. I have the right to be, because I represent the finest country in the world. More than one aggressive nation has tried to tie me down, but they felt the fury of this freedom-loving nation. Remember, many of you had to go overseas to defend me.

Take a look at the Memorial Honor Rolls sometime. Look at the names of those who never came back, and are resting beneath white crosses on a shore far away. Some of them were friends or relatives of yours…maybe even went to school with you. That's who you're saluting…when you revere me.

Is it now a sin to be patriotic? Have you forgotten what I stand for? Or where I've been? Valley Forge – Argonne – Anzio – Guadalcanal, Korea and Vietnam. Do you remember those who did not return – to keep this land free and under God? When you salute me, you are really saluting them for their sacrifices.

It won't be long now, until I'll be coming down the street again. When you see me, stand a little straighter and salute. I'll salute you by waving back and I'll know then, that you remember.

Veteran's Observer, June 1983

Seeing our flag in a torn and tattered composure reflects good times and bad. Worn but unwavering, patient and alert, our flag coupled with our nation's history could almost prohibit a silky clean, unblemished display. Ultimately though, our flag *is* at it's best, radiating in the sun with golden cords flowering red, white and blue.

Hearing our National Anthem before a ball game, even of the Little League essence, relocates me to a time that showed our nation's youth. And I reminisce with each note of our tune, of past military engagements maze-like, with tears and smiles that intermingle in an insane non-pattern that only a Picasso could oppose. The maze doesn't relieve me of my pride, although conflicts held therein return faithfully to embitter me, at times even as I nap.

And conflicts are best forgotten, but keep a small place open in your mind for them, much so they are not forgotten to be replayed again with some insignificant being or place, likely finalizing in a stalemate. Conflicts of heart and mind and soul are also lessons to be learned, "having to happen sooner or later" I justify to myself, just as the lesson of Vietnam conflicted the USA a long, long time ago.

Those who fought against the war *did* have a choice. As conscientious objectors, they could have served their country honorably with a religious conviction that prohibited killing a human being. But instead, they detoured the American Spirit onto a road of blasphemous asphalt, heating our fighting forces to the point of unintentional collapse, as removing a radiator cap from a boiling engine. It was something they felt was necessary to do to end the carnage and, being Americans, they inherited the right to protest, although most of them never really earned it. They were just lucky enough to have been born here, *and,* they were lucky enough to never experience the blistering heat, the near supernatural brain clutching stress, or the terrible longing for their homeland while being "imprisoned" in Southeast Asia; a most intolerable brainwashing with a steel brush minus soap.

Through all the experiences, changed lives and ramifications my service years dealt me, *I* would never change a letter in its sentence.

Emotion intervened throughout this epistle. Anger, depression, anxiety, all parts of the war, reclaimed me at times, but remembering my Girl helped to me continue and reach a conclusion: wars are fought for freedom and for the girls, so now, the girls I justifiably enshrine, one who sent me to the war, and one who waited for my return.

Certainly you must condemn yourself to the Vietnam experience to have chosen this writing, so interconnect with my testament of clanking treads and their crewmembers, Grunts and groans, and continue to wonder why we weren't allowed to end the war with more dignity.

I didn't over emphasize the deaths. You may already know: 58,000 us, millions, them.

Some names are changed or omitted, due to my diary's weathering and limitation of my memory in this non-fiction autobiography. A confession, if you will, that lets my mind and soul unleash feelings and trials that encompassed my maturing in the upheaval on the other side of our world.

And how it felt, tasted and smelled in '67 and '68 in the Republic of Vietnam.

Love of country lights the holy fire of patriotism, and a man's country need not be a certain area of land, but a principle, and patriotism is loyalty to that principle.

Fear of the next election is one of the most universal emotions among democratic politicians. To a large extent, it is the fear of the unknown.

Few announcements sent over the intercom at Morton West high school had more pertinence than, "President Kennedy's been shot! No further word on this development, but stop to say a prayer for him and our country, class, please."

I remember pens and pencils dropped on tilted desks, clinking on the tiled floors in the otherwise silent halls of learning. Girls and some boys sobbed, as the din increased. "What's going to happen now?" seemed to echo through the corridors of future America's assembly, and "What if he dies?"

I was 14 and shocked with the rest of the groups in the learning process. Principal Wright had not foreseen this calamity of course, so we were kept in class as though a regular school day, to sit and mope minus a learning ability that had been stricken from us by the assassination of a beloved president.

How could anyone do such a thing? Maybe I was just too young to understand atrocity, but it seemed as though Kennedy was loved and respected by all, while doing good for his country and fellow man.

God, the feeling was terrible throughout the world and in my heart, as a personal friend shot down cold. And the Globe *did* mourn, as the Press released the confirmed killing of the first Catholic President of the United States. Camelot mourned. A 5 block walk home from school ended sadly that day. Buddies, Bill and Bob, went their own ways; no stop at the bowling alley for pinball, no cheeseburgers at Cock Robin's.

Walter Cronkite had difficulty announcing the tragedy, suffocated with tears. All T.V. and radio stations were at a standstill with the catastrophe, as the U.S. and the entire world waited for the rest of the drama to unfold. And as I lay in bed that night, I vowed to be a patriot for my country when the time was right. Kennedy was assassinated while on duty in service of his country, and if need be, I felt it as a correct duty for *any* man. I enlisted when I was 14 and didn't even know it, and JFK's words drove me to the recruiter 4 years later; "Pay any price, bear any burden, support any friend, face any foe!"

I had to follow his example. It was just *me*. The way I was, impossible to change. Patriotism became my inner truth.

Graduation came in 1965, with friendships changing, disappearing, and with some, cementing and perpetual. My parents insisted on college for me. However, furthering my education was the least of my priorities. I just finished stumbling in Algebra and Geometry, making trig and slide rule in college impossible mountains to scale. I loved the freedom from the classroom too much to return to a lack-luster existence of inkwells and sarcastic scholars. Actually I had no goal in life except to party and see the world. Donna, my closest of friends was the love of my life, but it got to be almost impossible to see her more than once weekly, with her father holding his reins on her as tight as a convent on a nun.

We behaved well I surmise, for teens in the sixties, but never going too far and being responsible with her choking curfews didn't seem enough to her pater. Hell, it took 4 or 5 dates for her and I to finally suck face, her being the initiator. I guess my self-confidence left a lot to be desired.

And our year and a half together was most impressionable to both of us. We loved each other and had great times just being together, cruising in my Dad's '65 GTO up and down Chicago's highways and by-ways, while listening to "I got you babe" on AM 1000, WCFL.

She was one of my biggest sacrifices upon my enlisting into the Marine Corps. The other was the Goat.

1965 Pontiac GTO

They were both beautiful and state of the art. A black vinyl top with four on the floor

comprised one, while long, brown hair and blue eyes atop a Cleopatra form created the other.

"Oh Bill, how could you do it?" Donna repeated when I told her of my enlistment. "And in the Marines? Oh, GOD!" She shook her head slowly and gazed downward tearfully.

I told her that I thought that it was my duty as an American to go to war when needed. And I thought that she would wait for me, but as it turned out, her father insisted that schooling came first and that the Marine Corps would change me. Boot camp alone changes anyone into a killer, most laughter and all immaturity concluded, in the 12-week training course for warfare.

As we went our separate ways, I've often wondered how her life has turned out and if she's ever thought of me in these years gone by. As for me, I *have* thought of her. From the kiss I forced as we plummeted down the first hill on the Bob's roller coaster in the last seat at Riverview Park (an inner city amusement park, shut down in 1967) to the Halloween party that had the police stop me for driving while wearing sunglasses at night.

The grand fragrance of lilac in her perfume ran well, an elated fantasy. And the Prom at the Tam O'Shanter Country Club, followed with relaxation at Power's Lake and Bill's softball broken thumb, reminds, in May days.

My surprise going away party found a then close cousin playing the drums, later reaching out the side window of his car to barf out the beer his young body rejected. I haven't run into Ken much since then. Not because of disagreements, you understand. We just parted ways. That's just the way it is, the way things go.

For myself, my head was set table-ward, weariness derived from ale. But I walked out, and was poured into a waiting car with the help of my Dad.

The memory of the party and Donna's last kiss faded as I hugged my Mom and Dad for the last time before jetting away from O'Hare Airport on March 23rd, 1966. I told them "See 'ya later" in a naïve tone, but my Dad's eye's told me that I'd made a mistake. And my Mom's tears, well, they fortified his know- legible glances. Everyone said that I'd never be the same, and they were right.

<u>Patriotism, to be truly American, begins with human allegiance.</u>

The Marines' Hymn

From the Halls of Montezuma
To the shores of Tripoli;
We fight our country's battles
In the air, on land, and sea;
First to fight for right and freedom
And to keep our honor clean;
We are proud to claim the title of
United States Marine.

Our flag's unfurled to every breeze
From dawn to setting sun;
We have fought in every clime and place
Where we could take a gun;
In the snow of far off northern lands
And in sunny tropic scenes;
You will find us always on the job;
The United States Marines

Here's health to you and to our Corps
Which we are proud to serve;
In many a strife we've fought for life
And never lost our nerve;
If the Army and the Navy
Ever look on Heaven's scenes;
They will find the streets are guarded by
United States Marines.

I am a rock, I am an island…and a rock feels no pain, and an island never cries.

The plane's cargo thought of themselves as Marines. WRONG! We found out shortly, that a man must *earn* the title of Marine by suffering dehumanizing severities of boot camp Hell.

A corporal awaited our arrival with a pointed finger towards the bus that would take us there.

"MCRD right this way FREAKS! Keep your fuckin' mouths shut!"

Slight pause. "Look straight ahead and keep your hands on your knees."

It didn't take long for the mind of even the simplest recruit to decipher the future. I didn't move an inch as the bus drove through the humid night air to the Marine Corps Recruit Depot. I was petrified. *We* were petrified.

Our coach stopped at the main gate with "We got anudder load of scum here, straight from Chi-town."

The guard retrieved his clipboard with our check in, oozing facially, "Y'er all fucked, girls."

First impressions are important in everyday life, sometimes striking and incomprehensible. A question answered by a stranger can be enlightening by realizing inner self. So was the case of the informal introduction between a fellow 'Boot', and our near live-in, Head Drill Instructor.

We entered a room that was large enough to hold 80 men, standing. An array of tables presented cardboard boxes to be loaded with our clothing and all luxuries. "The Corps will take of you real good. You won't need a thing that you brought except your wallet, so send everything else home, LADIES!"

We stripped in about 8/10's of a second, loading each box with our scraps going home.

The "Voice", or sergeant, staff type, drill instructor, was pestered by a cocky recruit by, "Hey Sarge, where's the toilet?"

Sarge had a seemingly in-born hatred for us, who he would refer to as "Chi town punks" as he grabbed the would-be toileteer by the collar and proceeded to slam him against the wall, howling "You slimy PUKE! You will NEVER talk to me like that again!" His voice traveled the 1000-foot long parade grounds. "The FIRST and LAST word out of your mouth will always be 'SIR', THEN ask permission to speak to the drill instructor! Do you fuckin' understand me, SCUM?"

"YeYessir" was answerer feebly.

"WHAT? SIR was NOT the first word I heard! I hate you already!"

The D.I. pulled the boy becoming a man from the wall, then propositioned him with another thud. "You Chicago bad-asses'll be crawling before I'm through with you!"

The smell of the new utility clothing in that building still lingers in my nostrils. So does the building.

Reveille started with a recording of Call to Post. It's also trumpeted at horse tracks, to ready bettors and whenever heard, I remember boot camp discipline, sickeningly.

The hot blacktop readying to patch the cracks on Ogden Avenue in Berwyn reminds me of training sessions on the parade grounds, with tar's acrid aroma spread as we ran hour after hour, day after day.

Collars remained buttoned until graduation. Hair was cut short of bald, weekly.

We stood at attention or at best, at ease, (right foot planted, no talking, no movement) with no mumble, murmur, or eye roll.

And we challenged 2 or 3 obstacle courses daily, sometimes becoming too wishful for home life to care about becoming a Marine anymore. No one expected boot camp to be so torturing and rigorous.

Pugel sticks were padded bats used in competition with each other, mimicking strict bayonet fighting until one fell. They were about 4 foot long, hand grasp thick, with both ends padded but not terribly soft.

Two weeks were dedicated to learning the scope of marksmanship at the rifle range. 2 am reveille made the regular beat, and punish-ments included running with rifles and full packs. Another zapper was marching with the M-14 atop our out stretched wrists. When the first rifle fell, we all did pushups, then ran again.

Everyone *had* to qualify with the M-14 rifle in order to graduate. Soon, the state of the art killer was replaced with the plastic M-16. Our rifle instructor preached us the B.R.A.S.S. method for "Sure qualification at the range, as you <u>B</u>reath, <u>R</u>elax, <u>A</u>im, <u>S</u>lack (Squeeze the slack off of the trigger), <u>S</u>queeze (The trigger, don't pull it)". Still another instructor informed that "The gas mask will be your friend, and today you will learn how to use it."

We learned how to secure fit with fingers, then "Double time, HARCH!" We ran. For 5 minutes we ran with the masks on, almost completely cut off from air, then "Platoon, HALT! One, two!"

Tear gas is a common 'stabilizer' and, still gasping for air, we were rushed into a blazingly hot Quonset hut where "Boots, I will now ignite this tear gas pellet and you will realize its effects on unprotected humans. When I give the word, you will remove your masks and SING the Marine Corps Hymn!" The pellet spewed its smog generously. "SLIME, REMOVE YOUR MASKS!"

We did, and we sang and cried and choked and drooled and gargled our own fluids. It was a terrible, most horrendous session, with sinuses never clearing so well.

After completion of the rifle seminar and a one-week mess duty awakening, we returned to a most barren of lifestyles in training. The small P.X. offered only essentials. No candy, no soda, no cologne (some fools would drink it for the alcohol content), no deodorant (nightly showers were mandatory). Reading was limited to our mail and the Sunday newspaper.

No radio or T.V. No potato chips, just adulterated discipline. Period.

Cadence yodeled by all DI's echoed in our ears even as we slept, aiding us to perfect a marching rhythm of 80 personnel envied by schools of thousands in the deep blue sea, never bumping, never missing a turn.

Graduating boot camp sent Platoon 285 to Camp Pendleton, California, where all Marines spent a minimum of 18 days infantry training for combat. A Grunt spends a few months of his life learning how to kill and survive, and thinking that we were out of extreme physical training proved wrong. Humping over hill and dale with full battle array was almost worse than in San Diego, but base freedom cooled one off each evening.

Would-be Marines fired the 3.5 rocket launcher (Bazooka) at a dead tank, 2 football fields away. When fired, the 60-inch long projectile could be seen and followed through the air as it met its target. Impressive as it projected, its tail could be seen waving goodbye while traveling at about 100 mph. Also, there is no recoil (kick). The blast is released through the back of the launcher, not to be stood behind.

And, at 400 yards, the round would go through an 11 inch steel plate.

Before finishing I.T.R., all Marines, whether their MOS be machine gunner or chief cook and bottle washer, would also fire the B.A.R

(Browning automatic rifle), the .45 cal pistol, the M-79 (44mm) grenade launcher, and the M-60 machine gun while mastering the M-14; a league of extraordinary gentlemen.

We also viewed devastations of flame throwers, rifle grenades, incendiary grenades, smoke grenades, land mines, and threw frag-mentation grenades. Unlike the pineapple grenades of yore, the new frags were round like baseballs and could be thrown further, more accurately, with deadlier results.

Leaving all of my basic training behind in a cloud of dust in July of '66, I still dreamed about Donna and even sobbed a little to think of what I would do without her. I never realized that being a warrior meant carrying a cross of such terrible density.

Reaching home, my parents showed me their new '66 Mustang convertible, automatic. They traded in the G.T.O. for a Ford. Super car was gone forever. Cool to a teen, to be a Marine, to be a super man. To be able to stomp anywhere you please: to carry and fire lethal weapons, to kill or be killed. Responsibility unparallel. Terrible consequence: frightful, terrible, death, destruction, all for the taking, and I asked for it.

But I took leave, still with a hope that Donna and I would return to another 1965 with roller coasters and Halloween parties and little sisters and G.T.O.s. But she was too distant and I didn't know how to handle the situation. The T.V. news showed her what could be store for her and I, and in dying color. We were through.

So my best buddy, Bill, took me for a ride in his GTX after Donna and I called it quits, but though his "X" was excellent, my mind remained with the girl. Donna and the war had my mind in turmoil, mostly because I trapped myself into the situation. Self-destructive, I considered. Death wish?

"Beautiful set of wheels, Bill!" as he tooled us to some forest preserve's Polka gang tripping the light fantastic in midday.

"Don't look like nothin' much. I drove all this way, and no broads!"

A car whisked passed us on the dirt road, coating us with dust. Consequently, my reaction was released in the form of harsh threats and clinched fists towards the dust devil. There were two passengers with the driver, so I consider the odds in our favor.

"Damn, Bill. The Corps. sure did you change you, but take it easy Buddy, they're gone. No harm done. If you go to Vietnam, I think we'll win."

My aggression showed all too well, as I startled myself. I used to be a quiet joker type, often trying to find humor in a dark side style of misfortune. Never looked for a fight, but I realized now that I got what I wanted, what I went for. Marine Corps training had readied me for combat, giving me a thirst for the most dangerous file of life; hunting man. And it all frightened me more when I divulged deeper in thought. I wasn't afraid of Vietnam and I wanted to go. Sure, my family and friends are here, but my girl is gone from me. The first cut is the deepest. .

"Hey Buttski, wanna play some dime machines?"

"Sounds good to me."

Bingo machines were plentiful in the '50's through the '70's in Cicero, with some greasy spoon diners exhibiting 4 or even 5 of the "*No* Armed Bandits" produced by Bally. Bowling alleys and pool halls also had their share of the flipper-less pinball machines that elaborated beautiful color schemes and bathing beauties in over 100 variations for 5-ball entertainment.

The object was to line up 3, 4 or 5 numbers on the back glass. The playfield contained holes with numbers progressing 1 through 25, and skilled players could bump and grind for numbers they wanted off of adjacent bumpers. However, the tilt mechanism usually ended a player's anticipation of a 5 in a row.

Paying in excess of thousands of credits, proprietors would trade even, a dime per credit, if he knew the players.

6 card machines were just that; 6 bingo cards on the back glass, with 25 numbers jumbled in favor of the house, they were played by depositing one coin per card.

Single card machines could be much more expensive, the big 'come on' being the ability to move numbers to different positions if enough coins were deposited and *if* the "Magic Numbers" feature would light up. Also, more coins might advance scores for the 3 to 5 in lines to pay more credits. Other features such as rollovers and double or nothing buttons helped relieve paychecks from naive gamers. Even so, Bill and I considered the pins our greatest pastime besides girls, until poker machines evolved, making Bingos extinct in the mid '70's. And in almost 20 years of hard-core manipulating, we hardly ever beat 'em. So I left my best buddy and worst habit when I returned to San Diego for radiotelegraph school. The sun WAS hotter than the Beach Boys broadcasted, in August '66, and our instructor, Corporal Jones warned that P.T. became the order of the day if he considered any student insubordinate. So it would be just like boot camp all over again. One mistake and everybody pays. The threats were justified in that we were told that one mistake in combat can kill an entire platoon. Made sense, I guess.

We took a run in summer uniforms one day when our teacher asked for quiet and was ignored by one Marine. We had to run for nearly an hour, soaked through with sweat.

But most of our class sessions were conventionally professional, practicing Morse code, typing, and radio procedures. Most commonly executed communicator was the Prc-25.

The portable radio communications weighed 25 lbs and a battery weighed about 3 or 4 lbs, was strapped on the operator's back, and made him quite lethargic after squirming through swamp for an hour. The featherweight .45 cal pistol was recommended for maneuverability by the R.T. team.

To relieve us of the rigors of school and nostalgia, we'd grab a bus for the beaches to observe things untouchable: bikinis and their contents. Finding a "Friend" in this locale was nearly impossible, us with hair no more than a half an inch long and reputations rivaling Attila the Hun. And the Beatles, etc, made hairstyles less than shoulder length considered "square." Still, the benefits of daily off-base lib afforded us gave a spark of joy to an otherwise drab existence. With our graduation came orders for our next duty station. I practically feared getting stationed anywhere but the Republic of Vietnam, and another of my stupid wishes came through with flying colors. "FMF WESTPAC, San Fran, 1st Antitank Bn, Co. C, DaNang".

"The V.C. have tanks?"

"You're going with tanks?" asked Joe, a good friend who side kicked in school. Like Archie's pal Jughead, he slept with eyes partially open in the daylight. And, he needed to shave *daily* for the Marine Corps. I Wonder if he got back from 'Nam. I bet that my Dad had the same feelings when he got back from WWII.

December 1966. The Hawk of Chicago fame whipped bare tree limbs to intimidate nature. I drove to Donna's with that faulty backdrop, hoping and praying that we were making our life's correct choice. A teen's first love is the sometimes the greatest and most fulfilling, and as she opened the door the semi-smile showed her fear for me in war's sights.

"How've you been, Bill?" holding each other tight, answering that life must go on, which glistened her smile a tad. "You haven't written. We're still friends, aren't we?"

"Of course, Donna. You know that I'll love you forever."

"Gosh Bill, don't…" She pulled my hand. "Let's go upstairs. My dad wants to see you."

I couldn't imagine that after he almost encouraged our relationship be dismantled, he'd want to see me again. Tony extended his hand as I entered the living room.

"You're going there, huh. The things they show on T.V. should be censored, but at least you know what you're in for." He paused to light up a Tareyton. "We'll miss you, Bill. Too bad you didn't go back to school."

I left the room without reply to his opinion, tired of all of the roads people paved for me. I made my own choice, right or wrong. By enlisting I changed my future.

Donna's sisters were as pretty as she, running around the front room and bouncing off of chairs. 14, 10 and 5 years of age, they were putting on a finale for my exit, as youngsters might do at a company picnic.

"G' bye, Mrs. N" choked to their mom before I started down the 20 or so steps leading to the final doorway. I felt like going AWOL and never leaving Donna, but her hand on my shoulder strengthened me to do what I was commissioned to do.

"I'll miss you, Bill", her eyes fully watered while exchanging a light kiss.

"You'll be going to school then?"

"Of course. You know Dad."

"School isn't for everyone, Donna. If you don't want to go, there's no sense in pushing it. Right?"

She looked down in disagreement, me reflecting a college dropout finalizing for war.

"Well, I gotta try." Pause. "Do you have any girlfriends?"

"Are you kiddin' me? Donna, you've been my only one." My voice faded to black as the darkened hallway. Only the light clicks of falling ice crystals against the door's window fought the silence. I held her closer.

"I'm sorry Babe, but I have to go. Maybe in 13 months…"

"Wait, did I tell you? I'm going out with this really nice guy John. But you know, Bill, you can come by any time." Insult to injury. "No, you didn't tell me. I hope you two are happy."

Of course I didn't mean it, but I wanted us to part, at the very least, as friends.

With one last kiss, I turned and walked out into the blustery sheets of sleet fogging my glasses, still not knowing if I'd see her again or if I'd even return home. I got into my Mom's Mustang and looked, waved, but couldn't see if she was in the doorway to respond. I drove off with her in my memory bank, reserved, unlike most other amorous deposits. I could think of nothing in the world that Donna did to hurt me, except break my heart. And I still loved her.

The next day found me alone with my parents at O'hare. No girl. Not to demote the role of parents, but a girl is the last link for a boy: one last look at heaven before war.

"You are expendable to them, Son. Don't volunteer for anything. You take care of YOU!" We shook hands and hugged. I thought of our rabbit/pheasant hunting days back when I was 10 and upper deck seats at Wrigley's field.

"Goodbye Mom."

"Billy, Billy! Oh my only baby! Why did you have to do this?" she cried.

I did it because my Dad did it. That was my resolve to this entire puzzle, but no answer could mend her broken heart.

I hugged and kissed her and it was over. Too late to change anything, we waved as I back-stepped down the ramp leading me to San Francisco. I'm sorry Mom and Dad. When a ship cuts through the sea, the waters are always stirred and troubled. And our ship is moving, through troubled waters, toward new and better shores.

Lyndon B. Johnson

I'm leaving on a jet plane. Don't know when I'll be back again.

Early January '67 set me down in Hawaii to refuel with a 2-hour view of mountains, lobby-wise. No liberty, just a view. But at least I can say that I was in Hawaii.

The other Marines talked about the other wonderful view of mini-skirts the stewardess's displayed on board and/or the in flight movie that most of us slept through.

But the first major stop was in Okinawa to calibrate jungle tactic training, and physicals. We were restricted to on-base liberty because parties, drunk or sober, would wander off into the mountains to play Rob Crusoe, avoiding RVN, getting lost forever.

On 'The Rock', we were introduced to some corpsmen whose job was to stick needles in us wherever they saw fit, immunizing us from the plague, cholera, typhoid, flu, tetanus and a score of other natural 'Killer' killers. Yep, it was the last step in the fine-tuning the Corps presented to ready us for our final destination.

That is, liberating a people from a government they supposedly didn't want, and we were the 4th Country to try to wrestle Vietnam from an enemy's Full Nelson.

A few nights during my weeklong stay rested me in the enlisted man's club, where dime slots were plentiful and a bottle of beer ran for 50 cents. But who cared? I had other things on my mind, like "Does John Wayne frequent here? Will I be another Sgt. Stryker?" He saved America and Iwo Jima, and now it's our turn to save the world from communism.

19

Then I restructured, Sgt. Stryker died. He *DIED*! So be it.

I reached DaNang, Republic of Vietnam, January 27, 1967. The 1800 (6pm) arousal gave a smell of a sanitary district permeating our nostrils and minds as we deleted from the plane. The odor made the smell of the Stockyards on 47th and Damen rival the allure of Chanel #5. Yes, life is a cabaret and I fell into the toilet.

We waited to hear explosions and see the dead: nothing except a massive landing strip and 99% humidity that never seemed to quit.

Uneasiness inside continued, diagnosed as a nervous stomach and more severe than it sounded. It returns to me now and then as a reminder of future's past.

We were to be split up to our final company or platoon, and being a radioman I'd be assigned as an assistant, contributor or reinforcer for whoever, wherever or whatever the Marine Corps deemed appropriate. I always wondered why they performed a background check for a secret clearance.

An associate, Rich Pan and I were to be issued jungle utilities, M-14's, ammo, magazines (for rounds of bullets, not for reading) with pouches, and other 'junk' that would make our stay more survivable. The heavy helmet and flack jacket were also in our wardrobe, filling 2 sea bags each to the brim, against the E-tool (Entrenching tool; shovel), shelter half, medicine pack with malaria pills, canteen with pouch, utility belt, bayonet, K-bar, poncho, compass and a few fragmentation grenades. The Prc-25 and its harness would appear later.

Rich was called Mr. Clean for obvious reasons. On the hottest days, after the muddiest patrols, in a torrent windstorm, he'd still come out clean as a whistle with combed hair and a smile, clothing still creased. The smile deteriorated week by week or episode after episode, like all of ours did.

"Got a girl back home, Ski?" My label followed me through my entire hitch in the Corps, and his question gave me a heartache along with the heartburn.

"Yeah," I lied, in uncomplicated response. "Do you?"

"Yeah. Two of them want to get married, but I want them *without* marriage" he laughed.

"What a J.O.!"

I dozed off until a supply Private came in. He looked thirtyish, so he was probably a busted down lifer. I came to know a few of those poor souls who dedicated their lives to the Marine Corps, only to loose rank after minor incidents such as hair being a half inch too long for inspections. The Corps *is* a tight outfit, enforcing all regulations tout suite.

He encouraged us menacingly to follow him for our government issue. Hell, I thought, Rich and I both outranked this Private, having been elevated to Private First Class after completing RT school, so what's this guys problem? He was 'Salty' (non-effected, well seasoned), exercising his jurisdiction in HIS supply depot, to the max.

After our issue, "Go to the armory for your pieces." We were still piling the goods into our sea bags. "Something WRONG, PRIVATES? Go to the FUCKIN' ARMORY!"

We jumped through the tent flap.

"Whatta LOSER!" muffled Rich outside the shelter. "He's probably got 12 years in the Crotch (a discontent's nick name for the Marine Corps.), and just made E-1! Whatta joke! Oh, I love the CORPS!"

He was right. The Corps *did* cut off it's nose to spite it's own face.

Some Marines never fire a weapon in their 13-month tour. We were to be exceptions, later getting sent to Grunt platoons for radio backup.

"Keep it clean, try to keep it dry!" the Armor snickered as he handed the rifle to me.

"I'm a radio man. Don't I get a pistol?"

"If you want one, okay, but they're worthless. Unless you're looking the gook straight in the eye, you'll probably miss."

I nodded in agreement, sans smile.

We went back to our temporary billet, fully loaded with gear and anticipation.

"This shit's really heavy," complained Rich.

"Yeah, but it's free!"

The metal uprights were made for about 12 residents, with light bulbs of 50-watt strength, hardly enough to gaze upon the wealth Uncle Sam gave us. I was to find it luxurious to have but a candle to burn in the upcoming months.

"I gotta get a fan at the PX tomorrow. Wonder where it is."

"I wonder where ANYTHING is," I croaked.

I was in a deeper rut already. "Do we get any food here? How about C-rations?"

There was a mess hall below the hill, closed hours ago. I'd relish the thought of home cooked meals, for C-rations would be my menu for 6 months. Ham & eggs, turkey boned, beans & franks and 9 other meals in green cans. Ham & lima beans, nick-named Ham & mother fuckers was voted the grossest looking if not heated with the blue heat tab (if you were lucky enough to *have* a heat tab). Hardened white lard lay atop the ingredients to greet the patron as it introduced the so called ham beneath, challenging even the most hardened veteran to take a chunk. Lima beans were added to enhance flavor, but that and the heat dropped my weight to 160 lbs during my tour. Being 6 foot tall, 185 lbs looked more fruitful.

Completing a meal was a can of fruit, fruitcake, or the priceless pound cake. Instant coffee, sugar, salt and pepper, and powdered milk all in packs were availed, as were plastic eating utensils and an ounce of toilet paper.

Boxes of goodies from home didn't phase me too well either. Dated 8 weeks earlier, arriving mashed, smashed and partially open was a frail reminder of home. Green salami? Patooie!

I thanked my parents for the packages and insisted they put their money to better use since the pony express didn't fare well over the Pacific Ocean.

The next day a group of us listened to an introductory sermon from a Gunnery Sergeant who'd been punctured and ripped by enemies a half dozen times.

"Marines, this will be short and sweet! You will soon embark on your mission of peace, only to be hailed by metal from an enemy you may not see and who wants war. This is why I am here, this is why YOU are here. In the event of these bloodletting exercises, you MAY need to be revitalized with a transfusion. I'm telling you guys, you MUST give BLOOD! No ifs, ands or buts. You MUST give blood! IF you have AB blood, you'd best give THREE pints 'cause it is rare and you MAY need some!"

I have AB but gave only one pint due to regulations.

"Gents, you are ALL going out into the field, the field of battle, the worst place in the world that you will never forget! If you are wounded and there is no blood, YOU WILL DIE! It's as simple as that." He ended quietly, "Give blood. Thank you."

Leaving us somber, I had a chance to value a patriot's blood as the seed of freedom's tree.

I've thought about that Gunny at times, his speech echoing not unlike George Halas half- time rejuvenations to his beloved Chicago Bears. Strong, precise, no B.S.

For the good of the team, the Gunny wore a Purple Heart w/stars on his chest with the greatest of pride, exhibiting a bleak future in the field he fought for being even bleaker, without life sustaining blood.

After all of this, Rich was caught trying to leave without giving.

Outside, "The Gunny caught me at the door with another of his speeches, Ski! He squeezed my arm so tight that I HAD to give!"

I just laughed. "Slacker."

Sauntering to our billet, we saw the NCO (Non-commissioned Officer) club. It was for E-4's and above, but no one wore chevrons so I followed this "Eddie Haskell" type, right through the entrance.

"Rich, we could get busted for this!"

"Then they'll send us to 'Nam', right?"

I'd never been in a bar before 'the Rock' except in Wisconsin on vacation for a Nehi orange soda. My folks liked Hi-Balls but whiskey smelled revolting to me and still does. There I was, thinking of home again.

But, being 19, it was quite a rush to be able to walk into a bar without questioning at the entrance. The Falstaff was of low alcohol, almost cold and thirst quenching. Parched throats can attest to that.

"Ever drink much?"

What could I say? "Yah, occasionally, especially at my going away party. Man, we got WASTED!" I never really partook in drink until future years. Not much to forget about then.

The third beer got me giddy, relaxed, thoughtful, and sad. "I think that's all for me now." Rich was also showing his weaker state.

"Yah. I'm ready for the rack, too."

The night showed the importance of mosquito nets, with pest awakening bites and buzzes near ear. Nets were in the field minus clean water and electricity, a small price to pay for freedom I thought and still do, but the price inflated daily in 1967, the year with the most U.S. casualties to date.

Can you picture what will be, so limitless and free, desperately in need of some stranger's hand, in a desperate land...

"Who's Herstowski?" was my venomous wake-up call. I raised my hand.

"You got all your 782? (Field gear.) If you don't, get your ass in gear 'cause the colonel wants the 292 (Tall radio antenna for long distance transmissions) up ASAP!"

There go my guts again: anxiety and fear of the unknown, not an odd-couple in Vietnam.

The over weight corporal kicked the dirt around outside with a polished boot. "We're goin' to Chu-lai, so dump your gear in the back." He pointed towards the Mighty-Mite, a jeep of American Motor's fame.

I bid farewell to my drinking buddy, Rich.
"See 'ya in 13 months."

Steve popped the clutch, easily spinning the wheels on the dirt pavement, much as the G.T.O. would on any surface back home. Back home.

My stateside utilities were soaked through.

"Pretty hot, ain't they?"

"Yah. I'll change when I get to my rack. Is it always this hot here?"

"It's only January, Pal. Wait 'til April! And the monsoons! Buckets! You could almost drown in it!"

Ron sat as shotgun (passenger with a loaded gun). "You just get in country?"

"Yep" I answered, almost apologetically.

"Only 12 months and 29 days 'til you rotate back to the states. That's sad."

We slid over the road, lickity-split down a highway to hell. Dust filtered along unprotected sides and behind, ordering all six lungs to cough and spit abundantly.

"We won't slow down here. I don't take too well to these fuckin' snipers."

"GO STEVE GO!" I'd always prefer a little dust to a little bullet. Ron picked up the hand-set.

"Cantilever Charlie, this is Cantilever Charlie mobile. Radio check. Over."

Response was loud and clear over the strapped in Prc-25. "These Prc's work pretty good out here. You'll be carryin' one of these on your back, Ski."

I mumbled "Yah", now with dust being replaced by a mist from suddenly ebony heavens.

Rice paddies stirred with amplified water droplets and water buffalo hooves. Controlled with rings through nostrils by 60 lb children, their hulk mania was easily dismissed. Magnificent, witnessing the Far East Stone Age: incompatible with powered accessories.

The rain slowed our progress, with ruts from convoys serving as grooves for our slot car, allowing the driver to lean back and enjoy the ride, not that he could steer if he had to. Steve folded his hands behind his neck.

"How's this, Ski? Can't do this back home." Laughter without smiles. A frustrated cyclist journeyed a few hundred feet ahead. He appeared to be in his sixties, with a long, white and almost transparent beard that flowed in the breeze that his travel created. Probably going to a village for some beetle nut (A substance chewed by both men and women, creating blackened teeth and gums and perhaps a euphoric state) or rat meat for his grandchildren, he struggled in a downpour.

Steve slowed down adjacent to the elder, for the biker's safety I assumed. But in a flash, Ron extended his leg out of the doorway and shoved the man off of the bicycle, reeling him into the mud and water of his native land.

More than his back hurt, fist shaking was his send-off the to wrongdoers.

"I HATE these bastards! Took me away from home!" were the final words I'd hear from Ron.

Man's inhumanity to man, a war crime that I'll never forget. We were taught to keep the Locals on the side of the United States, to keep the welcome mat down using diplomacy; Brotherly love, a righteous tact, chocolate to the kids, a fatherly claim. But this blatant cruelty displayed a true concept of the war that these two fools ignored, friendship in the face of death.

I wondered if Papa San would now go to the vil for a weapon instead of food, to take a pot shot at his other enemy, Americans. After all, this is *his* backyard, *his* home, *his* country. Small wonder that solidarity dwindled with these episodes.

Quietly, we reached a roughened board exclaiming 'Charlie Company, 1ˢᵗ Anti Tank Battalion', with speed and rain subsiding.

"Welcome home, Ski. We made it again."
I ignored Steve and his low class auxiliary.

The title 'Anti Tank' struck me bewildered. Does the NVA (North Vietnamese Army) have tanks in their weaponry? I didn't hear so, then what in the world would a purpose of these splendid strength rendering machines serve?

Without an answer, I shifted out of the vehicle with a stretch and my belongings. Sighting the 'Company Office' sign with a sigh of relief, I was hoping to find my journey's end. Lights glowing and fans twirling circulated the clammy hot air as my footfall on the wooden floor announced my arrival.

"Are you Private First Class Herstowski?"

"Yessir!"

"Hold on, Herstowski. I'm not an officer. I earned my rank! Just sergeant, not sir."

"Yessir. Er, I mean sergeant." I answered loudly, gung-ho-ish, trying to release the qualities of a Marine ready to win the war.

"AT EASE ALREADY, but don't get too comfortable. We need a radio operator at Charlie One. You ready? It's out in the bush (Isolated, in the field). Kinda hot sometimes."

I nodded. What the hell is Charlie One?

"We'll get you a ride out there ASAP, meanwhile, out the door and to the left is a hut you can rack in for now."

I got to the screen enclosed, metal roofed stay, trading sweat soaked bindings for proper jungle garb.

A smirking corporal walked in. "Hi. You Ski? I'm Yelle an' I'll show you around. Sarge told me you'd be going out to the field tomorrow, so I'll answer any questions you have. Indoctrination, if you will."

"What's an Anti Tank supposed to be?"

He became solemn.

"I'm going home in a few days." He sat on a rack with a half inflated air mattress ballooned, on either of his sides. Breathing a melancholy sigh,

"Look, you know what we're trained for, so I don't have to tell you what Anti Tanks do. How long you been in?"

"Almost 11 months."

He grinned. "You got a long way to go. You're about 18?"

"19, last November." Yelle looked about 30.

"Follow me."

We walked outside behind the billets to what looked like and what kids called, an army tank. Memories of a Monogram kit of plastic, for assembly, back home. Back home.

But it beheld 6 long rifles.

"This is an 'Ontos', Greek for 'The Thing.' It broke a track, so they brought it here. Ever see one before?"

"No. And I'll be part of THIS?" I glowed inside with my mouth wide open like a 9-year-old boy. Yelle semi-fondled one of the six, 7 or 8 foot long barrels, extended atop the masterpiece of control.

"These are recoilless rifles, so NEVER stand behind one when it's being fired. You'll fry like a chicken on a grill. They shoot 106 millimeter rounds, and the army disbanded them so the Corps picked 'em up after Korea at a discount. One weakness is that it doesn't have a turret like a tank, so when firing, the whole vehicle has to be turned towards the target."

He pointed to the top center, about 8 feet high. "There's 'yer .30 caliber machine gun. Shoots faster than the .50 cal., but slower than the M-60. Hell, I hear that they want to replace two of the 106's with .50 cal. Those things are made to shoot down airplanes! AND, they shoot slower than any of 'em. I don't know what the hell they're thinkin' of Ski." Pause. "Yep, we could sure kick some ass if they'd let us."

With a depressing silence, I thought that after training with these weapons of destruction and using them, we were released after our tour back on the streets of Hoboken, like nothing had ever happened.

"The radio is inside, but usually a crewman takes care of that one. You'll be responsible for your own and you'll have to keep radio contact with us in the rear hourly, daily or whenever necessary."

Drizzle began.

"We call them Pigs and they break tracks at about 30 or 35 mph. They weigh 9 and a half ton." A 10 second gaze at the guns. "I guess we can go in now. I can't tell you much more."

The corporal looked saddened as he turned back to the huts.

"I think I'll stay here a minute or two." I was like a kid with a new toy.

Yelle stopped a stones throw away and turned. "Pigs aren't too heavily armored. Rockets take 'em out real quick. Oh, don't forget to take spare batteries with 'ya. And the rounds are about 3 feet tall." Pause. "I never measured one."

I stared, circling the tracked killing machine. Who ever thought of this, I wondered, then I made my way back to the rack.

More transients were there, discussing their novel approaches to victory, home lives, cars, and of course, how many girls they 'had'. With different outlooks and backgrounds, it was as a united nations. And most of them were Grunts, straight infantry with no more Marine education than killing: the backbone of the Corps. When I told them that I was radio telegraph, "WELL, la de DA! Ha! YOU are going out to the field with US! All you need is a strong back. No Morse and no mistakes, school boy!"

One by one fell asleep, awakened by the sun and anxiety and "Motor Transport has a beer party!" loudly. "C'mon, let's go!" sounded like an order, and outside was a 6 by (Large troop transport truck. Seats 6 on each side of the rear bed, plus more room to stand in the center) with a 55 gallon drum filled

with ice and beer cans and about 25, M-14'd Grunts in shorts. Green towels wrapped around each neck gave me to expect dancing girls to emerge from foliage at any given moment. I came to realize that this wasn't really the fighting zone, just the 'Rear',

used for supply and paper work and enlisted man's clubs with full-length movies nightly.

I saw Yelle waving from the cab for me to jump in, so why argue? The Budweiser looked good, and reaching the un-manicured beach, I decided to just go with the flow. The sky was clear with the temp in the 80's. Winter was hard to forecast here, as was Chicago's.

In this heightened insanity I noticed the coastline of the South China Sea closing in. Sand dunes prevailed, as did some skittering lizards of unknown species, adding still more omnipotence to the prehistoric landscape. It became more of a sin to me each moment, to disturb even a grain of sand in this seemingly virgin territory.

Smells of charcoal filled the air as the truck disbursed us on the beach. 1100, and the steaks were already being burnt, as 'Cooks' sat on lawn chairs, half schnitzeled with Bud.

Another short-timer, Mahovolich joined me towards the beach. "They call me 'Ma,' for short."

"They call me Ski."

I'm goin' home tomorrow. I feel sorry for you, Ski. Make the best of it, though." He stopped, took a deep breath and stared at the sea. "What the hell's goin' on back home? I hear there's a lot of crap goin' on there."

"Never noticed any, myself. I was just anxious to get here."

"Hey you guys. C'mere!" He must've had some 'pull' in the outfit, because 5 or 6 "Grunty" looking individuals swarmed around us with his order.

"This guy Ski here, he was in a hurry to get here. Your name isn't John Wayneski, is it?"

His question created frowns and moans from the group. Myself, I was gouged. I looked at myself as a real sucker now, with fellow Marines showing no respect for the 'Gung Ho' spirit that was supposed to help win the war. One of the spectators, speaking with a foreign accent, remarked, " If you're goin' in the bush, you might wish yourself dead, comrade." Then they all laughed at each other and towards me.

"We're just screwin' around, Pal. You know what's happenin' here but if you don't, you'll find out soon enough." He downed the can of beer like water, and then reached into the 55-gallon drum for two more, telling me that he was an E-5 and this was his second tour. "I'm leaving country in a few days and couldn't be happier. The first tour in '64 wasn't shit, but now? Jesus, they're building up for something REALLY big! I want out! I re-upped (Reenlist) once, but never again in the Corps!" He started a drunken stare towards the water again, with eyes mostly closed and a mumble through his lips. "Hey, let's go in!" caused a near stampede to the brine.

The water, churned and chilly, felt luxurious in the baking heat. My mistake was not keeping my eyes closed. "This water's SALTY!"

Sand violated every inch of flesh, pounding into my new jungle pants and practically pulling them to my knees in the surf.

"Didn't they issue you shorts?"

"I didn't expect to get shorts issued for a war!"

Waves knocked everyone back to the shore for another beer and beef. We found shade under a shelter half to eat our lunch while counting the waves rolling in. The steak was crispy, but I never was too fussy an eater, which would lean to my advantage in the coming months. "Want another one, Ma?"

"Yah, Man" he muttered, as he booted his beer over in the sand. I returned with two more filets, but had to eat them both, as he passed out, probably dreaming of home. He came from somewhere in Virginia, but I hadn't noticed any accent with mumblings that sounded like "Boo ridge…"

We got back to the compound at about 1600, my shoulders and back as burned as were the steaks. Like a surfer in California, I felt that I was immune to the sun's rays, but I'd pay for it for the next few days.

"Way to go, Ski," the company Corpsman winced. Here's some calamine. Don't be so stupid, ya' know? This is a tropical zone and temps'll reach 120 degrees, so keep your body covered! Your Corps' been known to court martial people for being sun burned 'cause they can't perform their duties."

"Thanks, I needed that.'"

Corpsmen were doctors in the field, patching up wounded Marines and themselves. Originally with the Navy, they were unlucky enough to be transferred to the Marine Corps to witness the hell of the land.

Most of the corpsmen I met were fine people. One I met at a Viet Now meeting back in the early '80's was a real wreck from battle and beer. It was a tough job, mending mutilated, young men.

I went back to my bunk and sat around with nothing to do until I was ordered to the duty hut for a guard duty assigment, which added another hat to my already growing list of Marine Characters. Weave was his name, a Pig commander, E-5. "Yer Herstowski, right?"

"That's me." I could tell from his southern drawl that he must have came from Tennessee or the whereabouts. His grin became him.

"Well I'll tell you what, Ski, you get the 12 to 4 shift in the tower at the north end of the compound. You KNOW that you can't fall asleep on guard duty, and the Officer of the Day will be around to check every post at least once an hour, so be on the alert. You have a good view up there from the tower, and the vegie's been Oranged (Agent Orange. A carcinogenic defoliant), so any movement out there will be fair game but call it in first. Understood?"

"Right. There's a phone up there?"

"Oh, yah. There's a phone in case you see something. If you DO see movement, pick up the phone to report it. It'll connect you with Command and they'll tell you if you should shoot or not."

"Where's Command at?"

"They're back at DaNang."

Dogs barked.

"There are friendly villages out there, and some villagers might be roamin' around in the dark, lookin' for a dog for supper. There's plenty of concertina wire strung about, so it'd take a battalion to break through to get you. Just stay awake! And at 0400, the O.D. will bring around your relief. GOT IT?"

"It's my first night here, so I'm a little jittery, Sarge. And isn't a watchtower a great target? Like a sitting duck?"

Like a STANDING duck, Ski. And don't call me SARGE! Just WEAVE!"

I left the hut, feeling that I'd insulted Weave, but I was more concerned with my upcoming duty in the watchtower.

I got to my bunk and fell asleep. My first dream there held volcanic explosions of my X girlfriend shaking her head over my flower abound corpse. I'd read that dreams last for only 40 seconds or so, but this one seemed to last for hours.

The O.D. woke me up as I lay in a pool of sweat, at about 2330. "They told me that Herstowski was in this hut. That you?"

"Yes, sir." The full moon shone brightly for us, otherwise he'd have searched for me 'til the cows came home, since his flash light batteries were near dead.

"No saluting around here, Ski." I already felt welcome being called by my nickname, by an officer. "Don't salute any officer in this country unless you want him shot at. I'm Lieutenant Beman, officer of the day. Put your flack jacket on and grab your weapon."

I prepared under the light of the silvery moon. The humid night air requested me to wear but the sleeveless flack jacket weighing about 15 lbs. They held no candle to a bullet, but were good for shrapnel resistance. Word was, if metal penetrated to a body through the jacket's plastic, surgeons had a tough time removing the plastic: near invisible flesh colored pieces causing wounds.

Enemies must have rolled in laughter as they hid in bushes while we passed in cumbersome attire. 120 degrees and up, Westmoreland ordered his boys outdoors wearing everything but insulated socks.

The Lt. had his left hand resting on his holstered 45. With limited lighting I tip toed comically and lightly bumped into him, wiping a sweaty arm against the back of his shirt.

"Trouble seeing, private?"

"Yes sir. It's DARK."

"Well, get used to it!"

My post was a few hundred feet ahead with choruses of native insects complaining with their timpani. The noise could lay cover for one to crawl quietly for a cutthroat kill.

"Crawl up the ladder. I'll follow."

Leading the way to the top, I counted 15 rungs. Or was it 13? I slid my 14 across the wooden deck, hitting an obstacle that sounded like a beer can.

"Now, here's the phone if you hear or see anything outside the wire." He pointed to the handset encased in a canvas bag. "NO firing without permission!" he emphasized.

I was left alone with the thought of a war with permission only. Then came the all too frequent thoughts of an icy cold Pepsi, G.T.O., a warm shower, a Baby Ruth bar, and Donna. And, what was moving in the bush? It resembled a man guiding a buffalo with a cart so I dismissed it as a commoner. Recreation on watch or guard duty was bending over to light a cigarette then cupping it for a puff. Helps to pass the time and quench nicotine fits.   My relief arrived none too soon.

"You Ski? I'm Larry. See anything tonight?"

His twitch reflected jangled nerves and he shook like a 12 year old Chihuahua. He needed to return home pronto.

"Yah. There was a figure dragging a boo about 100 meters out."

"Did you report it?"

"Nah. I saw him for a second then he disappeared in the bush." I pointed out the area.

His squealing response was irritating. "You DIDN'T call it in? What the HELL!" 10 seconds of silence. "Where you from?"

"Chicago."

More silence.

I bungled to the ground, thinking that warriors should have a closure relationship than the one just displayed, but not in Vietnam, in 1967. Marines served 13 months minimum in the Long Thin Country unless wounded or dead. I never have figured out that rule, though. All other branches served 12 only months.

So knowing that you didn't have to stay for the duration of the conflict made it everybody's business to count the hours and days remaining before rotation, thereby making tours more like a run of the mill stay over. And the many lulls as in all wars justified the ends to be merely subtraction.

"We have reports of enemy movement within 5 miles south of us. Stay near this tower and expect anything!" Lt. Beman sounded punch drunk, probably from lack of sleep.

"Prop up against those sandbags and keep watch."

"Yessir." Hell, I thought again. I just got off watch and I need some sleep! Whoa! I forgot that I was in a WAR! God! How could anyone keep this up for 13 months? Drizzle started and dust clouded as I sat down beneath the tower. Dirt emancipated reminded me of my pooch Fritzi, who scampered roughly in our Chi-Town backyard play ground. I'd lay on the ground with him circling me with incredible speed until he'd close in for 'the kill'. For a small terrier he'd really way lay a 10 year old. Finishing our playtime, he'd dig out a spot of dirt to lie in. Just like me now, and a million miles from 'the world.'

I rested there not sleeping, when rolling Thunder exploded me to my feet, yelling, "What the hell is that?"

"Sounds like another B-52 strike. A lot of them lately."

"Big bombs?"

"BIG!"

For a minute I thought that the crashes would never stop. Then, silence. We could see dense smoke rising over the tree line, and could guess the strike happened where the Lt. told us to watch. It lasted about a minute.

"Did you sleep under the tower?"

"I was there."

"That's a Vietnamese cemetery, Ski."

He snickered, turned back to the jungle and its offerings, and then picked his teeth with a piece of wood.

"Who cares? The people down there are dead."

No laugh. No response.

The sun was on the rise, and we were both ready for a good day's sleep when, "All secure?"

"Yep, but Ski-boy here didn't call in movement last night."

Weave's eyes slanted inward. "Let's go. Big search and destroy mission startin' and we're all gonna be part of it." He smiled.

Rain fell heavier. It got colder.

"Weave, I thought I was getting transferred."

"Well, guess what. You ARE! Westmoreland needs you to carry a radio for him in the paddies. Any objections?" Another grin.

"I grinned back, "Lemme at 'em!"

Polish your guns, your own self be reflecting.

***Out here in the fields, I fought for my meals…don't cry; it's only
teenage wasteland.***

I crawled slowly up the 6-by after being handed two frags. Like, I really needed 2.5 more pounds to lug around. All the combat gear plus the Prc-25 made an unimaginable heavy, even for a Marine aged 19. It would be the first time I'd toss a firecracker like this for peace and survival, and I became a trembling mess.

Looking around wide-eyed, I could see grand palm trees, and youngsters like myself readying for battle. Is anyone else looking at us? Will there be a parade? Will we all come back alive?

The truck's canvas roof was removed, but not for a beach party. For this, we faced outboard with weapons locked and loaded and paranoia, driving to an unknown assignment in this ever-confusing theater. I asked a cigar smoking lance corporal if we were on an operation, while counting over 10 trucks in convoy. His tobacco-juiced lips answered "Yah", calmly, coolly. The limo bouncing in and out of potholes had us adjusting our sink-like chapeaux while bumping into each other helplessly like Mexican jumping beans. White feathered Quackers escaped tires time and again, with chickens pecking duck-ward with piercing beaks. Choppers (Helicopters) whizzed by sending a message to friend an enemy alike, that the Marines were about to land. Their bursts of fire exported a conveyance of seek and destroy, not an ineffective exercise. I began to feel patriotic again, but felt alone as I looked at the other passengers. I knew not one of them. We were side by side, perhaps to die, and we were complete strangers.

And, was I the only Yankee Doodle Dandy on this bus?

With mixed emotions of terror and fervency zip-snarling my mind, the diesel rumbled "*Out of my way*", as it skidded through small settlements too fractional to be called villages. They were populated with families down to the last cousin, likable, minus the marring of war.

Our driver held 3rd gear while passing the lead Mite. It held a man of Colonel age, standing with an almighty look and an arm that waved us forward to the area of the great crashes made by rockets expelled by the choppers.

The truck stopped and the driver jumped out of the sand bagged cab to drop down the gate for us to "GET OUT!" A sergeant ran next to the convoy yelling "MOVE IT, MOVE!", his un-14'd arm waving crazily.

Exiting with a 5-foot drop, we bumped into each other with our war accessories as a silver ball against 'Jet Bumpers.' Without peripheral interference, I would have fallen flat on my face.

A corporal, recognized as our leader, waved me to the slimy side of clay embankment. "Who the hell are you? You ain't been with us before! Jesus Christ!"

Sniper rounds thudded in the ground nearby. Arm waves sent the 12-man fire team slipping, sliding and crawling to the opposite side of the road, as the enemy held the adjacent tree line. Unknowns fell.

"Keep your head down!" a seasoned one warned, with rounds hitting low on the road surface spitting clay and mud in our eye; spittle from the enemy.

Corpsmen rushed with aid.

Choppers attacked unashamedly, with mini-guns (machine guns, shooting thousands of rounds per minute) a blazing. Even in daylight, streams of fire were seen as in a Greek fire celebration a hundred feet over our heads. Palm leaves fell, heartburn elevated to my tongue. Mortar rounds exploded behind us in the paddies, their jagged and pointed metal casings digging the embankment we lay on. "Follow me" was the call. We crawled in unison and mud, as mist began covering the sun and terrain. When rain fell, you stayed wet, and misery was contained with cold, and you stayed cold. After the operation, a tent awaited without a heater to dry you off. And a cold shower rarely returned a smile to a face.

I guess no one took the time to read a map of this country before moving in with foot soldiers. The landscape was enough to dissuade a smart commandant from entering a war in this country, expecting victory. That is, IF he could read a topographical map. Too much foliage, too many mountains to climb, too many paddies to wade across, too much heat, too much wet, too many insects.

Island fighting during WWII should have been lessons for the future. Snipers and booby traps abounded, just like in RVN. I figured out our pitfalls rapidly on this first Op I attended. Save a full land cover by our Forces, our involvement would end deadlocked at best.

I had read that President Johnson couldn't stand losing, especially a war. Combined with racial tensions and war protesting, his lot in life and office became quite negative. But in running the war with *my* tactics, or evacuating the entire Vietnamese populace, he may have turned the tide in his favor. With resistance stifled in Vietnam, America may have congealed to the point of much lesser racial tensions, making Johnson a hero to his people. I say it *might* have worked, but Mr. Johnson's playbook didn't gather him a winner.

As far as his protestors, it was their way of shaping America. They enjoyed the bennies of a free society while bitchin' about their government's use of their youth. I was appalled at their conduct, but now, I don't know who was really right. God bless America.

So there we were, sliding off the roadside into the paddy 6 feet below, not knowing where we were supposed to go or where the enemy was to shoot at. We were pinned down, which was really pissing me off. All of this power and might, I thought, and 'nowhere to go!' Just then, an Ontos eating up the treeline expressed the power down the road.

A Grunt next to me, "They're using flachette rounds on the trees." We stopped crawling, and waited for explosions to subside. He lit up a Lucky and offered one to me. I took it. My pack was soaked from drizzle.

The deafening blowout continued, and as I peeked over the road it became apparent that we were destroying Mother Earth in our process of elimination. Trees were splintered and all denizen in the forest, annihilated.

Firing ceased and we remained in the mud, our utes (Utility clothing) soaked with rain and paddy sludge.

"What are flachette rounds?" They sounded menacing, and I had to find out all I could, even with embarrassing questions.

"You're new here, huh? They're 106 rounds with darts in 'em. Antipersonnel. They make 'em JUST for the gooks." He spit out his wet Lucky. "The rounds can be set to explode when the crew wants 'em to. Pretty shifty, huh?" He laughed deeply, as his gaze returned to the tree line.

I saw flachette rounds later in my tour. The 'bullet', if you will, must've weighted 75 pounds. Just a guess, but I did carry a few to Ontos' now and then. They were tipped with a dial to set for maximum efficiency in release of the aluminum darts. After the round was fired, the projectile would explode the 1" long, aluminum darts to the air at whatever distance the dial was set. 100 meters, 500 meters or whatever distance the crew chief deemed necessary; one hell of a payload. After the terrible barrage, we were told to get to the ready. Hand signals sent point men (first man in a patrol) from fire teams to advance towards the tree line. It had been quiet for a few minutes and anxiety mounted. I was nervous, but still ready to take part in the movement.

My fire team and a few others were held back to keep the road area secure. Small arms fire continued to eliminate resistance in the rain forest, making it difficult to distinguish friendly fire from enemy incoming. More explosions echoed from the woods, hopefully being our own grenades. Then more firing, more explosions and pha-taks from machine guns. We hit the deck again, crawling to the far side again, readying again, and wishing I were home, again. The smell of gunpowder became sharp, mixing with the stench of death that I felt would greet us soon.

"CEASE FIRE," came from the tree line. A radioman ran behind an officer who talked into his handset. They jumped into the tall elephant grass like it was a swimming pool, under fire. Still, there were snipers shooting from their jungle sanctuary. THAT, I couldn't believe! The terrible onslaught we prevailed didn't work! Mini-guns, small arm fire and 106mm didn't clean the area. We lay in the mud and rain another ½ hour with infrequent thuds in the road ahead of us and spurts in the rice paddy to our rear.

Choppers returned for medevac.

The rest of the teams were high tailing out of the black forest, and we opened fire again. The place went deafeningly insane. Discord in unison, like waves at the sea 24 hours ago. The smoke of the weapons lulled in the rain as a Grim Reaper when bodies were pulled out of the jungle.

The fighting finally stopped as we all moved to the tree line, witnessing the enemy bodies dragged out unceremoniously, to be set aside for flies to inspect as our wounded and killed were lifted out in air ambulances. Other Marines with minor injuries waited for the next lift, with cigarettes burning. We walked through the 200-foot long village with a lieutenant broadcasting, "We'll be here through the night, so SECURE THIS VILLAGE!"

I was supposed to be a radioman and somewhere else! What the hell is going on? Live and learn the saying goes. Take notes, Ski.

We filed through the village, my second or third day in country. I'd already forgotten how long I'd been there. And I was face to face with seventy-year-old prophets and half naked 3 year olds running in their streets. Most of them didn't even have shoes, much less 3 squares a day. I pitied them, and later in the year, I felt apologetic for our intrusion with their life and loves.

No opposition was found in that town, from the KNOWN enemy, that is. But the village people were VERY disturbed as was expected. One of their little ones was scratched and bleeding from her leg, from metal haphazardly airborne. A corpsman was paged, seemed quite sympathetic to children's injuries. He turned to, at the sound of the child's remorse. The wound superficial required only iodine and wrapping gauze, but the red pigments caused her to screech, squelched only with C-ration candy substitute.

We were about a half-mile from the main contacts when another firefight broke out.

"When the fuck are they gonna call in the air!" calloused out our platoon leader. "Joe, find out our sit rep!" (Situation report.)

Finally, news of an upcoming air strike in the woods. It seemed that more enemy contact was being made, and the colonel was tired of men snipped off, one at a time.

I followed the leader out of the vil and right into the rice paddy. I was freezing wet, shaking. Or was it nerves?

Ribbons of celebration that the people had strung up connecting their grass huts were torn down and twisted. Some words were, "DUC CHA", the rest were obliterated and probably wished a "HAPPY NEW YEAR!"

When the jets were heard, the natives realized the reason and started in our path. We were just far enough away from the tree line to not get melted. We hoped. Napalm was their payload, contents of fire breathing bombs that spewed forth jelly not like Welch's. It was terrible. Ruthless. Hell. Phantom Jets from Hades.

If ANYTHING lived through that storm of flame I thought, we might as well ALL drop our arms and return home with our tails between our legs like a Fritzi-dog.

The jungle was tranquillized, distracted periodically with snorts from pigs and late falling palm leaves.

We regrouped with two other fire teams and followed their way towards one of our steel bridges. It crossed a river and led us into the woods, miles from our drop off station. No one knew if the area was secure, so again, we became guinea pigs, staying spread out in our patrol, waiting to hear a shot fired to fell a warrior in our path. It was slow travel. Scary. Heartburn.

And we trudged through marshes, just as my drapes were beginning to dry. No matter, mist returned. My M-14 was really getting the best of me, the rest got heavier with every step.

Finally, the long awaited hand signal that called for a break in the action came to be. Moving to cover for a flop out in the muck and mire, we were convinced that we were in the worst place in the entire galaxy. The mist turned to light rain, then a heavy downpour. God, I thought, where IS the glory? Only in the old, black and white 'talkies' was glory injected in the players, overflowing with propaganda and laced with Stars.

The 15 minute break flashed by, with more hand signals pointing forward. No wonder wars are for the young. The stop was good, but my back felt broken the instant I stood back up. Almost with a moan, my feet were back in gear, to pain another few hours.

1600 found us at rest stop, and I hoped we'd stay for night's rumble. Small groups huddled in the bushes listening for the situation report and to the gurgling of a river close by for our night position. Paired up, we'd take turns watching the jungle across the water.

I teamed up with the Joe who didn't talk much. Not that he was shy, but he was split up mentally from the war and the Marine Corps. He said he never slept much, attributing it to the wars back home. Shortly after we set in, an Ontos arrived for H & I (Harassment / Interdiction) fire across the river. The water expressed a brown hue that looked comprised of human waste and blood. It smelled the same, with decomposed night crawler toilet water thrown in.

The crew began to load their arsenal as 6, 106's prepared to mow down a path. One of its members became a best buddy of mine through his stay, Luke, a driver.

"You guys ready?"

"Fire when ready", stereoed.

I was ready too, with fingers plugged both of already damaged eardrums. A resounding boom broke the silence and unprotected hearing cups. Then another ground beaker erupted, with the fiery missile tearing over the river, into the tree line a few hundred feet
away, eclipsing matter few have seen. A shock wave winded with each demolition. Branches, coconuts and palm trees themselves were mitigated from their bases. We of the West had the power.

Luke told me that they were using HEP (High explosive) rounds. Flechette rounds were used when personnel were in view, too costly to use on targets other than human.

Night consumed the Earth as a bulky spoon, making us almost blind, with sounds of the stink-ridden, gushing river prevailed only by mating calls of eager insects and rustlings in the shrub by things that go bump in the jungle. The sounds duplicated in my helmet liner. For fear of a well-placed bullet, the helmet remained.

The thought of death didn't usually bother me. I've always felt that when one dies, they rest naturally. Meet God for a final reward, with no more pain. And it can't be hell, because I've already been there, man made.

So I thought in the dark and the mud and the rain, graciously of a sidewalk to ride a bike over, the Rolling Stones, clean water and a clean glass to pour it in, smelly fresh linen wrapping a firm mattress, a movie theater selling buttered popcorn, a Pine Lake setting, just being 19 with Donna, a 19¢ MacDonald's with fries and a vanilla malt, fishing with Dad, dry socks, the Church, smells of a newly mowed lawn, Christmas trees, and Ron Britain on WCFL, AM, Chicago.

Then POP! The lights went on as Joe kicked me in the leg. "GETUP SKI! A-A Across the River!" he stuttered. "B-Black pajamas!"

Three hundred feet ahead we viewed a silhouette easily, even with the limited scourge of a pop flare. Joe started firing his M-14 while I crapped in my skivvies. He emptied his magazine while I shot hesitatingly on semi. The other teams opened fire to movement across the 'street where we lived' until "Cease fire" was mumbled. Staring resumed.

Score, act one; one hit by a sniper round, one cry of severity, one eruption by the USMC. A thousand orange fireflies, a thousand bombs of Ontos descent. God knows how many they lost in the last 13 seconds, but *we* lost one as drivers hustled their Pigs further apart, with the Top Dogs (Ontos Commander) jumping to the .30 calibers to heat up the barrel. The driver on C25 lined up for fire, as the muzzles were loaded. "Clear and ready for play."

Flares from Gun Ships revealed the landscape as the battle continued. I trembled from the rain and idiocy of war. It's unfeeling to shoot at each other, don't you think? Hurt or kill each other for land or ideals?

Heavy clouds of gun smoke dense came from cronies to our right.

Ordnance; peddling their wares.

None too soon, ebony water continued sloshing, bugs kept bugging and we fell into another morbid peace. Parachuted flares still soared as eyes strained for direction. My head leaned down and I thought that I could throw in the towel any minute now. Not much sleep in the last few days, the great outdoors and a hundred pounds back-wise lent me to disillusion. But I fought it off as we all did, misbegotten days of our youth. We were in a war, not like the movies or the views in the 6 O'clock News.

Quiet seemed to cue to Buddha to help our enemy. "Rain upon these hateful invaders", an imagined Ruler enlisting the clouds. Less than a week in country found me considering my breaking point.

More flares burning the pitch black, expired, leaving the environment shaded in a way only the blind realizes. Sounds of nocturnal chase added to bombshell's fitful explosions a short mile in the distance. We were scaring the snakes, too.

Now with fog and sustained drizzle in the dawn of a new day, a 'Bugle Boy' told me to report to a Sergeant Jame.

"Hi. I'm Herstowski."

Jame was the crew chief of C25 and straight out of New York City. "Just throw 'yer stuff on the pig and we'll go home." He spoke through a degenerated smile.

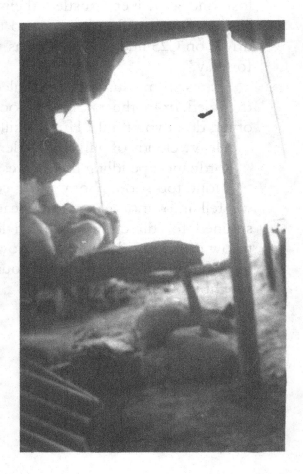

HOME? We're done here? The area is secured? We won? Nobody knew. We just moved onward.

"So you're Ski, right? It's to Hill 22, non-stop. Hop on the left guns. You'll be the farthest away if we hit a mine." The enemy, in roads and on trails, planted land mines, dud artillery and B-52 bombs.

Luke started the diesel burner at the touch of a button.

"Goin' my way?"

"Sarge, the rest of my stuff is at Battalion. Can we go for it?"

"Don't be a pain in the ass. Maybe *you*'ll go tomorrow."

He pointed towards a Marine who

didn't look the part. Skinny, maybe from the physical and mental climate, with front teeth not unlike Disney's Goofy. "There's George. He's a loader, but if he drives, hold on TIGHT! He's nuts!"

George came over with a smile. Nuts, is right. How could anyone smile after the firefight? We nodded at each other as I straddled my front row seat, reminiscent of a carnival duck to be shot at, 8 foot high.

From atop my perch I could see how tracked vehicles are maneuvered. Applying pressure to left or right braking handles directs to corresponding side.

And Luke did it well, through winding sands and over obstacles with finesse. I bent to miss tree limbs and palms, hearing Jame's "Yahoos!" sounding like Roy Rogers Saturday morning serial without Post Cereals.

Luke yelled "TOO ROCKY!" and Spanish obscenities.

In about an hour we reached a beaten path. Not a freeway by any means, but it served our purpose better than clumpage cursed near the river. And the scene held a foreboding air with jungle closing the shutters with a ceiling of green.

"These are the hanging gardens of Chu-lai. Keep on rollin', Luke!" Jame looked timorous as he handled his piece.

We were a support unit, but there was no support for us, and it was crazy to drive this route solo. Like the first ride on a midway's "House of Horrors," you never saw the creature before it was too late. Apprehension was foremost, with a monster around every corner, or maybe not.

We made it to the main drag, breathing a sigh of relief. No confrontations.

A mama-san marched down the graveled road, laundry baskets ending on a pole precariously balanced on a shoulder. Ducks floated in paddies, waiting for killer chickens to retreat. Pungent powder smoke clung in the air like stink on shit, entangled with cooking fires of villagers.

A mile or so turned us to another of ill repute, one that was christened

'suicide.' I'd travel it a hundred times during my tour. An uncomfortable Roosevelt Road in Berwyn. Every curve and run-out, I would memorize. Bushwhacking arenas contained would be met with pedal to the metal. Villagers I would come to know would try to win the domestic war.

That hardened path from DaNang to Hill 22 rose and fell, only to rise and fall again with Luke keeping a steady pace of 25 mph max.

Not to be outdone by a rocking horse under the Christmas tree, Ontos rocks in defiance on uneven surfaces. Luke hit the brakes preparing for a curve, nearly plugging my head between
the two top guns beneath me, from momentum. Jame chuckled while he plugged an ear with a finger. He ALWAYS had a finger in an ear. It took all types.

The last curve before the outpost posed a threat as soon as I saw it. A sharp turn with a steep hill spells out dangerous deceleration, but this one? The driver had best be able to slid gears quickly.

So at long last, the hill that was 22 feet above sea level. It resembled a pile of sand and clay, with tents and sand bags scattered randomly. Topless warriors strolled casually on the 250-foot wide bush less hill, wearing only shorts and stares.

"Here we are, Ski. Hill 22! No P.X., no running water, no electricity, no Club, no movies. BUT, we have plenty of ammo." There was no trace of gaiety in his voice throughout the introduction.

I followed Jame to an open tent flap.

"Dig up a rack and put it on sandbags."

"How far is the P.X?"

"DaNang, 10 or 15 miles. The radioman does the running for us, and YOU are the radioman! You get to get off this hill almost every day, and the Mite has just been overhauled."

"I don't have a license."

Jame returned, "Don't worry, you'll get one."

After setting up my area I went outside to see the terrain. Some high foliage that could hide unwelcome visitors, with bands of concertina wire (circular barbed strands of wire) preceding a trench line reminded me of WW1 photos. Grass huts 1000 foot downhill reminded me of Vietnam.

"That's a friendly village, Hamberski. Don't take any shots at it."

"Okay, George. And it's *Herstowski*!"

He laughed "Okay, Ski", as he rammed a rod down one of the barrels of his Pig to start a P.M. (Preventive Maintenance. Cleaning.).

After a few days with this crew, I would conclude them to be as content as possible, given this situation. Spending a tour with them would be tolerable compared to others I met, who were mentally disturbed or just malevolent. Those were the disloyal, bad combatants.

Luke pointed a tent. "That's the Duty Hut." It had a red and yellow sign proclaiming 'ENTRANCE' where the door would be. On hotter days, all tent flaps were rolled up for ventilation, so anywhere could be the entrance. I removed my cover (A Marine's cap) and walked in to announce the arrival of the hill's new radioman.

"Herstowski?"

"Yes sir" spewed forth. I was exhausted and the captain could sense it.

"Just got off the Op? Well, we have work to perform, but some things can wait 'til tomorrow." Captain Morgan read some of my duties, like the P.X. run.

"Sir, I have to get a driver's license."

"You'll get one tomorrow" looking annoyed, over the top of his glasses. "Get some rest. Dismissed."

Jame and his crew tended their Pig as I stepped next to the guns. "Don't you have some radio work to do? We take care of the Pig's radio, but you have to take care of your own gear."

I was still dazed from prior days. "I'm hittin' the rack. Do we have reveille?"

"HELL no! We're up at all hours. No reveille, no Monday, no Friday. Every day is the same, except on Sundays the Chaplin might come out for mass. Sometimes."

I went to my area for some positive shuteye. No Fridays, no Donna. Luke came in with more rules.

"No mustaches or beards. Keep your hair cut short. Inspection every morning."

"EVERY MORNING? I thought that we were in a war zone!"

"We're Marines, Ski, and the petty shit never stops. How long did you say you've been in?"

"Almost a year." I was embarrassed with the crib time I served.

"You're new, all the way around, so don't act too salty around the Grunts. They get crazier and madder by the day when one of their own gets ambulanced home. The road to this hill gets mined a lot, and they have to clear it every morning. They take the guff and sniper rounds and are damn sick of it. Somebody shootin' at 'ya and you can't find 'em.'"

My area was near the imaginary door. Our clay floor was covered with dust-powder that resettled with after whisk of wind, covering half-used cans of C-rations and footlockers.

"Don't forget to mark your name on the rack or somebody'll steal it." It was usable but brown instead of the manufactured green, and I was already half asleep in it when Luke told me he'd show me around the perimeter.

He led the way into the trench line, and being about 5'8", he had to stand on a sandbag for a better view. "Trenches surround our tents an' we've jumped in 'em a lot these last few weeks. Don't wander into one at night. Might break a leg."

The 'protections' were about 5 foot deep plus a foot of sandbag. Good combat cover. "The barbed wire is pretty thick, and see the patches in the sides of the hill? They're for claymores (anti-personnel mines detonated by an electrical firing mechanism). Ever shot one?"

"Can't say that I have, Luke."

"Make SURE that they're facing outward! A gook snuck through the wire just to turn one around. When it was shot it blew one of us away."

Claymore mines were about 2 inches thick, a foot and a half long and maybe a foot high. They deliver steel fragments in a fan-shaped zone 6 feet high and 100 feet wide. Back blast occurs, making it imperative that the mine is mounted with a barrier behind it. "The mountains and hills fill with V.C. now and then, but our government doesn't want to disturb the environment. Crazy, huh."

We walked to a further side of the hill. "Down there is supposed to be a friendly vil. Sometimes we group up and go for a cold bottle of Coke. THEY have ice, we don't. There's a well down there. On the hotter days we go for the bucket. The water is cold but it feels good. And it stinks."

"Right!" I was so shaky that I thought I'd never leave the concertina's safety.

We went back to the tent but clanking treads awakened me to stare at our green ceiling thinking about barbecues back home. And Riverview and Donna. I turned for a towel to wipe my face and viewed insects from the Jurassic period. Some had 100 legs, others with 20 eyes and 5 tails claimed towel ownership. Add creepy crawlers to a heartbroken mind, with home melancholia.

From utter exhaustion and mental stress, I reentered Sandman's domain.

In short, we must be constantly prepared for the worst and constantly acting for the best, strong enough to win a war and
wise enough to prevent one.
                                        Lyndon B. Johnson

Hats off to Johnny Freedom...he's the spirit of America, our country's pride and joy...you can read on him on each page of history...

First light and a clammy sweat that would've put Sugar Ray Robinson to shame interrupted my sleep. I sat up and put my bare feet on a dry clay floor to a reception of, ironically, an army of aggressive *red* ants, smashing them for their due.

My feet no longer attended, I slipped them into my brand new jungle boots of mostly leather, with canvas sides for maximum ventilation. I needed to make a head call, but large beetle-like vermin in the bottom of my footwear almost had me deliver my load in my rack.

With bugs bested, I went to the pipe Sergeant Jame identified as "the pisser." It was a pipe of maybe 10" diameter, dug into the ground for male use only. The 'crapper' next to it was not unlike the out houses found near the Wisconsin farmhouses in the 50's and days of yore, but it had two holes to sit over to release one's tension and waste, with screening to provide a beautiful view of the landscape for the visitor. Below sat semi-55 gallon drums filled with kerosene, burned with gasoline when the 'toilet' filled. And everyone took his turn burning the residue, everyone except officers and E-5's and above.

I returned to the empty housing, wondering where the other tenants could be. Luke came around as I stood there with my hands on my hips.

"Get dressed, Ski. We're going on a P.X. run, and you can take your driver's test."

I slept in my pants, so I dug a shirt out of my sea bag. Pulling my shirt on, Luke noticed a dozen insect bites on my back and arms.

"Man! They sure came around last night! You'd better get a mosquito net right away, or you'll get malaria, for sure."

"I thought those pink pills I got were supposed to stop that."

"Do what you want Ski. Do you like to itch?"

I turned my mouth down, looking his way. "Hey! When can we get to Battalion for my other gear?" I'd already forgotten what I left there.

"We'll stop there on the way to DaNang. I told the Cap where we're goin', so lock an' load and let's go!"

The Mighty-Mite sped down the dry, gravelly road, dust infusing every square inch of our air space. "They already swept the road this morning, so we should be safe from mines" said through unsmiling teeth. This drive through the molested pageant would be one of few that a self-proclaimed naturalist like I could enjoy as a Shotgun. It was a beautiful masquerade, this green cover of the earth, smitten with towering clouds of smoke and dust.

The Vietnamese seemed immune to the sweat syndromes that I and all other teenagers experienced during our treks through their patches.

Nothing Hollywood historicized with their cameras, fondled the utter exhaustion felt by an old teenager strapped with an overly protective suit ignored by Gentlemen's Quarterly. "Too constrictive!", editor protests. Lecherously hot days melted our eyes into our brains as body's oils poured like an opened oil plug, releasing, from a 327 Chevy engine.

We all felt our muscles stretch as a rubber band, contracting with tension released while piling onto the ground.

So I enjoyed this Utopia while I could. "Like, we almost there yet?" The road surface was almost always intolerable, and the racing springs on all of our government vehicles gave proof to a galloping rhinoceros.

"A few more minutes, Ski. We'll pick up your gear at Battalion, first,"

"You look like you know these roads pretty good. How long have you been here?"

"I've been here about 5 months now." It still beat me that *anyone* could smile while they were here, but Luke did. Just happy go lucky.

Blind corners of our route showed more beautiful floral arrangements, disputed only by Amling's Flowerland. Most colors of the rainbow blossomed extensive reds and yellows, colors adopted by the U.S.M.C.

We picked up my 'lost' gear, and I proceeded to take my driving test that licensed me to a 2.5-tons.

The toughest part of the test was getting the truck out of first gear, but I'd already mastered that with Dad's G.T.O. back home. Back home.

Luke took us the mailroom, where I'd pick up Hill 22's deliveries. A flag draped near the front entrance and another red and yellow sign announced the mail call hours, which seemed conservative, considering the amount of actual work the mail boys had to perform. "Be nice to these guys. Don't get 'em pissed or the mail WON'T go through! Don't rush 'em, and everything'll work out fine."

Post Exchange runs had me returning with cartons of cigarettes @ $2.00 each, comic books, Barbasol shaving cream, blank reel to real tapes for correspondence with the girls back home, an issue or two of the latest Playboy magazine if available, for inspiration, cases of hot Coke Cola, and nickel candy bars, melted.

I bought a Yashica 35mm camera, relieved of promptly as the P.C. (Personnel Carrier, ¾ ton) had to be slowed to a crawl in a traffic jam near DaNang. The back window was a good place to hang the camera out of, and a youth hopped on the flat bed to dispute this claim. He found a souvenir. I had the truck crawling, so the irregularities in the road kept me from noticing the additional 50 or 60 pounds of the thief. I did feel his exiting though, but only feigned a chase, as a pursuit would have surely had my vehicle stolen. We had no keys to start the engines, only ignition switches.

"Here's the mess hall. Just show your Geneva Convention card when you come in and you can get a hot meal if it's chow time."

We had a meal called lunch, consisting of what tasted like a canned hamburger casserole. "Let's go back to the boon docks, Luke."

"Yah. This stuff tastes like C-rats." So we left for our return trip.

An Idler can relish the vista, but as a driver I became more aware of the obvious pitfalls that befriended every curvature fruitful with papaya, each hill geometrically hindering a non-racing jeep, and every inch of a mudded or dusty drag way too slick to dominate.

We neared the compound, with the final curve accompanying the final acclivity, giving me another lean towards insecurity. Along with the mountain hideaways the turnpike became more and more tantalizingly derisive to me in the months that would follow.

Sgt. Jame stood on a back step of C25, wiping the 30 cal. down with an oily rag, drying it with a clean one. With his cover on backwards, he reminded me of some of my boyhood friends at Lawndale Park whom I competed with on our Little League teams. If we won, we'd turn our caps around as if to show an air of defiance in victory. "You expecting to win, Sarge?"

"Huh?"

"Nothin'. Never mind."

"Luke," he started, "Did you bring me some chocolate?"

"Awww! I forgot!"

"What?" Out there, if an item was ordered, forgetting to pick it up at the P.X meant another day or more without. No candy machines.

Luke tossed a Hershey's bar and both men grinned ear to ear.

"I'd a killed ya, Luke!" He unwrapped the bar and threw the wrapper on the ground and returned to his gun cleaning.

I went in to clean my weapon. "Luke, where's everybody at?"

"Some are on R & R, some are off on patrols, and some are on their way home."

I didn't ask him in what condition they're going home under.

"What are the patrols like?"

"You carry the radio for Lt. Berm. They last for about 2 hours, all around our perimeter. Patrols check for enemy movement and supplies and make sure Charlie's not diggin' in and getting ready to overrun us."

"Ever have trouble here?"

"We did, a few weeks ago. That's one reason they brought you here. The last radioman went home, sniper fire at night." His head turns towards the road. "The engineers blow up mines once in awhile."

Roads were engineered 3 to maybe 6 or 7 feet high, and the enemy found it easy to dig in the sides to plant their mines to hardly leave a trace of digging to be found.

"MINES!" I quivered. "And I gotta drive over this road EVERY day?"

"Not EVERY day, SKI. And the engineers find most of 'em."

I sat awhile, staring again at the minuteness of the procession of ants crowding the existence of a foreign interloper in their sphere of influence until they finally apprehended him for dissection.

Clattering tracks sounded the entering of another Ontos on our dirt outpost.

Luke bent under the tent half. "It's Weave."

I followed him out the door, knowing I'd learn more before the day was through.

We reached the Pig and its crew, Tex and Bravo.

They were brown with dust as was their vehicle. I always wondered how we weren't blinded for life from the chronic dust that prevailed from the roadways. And our lungs! We're worried about smoking?

"He's the new replacement?" came from Tex, pointing in my direction. He was about 5' 7" and looked to weigh in at 140 pounds. His drawn out face showed 50 years, but 25 was my guess, and an almost toothless grin made him a candidate for a Beverly Hillbilly's comic.

Bravo talked with an accent from south of the border, Mexico he said. His hair was on the long side for the Marine Corps and it looked cared for it with Vitalis and axle grease.

"What the hell you been doing, Herstowski?" Sgt. Weave bellowed.

"Me and Luke went on a P.X. run. I just got my license."

"You're SUPPOSED to take care of the radios in the Pigs, ya know!"

They, or rather, SOME of them expected new personnel to fall into their duties as though they had done it all their lives. It was like that in the Corps, no matter where. But I was too 'boot' to the 'Nam to complain or resist, so I acted like I was working and went to remove the Prc-25 from Jame's Pig.

"Herstowski. My Pig just came in from the field, right? So don't you think that MY Pig needs a cleanup more than Jame's?"

I set the radio on the top of C25 and moved to the other vehicle, hearing Weave mumble something to his crewmembers for a laugh.

"How many of these radios do I have to take care of?"

Tex was the closest one. "Well, usually we have 5 of 'em in a platoon. But we're down to 2. One hit a goddamned mine last week. The whole crew was thrown through the air. We didn't get the word, but 2 of 'em gotta have been killed. The Pig didn't look like a Pig!"

I already felt desensitized. 2 got killed? Oh, well.

Tex dropped his .45 on his rack. He went straight through the tent to the lister bag (a canvas bag about 3 foot wide, 4 feet tall, hung 5 or 6 feet high from a tri-pod to dispense water from plastic nozzles near the bottom. Iodine tablets were dropped in to kill germs and make the water palatable, with a crappy taste). His mates looked towards me, exchanging words. They sure didn't make me feel like a part of the family.

Our shower was a 55-gallon drum mounted on a platform, if a 6 by came to fill it with water. If not, we'd wander down to the village well for a bucket bath.

"Hey! Da shower's EMPTY!" discovered Bravo. He yelled to Luke in Spanish, making everyone laugh but me. I had French in school.

"Am I invited?" I asked those, throwing their 'muds' on the dirt floor.

"Wrap 'ya a towel. We ain't waitin'!" was Weave's okay.

"Don't forget your weapon."

I followed the team of bathers through the wire and down the hill towards the vil. It was a 2-minute hike; the least expected looking of groups to fight a war, jungle boots and bath towels waving.

"You go first, Ski! And don't take all day!" Weave wasn't being polite, he just wanted to see my expression as I doused myself with the first bucket of icy water. It froze my nerve endings initially, but wanting to be one of the boys, I performed quietly, ending with "This water stinks!"

Some snickered as I moved to the circle formed for security as another bucket dropped in the well. The Village's girls sat by their wares, rearranging cans of Coke then looking up to point and giggle and rearranged their 'Viet Nam' photo albums, melted candy bars from U.S boyfriends, C-rations from passing Marines and other miscellaneous trivialities in their bizarre bazaar. We rallied to the tables with showers of "You numba one, G.I!" Weave took it as a personal greeting to him alone. After he gave a girl a can of peaches he expressed his first smile.

Jame got pissed. "What the FUCK you doin', Weave?" You KNOW we ain't supposed to give the gooks ANYTHING!"

"I'll do as I please, Jame! And don't call 'em that!"

Jame walked back to the hill to avoid a sure confrontation, expanding my education by the hour. No respect for the natives or each other, only a bucket of grimy water and Vietnamese girls, black-marketing.

The sun, just a bright spot in the nighttime, made its way behind the mountains and guard duty came into focus.

Comparing this wasteland to the splendor and safety of the North Woods back home, I wondered how terrible it would be if one had to sit guard in his own backyard just to live another day. The Civil War came to mind. THAT hell was worse then this one, so the history books rendered.

Guard duty broke up the boredom of a good nights sleep, and those nights, in this deep and dark winter, froze one to the bone. Probably dropping to the low 60's, a night with a full moon seemed cause to expect a sudden snowfall, as a motionless body lets the blood sit without warming one's extremities or innards, having the guard want the thermometer to rise to 99 again.

"You can sit on Charlie 25 with George tonight, Ski. Make sure ya stay awake. Dig?" Sgt. Jame recruited me to his Pig because of the words he had with Weave, earlier. Having one less guard made Weave have to pull a watch for himself, so Jame was getting him back for the argument. "If you get cold, DON'T walk around too much. Victor Charlie might put you away."

George was sitting on his Pig. "You can watch from midnight to 0400."

"God bless the USMC, George."

"Unlimited shit and mass confusion?"

The night as most flowed uneventfully. I crashed in my rack at 4, with Luke taking over on the Ontos' 30 cal., peacefully.

I felt slightly more rested at 0730 when I was awakened for our daily inspection. We stood at attention while the Captain walked passed each one with a glimmer in his eye, trying to find a dirty weapon or unpolished boots. No problems, but he requested my presence in his tent. The sun had his billet heated, even early in the day.

"Herstowski, stand at ease. I haven't had time to talk to you about your duties here, but with an MOS of 2533, you know that you have to maintain communications with Battalion and keep the radios clean and in working condition. If you assist in patrols or mine sweeps it'll be for killing purpose only. I don't want you to carry a radio because I have infantry personnel that do that for me. YOUR main job is for comm. with Battalion, and no cursing over the radio. Understood?"

Vulgarisms broadcast over radio waves were unlawful and superfluous because they could be misunderstood or possibly prevent transmissions containing lethal actions. Again, lives were at stake.

Before I could comply, "You will also be in charge of mail pick up, P.X. stops for hill personnel and P.M. of the vehicle. Questions?"

I thought for a moment. Standing in front of an officer and his authority made me nervous. "No sir, no questions."

"Good! If you have any, just talk to Sgt. Jame. He knows his shit!" I was glad he didn't mention Weave.

"Carry on, Private."

"Aye aye, sir." I pivoted out of the tent, smelling a diesel engine riving up.

"Say, Sgt. Jame, when am I supposed to go for the mail?"

"Usually when the sweep team comes back. Ask Luke, I gotta retune this engine." George sat in the driver's seat pumping the gas pedal while Luke sucked on a Lucky Strike, poking at George with a stick.

"You need company for the mail run, Ski?"

"Yah. WHO RIDES SHOTGUN?" The engine roared, so I tried to beat its combustions.

"HUH?"

Luke came by me when I waved him over from the noise. "Do you go on all of the mail runs?"

"Naw. Sometimes others have to go in for maybe a dentist visit or whatever, you know."

"When is the sweep over with?"

"Don' know, maybe 9:30 or 10. You'll see them returned in the 6 by."

I saw the truck returning, to the right of the hill. The road semi-circled the hill, making their distance look like a 2-minute break instead of the 5 it really took.

I walked over to my Mighty-mite to check the fluids. WOW, I thought. It's MY vehicle! Good, and bad. An okay responsibility but hell to pay if something goes wrong. Again, I thought, I'm a radioman, not a cabby!

Luke came out of the tent with his 45 holstered.

"Hey, how come YOU get a pistol and I dig up an M-14? Hell, how am I gonna carry this with all the radio and gear?"

"T.S.!" Luke laughed. "Go to the battalion armor and trade it in!"

"Yah, I know. But when I'm driving?"

"Aww shut up and let's go. The sweepers are here." Dust from the truck's zephyr hit us in the face.

"Cap told me to get us a block of ice. We'll get it on our way back."

"Wanna drive?"

"NO, SKI! It's YOUR job!"

As I drove out the front gate of wire I wondered if I'd hit a well hidden mine or get ambushed. I wondered that for over 100 times going and 100 times returning.

No sundry from the P.X. was ordered, mail and ice our only, but valuable, commodity.

I gave Golf Company (Infantry assemblage of about 100 men) their sack of mail, and the rest to us in the Ontos platoon. I get none, since my address changed twice in three weeks, and home wouldn't get their for at least another week, so here I was, in a hell of a purgatory. But once I DID start getting mail, I became more homesick. Then, I was enrolled for morning patrol.

With tent flaps were dropped for the night, I lay in the rack, hypnotized by the flame on Bravo's candle, thinking about my first patrol. Curiously, I reached my head out of the flap out for a weather forecast. Stars were hiding, but I wished on the few glitterers visible, and I hoped that they were being wished upon over Second City. I wished. Donna…

But partial constellations weren't amazing enough to outshine the gunshot I heard from a hedgerow bushing Hill 22. A millisecond passed when the next sound heard imitated a bee buzzing at supersonic velocity right passed my good ear.

"Shut the goddamned flap, Ski! Do you want to go home early?"

I closed the flap and fell to my rack in a state of justifiable shock, breathless.

The Grunts caught duty, so that set me to thinking about what could happen if someone fell asleep while on guard. With that in mind, a restless night fell ahead with a melody of insects and paw pandering.

Courage is the price that Life extracts for granting peace.

...better run through the jungle, and don't look back.

Rest the soul of the Point Man. He leads patrols and therefore, is the first to trigger booby traps in the pathways least taken by the sane. The most likely to die, the least likely to return home unscathed.

The cowardly but precise act of ambush by trip wire ended many a career and life by an enemy not even present.

Usually a hand grenade was used, but punji stakes (pointed sticks) smeared in feces, propped up in a pit, was a popular and economical way of scratching point men from the scorecard. The grenade 'trick' would damage 2 or more fighters, in the flick of a switch. A wire was tied to the grenade pin with the delay removed, so that when tripped, immediate concussion, and medevac homeward bound.

My previous experience on patrols was at Camp Pendleton, California, and on my 3-day stop at Okinawa's final testing grounds. Being trainees, with the element of friendly turf without killers present, our false sense of security linked with  a nonrealistic bravado may have done more harm then good in learning the skills in the bush. A person could be shown how to rebuild an engine, but didn't really know how to do it until he got his hands dirty.

So at first light and suited for the party, I met with the group in the C.O.'s tent for my indoctrination. No one wore chevrons, so the man in the middle of our baker's dozen was presumed to be the leader.

"Herstowski?", you walk in the middle, behind 'Skeeter'. This is your first patrol, right? No talking out there. Jay, give him another bandolier. Here's a frag."

What a way to make a living. I didn't know any of these men or their names, but we were going out on what could be our last mile. Daily.

I already called in our sit rep to Battalion, now I was doing my second duty 'for God and County.' My third duty of the day would be my run for the mail.

It was already hot enough to leave my shirt clumped up on my rack, with a flack jacket being my suit coat as we filed through the wire as the leader of the pack ordered "Lock 'n load!" Caustic clicks of metal slides and rounds chambering were liberated with the hollow sound of an M-79 grenade launcher readied for the kill. Strength personified, chambering a round. Immense feeling, quite, carrying a loaded rifle, in a jungle, in a war.

The M-79 gave an appearance not unlike a sawed off shotgun about 2 1/2 feet long, single shot, manually fed. The Hep round looked about 4" long with a 3" diameter. It wasn't shot straight like a rifle, but elevated, as the round would be projected at only 250 feet per second. It was escorted 2 players ahead of me.

Behind me was a machine gunner, with his ammo carrier, the rifleman, behind him. They were in heavy metal boxes, these strings of 7.62 mm rounds, the same size rounds that flowed from M-14s. The M-60 weighed over 20 pounds, making most of the runners I saw have to carry it on a shoulder unless they owned 18-inch biceps, in which case they'd still have to trade arms periodically for strain relief. It shot 550 rounds a minute to devastate ground troops. The corpsman carried a .45 cal. and bandages, the rest of us had rifles.

Our hide glistened in the sun as we walked the worn down dirt path to glory. I questioned the tactical gratitude of using a worn pathway. Later, the leader told me "You wanna walk through the jungle, go ahead. YOU can take the point, but WE'LL still walk the path. We don't fuck with Charlie, so he doesn't fuck with us. Get it? If we don't fire into the woods around here, they don't fire at us. It's kind of like a truce in this area. We take care of each other like brothers." He finished with a resentful laugh.

So we angled forward on the beaten walkway. High grass was on either side, close enough for the enemy to reach out and shake our hands through cover galore.

After continuing for 15 minutes, we entered a tree line of dark green excellence. It was a haven from the sun, but in reaching it, the temperature rose, hothouse-like. Gigantic branches resembled arms with open hands, made to foster the dampness and cause an eerie shade with riveting slices of sunlight escaping through their fingers to the ground; again, the Jurassic Era.

Our procession continued, now descending enough to allow me to see the point man descended, fording a stream about 20 feet wide. I got to the moving water, stepped in to feel its chill, and imagined the Spartans landing on the beaches of Iwo Jima; hardly comparable, a teen hero's thought.

The cooling creek was the nadir of our trek. Ascending after wading, the temperature seemed to rise with every step, until I felt that I could hardly breath the 'water-air' in this garden's atmosphere.

No one explained to us in our training, that during the summer here, a person could expect to perspire 24 hours a day, three or more months straight.

We slowed to a stop, with the word being passed to brake for a break. I sat in the weed bed next to the path, wondering if I could do this at age 22. I lit a Winston and said 'NO', to myself, I could NOT do it at age 22!

No contact was made on this patrol, but I wouldn't volunteer for this kind of stint, EVER! Mosquitoes were unbearable enough, let alone the stress factor involved with each step. And the turnaround point was a swamp, next to an almost mountainous incline that held fetid water up to my armpits. All weapons had to be held over our helmets, and an attack would have meant a sure ending of our tours.

We all dragged our feet as we welcomed the sight of Hill 22, just for rack of it. No soda machines or television, no glamour or girls, no water for showers, no fun in the sun. I HATED it already, but loved the pride I felt, doing this for my country.

We assembled in front of the Cap's tent, without a word. The leader went inside, and came out with our Superior dropping a case of Bud off his shoulders, onto the clay. "No contact? Good! Have a hot one, on me." With yesterday's block of ice melted overnight, he went back into his tent while we all stood in the sun waiting for another block of ice to fall from the sky to cool our brew. It didn't happen, so the leader picked up the case and walked to the Grunts tent with the rest to follow. I wasn't invited and felt slighted, so I just went to my area for shade and a nap.

The six were B.S'ing when I fell in the tent. "Good morning, SIR! Kill anybody today?" came from Bravo, snarling. I didn't know him well enough to take it as a joke or an insult, so I didn't answer him as I crowded my rack.

"Hey, Ski!" George called anxiously. "Where IS the mail?" I thought I'd be excused from the rest of my duties with the patrol and all. Uh, uh.

"I'll go along today. I wanna get to the P.X. Here!" He tossed me a can of Black Label that felt like it had been in an oven.

"Thanks, George." "An' here's the church key." (Can opener.)

Close to half of the contents sprayed in my face in a hot lather. Then, worse yet, I took an unbiased gulp of the ale. It was so hot it felt like whiskey going down. Try it sometime.

I poured the rest in the dirt.

It's Miller time.

"GOOOOOOOOOOOOOOOOOOOOOOOOOOOOOOOOO OOOOOOOOOOOOOOOOOOOOOOOOOOOOOOOOOOOO OOD MORNING, VIETNAM!"

"I'm Army Specialist…" broke air on "Dawn Buster" from little Sony's each morning at daybreak, for those in country to growl at as they threw radios against crusty decks beneath them, or for those in the rear to decompose for another 40 winks.

The Specialist in a controlled climate would stretch "GOOD" for a good 15 or 20 seconds mockingly, to those fighting in the fields and to those spit shining their boots for inspection in areas of 110 volts. I got a kick out of the black humor at first, but it wore thin as the days died on. Nothing was very humorous anymore. The heat found us sweating in frenzy, bitching about all inconveniences and picking fights with even the closest of friends. At times, it became impossible to live with each other.

Sgt. Jame eyed me, hunched over on my rack as he cleaned his pistol. "When you gonna get C25 a new handset? An' if you're sick, go HOME!" He tried to spread cheer most of the time, but this time as most others, nothing could stir me.

"I'm just beat from the heat, Sarge. I tried to get you a new handset yesterday and Battalion said they were on order."

"I understand," he replied congenially.

"You know, I tried the thing earlier and it worked okay for me."

I tried a radio check. "Cantilever, this is Cantilever Charlie One (Cantilever being the Battalion call sign, Cantilever Charlie one, the call sign for Charlie Company, first platoon), radio check. Over."

A few seconds passed, then I made a re-call. The answer came shortly. "This IS Cantilever Charlie, I hear you loud and clear. How do you hear me? Over."

"I hear you loud and clear. Break (Changing subject). Did a new handset come in? Over."

"No new equipment has been delivered here yet. Over."

"Roger. Out."

Jame saw me shake my head as I pulled the radio out. Strapped down near the driver's compartment made checking the power supply a difficult chore. "I'll get a new battery. A weak one's been known to cause transmission problems."

Luke was checking the tracks for weakness or hairline breaks. "Did you ask if any mail came in?"

"I forgot!" After recalling, "Yep, it's in."

I got mail from my parents telling me that I should forget about Donna and that they never hear from her, but Luke? He must have had a fan club, because I distinctly remember his share being at least 3 letters or packages at an average mail call.

"Anything for me?"

"Of course, fur head!" Curly hair gave him more than one nickname. "Why the HELL don't you just move IN at the post office?"

Jame laughed with his driver, curbing a touch of my animosity. My feelings stemmed from the war and from a girl I left behind.

With amour in my heart and mind never seeming to weaken, I jumped into the jeep for a ride to Battalion, not even thinking of taking a rider with for Shotgun. I was lucky to have taken my 14 along. I made a quick run, returning to James' waving hand. "The CAP wants to see ya, Ski. Where's yer Shotgun? He wanted to go in with ya, and now he's PISSED! Better get yer shit together, boy!"

"Where the hell did you go?" greeted me in Cap's burrow. "I wanted to go to Battalion today, damn it!"

I couldn't think of anything else to say. "I forgot, sir!"

My mind was reeling again, and now I knotted up my life a little more.

"Listen, Herstowski, you've been here 3 or 4 months, right? Problems or something?"

Sincerity started me. HE is going to worry about a PFC? I told him my story.

"Well, YOU aren't the first one to have loved and lost. You'll lose your life here if you don't think straight. Get back to your area and rest whenever you can. GET OUT!"

"Yes, sir" ended our conversation. I straightened out and flew right the rest of my tour, at least enough to get me home.

"How'd it go, Ski? Did you get Office Hours?" (Informal court martial).

"Luke, why don't you take a rolling fuck down hill with a donut?"

No one is born evil, and I excused myself at the same time. People and their environment influence one's mental geometry, no matter how slight or coarse the brotherhood co-exists. No apologies were given and none would have been accepted. We posed as rough, tough Marines who hated everything and everybody known and unknown. If the *CORPS* didn't corrupt us this way, the war and it's reprehensive cloak of doom and gloom certainly would. And even if there wasn't war, and we weren't calloused, murderous beings of the Corps, the Fighters it produced would have been inefficient collateral, disbanding in it's own "glory."

"Do you know what today is, Luke? Easter Sunday!"

I graduated Epiphany, a Catholic grammar school on the southwest side of Chicago with attending nun's chutzpah opposing Genghis Khan's. Required to attend mass on Sunday's, Holy Days of Obligation, Friday's (from our classroom), with a written explanation of WHY we didn't go to holy communion Sunday with the rest of our class, I felt myself as a model martyr, practicing all sacraments allowed me.

And now I'm here, with a mean disposition, forgetting the resurrection of Christ. The article I read in "Stars and Stripes" was a reminder from the Lord, in print, with an accompanying article below in read, "1967, worst casualty count yet!"

"Relax Ski. Easter was LAST Sunday, you dumb ass!"

OMIGOD, I said to my unholy self, and stepped outside the tent for a look at the sunset. Far off, over the hills, misted a rainbow in the blue, which must've reincarnated me with that view of nature's colors. In a few moments, I felt better, like, maybe a few years ago in a roller coaster, without a worry in the world. The Eye in the sky would forgive me, all my sins.

I shuffled dust, walking around the tent to let the flaps down, causing a stir amongst the tenants. "Keep the dirt down, Priv!" scolded Luke. "C'mon in 'n' play cards." It was time for our Black Jack seminar.

Cards and funny money (American money used in Vietnam, valued as American, though resembling Monopoly game script) traded hands freely, eminently grouping in the dealers favor.

I stood behind Luke, pestering him with a poke in the neck or hateful 'hisses' in his ear as each card he was dealt promised demise. The game was an easy one to learn just screening their play, but the trick was to try to memorize the cards that were already dealt.

Black Jack became a favorite pastime of my war years, especially dealing to Luke, who became my favorite customer. I pulled a few hundred monthly, dealing with a straight deck, never cheating a Dude. Luke left country owing me $691.00, leaving me an IOU for cash that I promptly tore up for posterity.

"Deal me in! How much goes in the pot?"

Bravo began re-shuffling the cards.

"Ski, we're playing BLACK JACK, not poker. ANTE is a quarter to a dollar. Just put your bet in front of your cards, and I'll deal."

So commenced my first hand of Black Jack.

"There's a KING! And a 9 in the hole? Good start, Ski!"

I felt good, until Bravo dealt himself a Jack and a 10. He slid my quarter to his pile, and I put up another 25¢.

"Last of the big spenders eh?"

"This is my introduction to the game, Gents. Please act accordingly!"

"Oh, a virgin shark, eh?"

I lost $5.00 in change when rain started to pelt our canvas.

"Sounds like big drops tonight."

"Weave, we got storms back in Texas that get close to these here. Not quite this bad, though."

The sprinkle stopped a minute then roared into full gear. Tex and me went to the door flap to hear, not see, the downpour. It was black as ink out there and the mild breeze that we left into the tent blew out Weave's candle.

"Can't you a hole's leave that fuckin' door shut? Jesus H. Christ, I feel like bustin' somebody's head." He staggered out of his rack and tripped over an uneven deck of earth.

Sgt. Jame remarked, "Well, looky here! Mr. Weave faw down, go BOOM?"

Weaver rolled to his back with an inebriated gurgle.

"Just you wait 'til I get up, Mr. Jame!"

"Tomorrow morning soon enough, MISTER Weave?"

His answer was a bubbly snort.

Deciding to leave the eyesore lay in the middle of the floor, our flames were extinguished until the next tutorial.

An operation was the talk on the hill, but no one knew where or when. I still thought about glorious interventions with the V.C. or NVA, knowing very well, that as long as the war was fought as it was, no glory could be retained, and honor was becoming a word without meaning.

And could that honor flooded into my brain be lost? I JOINED the Marines. I wasn't a draftee, falling in with the scheme of a typewritten announcement. We must honor ourselves, for personal victory. Rain's roar of resistance met by the canvas top lulled me to a 3 hour rest.

You have to know when hold up, know when to fold up.

I realize that patriotism is not enough. I must have no hatred or bitterness towards anyone.

"C'mon, Ski! They need another Rifleman for the patrol. Suit up!"

"Why is it always ME?"

"'Cause we're friends, remember? I volunteered you, buddy!"

I sat up quickly, with one of my claws scratching at his face for payback. "Thanks a million, slimeball! I'm getting short, and this is how I get treated?"

"HA HA! SHORT? You got 9 months to go!"

"SOOO?"

"Just get ready. We're moving out in 10."

I had all I could do in preparation for the walk in the black forest. Knowing that Luke was told to get me ready, not recruiting me, kept me on speaking terms with him.

I'd engaged with a good handful of these collections now, so I was beginning to feel the salt in my torso mix with the salt ON my torso.

Ol' Sol curved over the horizon, making it bleeding hot for the total force, rallied with "Enemies have been sighted S.W. of DaNang, 15 miles, right around these mountains. 150 of 'em Battalion estimated, so be alert. Don't let me catch anyone smokin'!" The 14 of us trudged again, through the wire down the hill. And the same ol' way we went. Luke ventured two men ahead of me, and I was in the middle. About 15 minutes from our mound of dirt, I lit a Camel from a complimentary pack.

The still, hotter than hell day afforded drops of sweat down my arms through the length of my weapon, for which I'd use an oily rag to wipe my salt off. Rust on the barrel will get you failed inspections, and killed. Chest and back sweat contained on the trousers belt line.

The point man reached and entered the jungle in our way, as count-full times before. He was relatively new, his experience limited to classroom and books.

Then the mutilating crash was heard from up ahead. The Camel fell from my mouth to my sweat-ridden belly with a burn, suppressed as soon as my body fell into the weeds off the side of the trail.

Weaponry fired to our right and hearing the point man's echoing screams, we were pinned down in the weeds. But for not the weeds, we would have been unhidden from the automatic that was trying to end our cause. My body vibrated from fear and recoil with ears deafened from my own rifle and the M-60 machine gun 20 feet away: thuds and booming all around us.

Incoming fire tapered off, but we continued to rattle the ambusher's cage with pot shots. As usual, we couldn't pin point our antagonists, but the smoke from their weapons gave us a general areas to shoot at 'til "Cease fire!" came from the head of the team. It quieted, excepting crying moans from the tree line.

20 minutes or so crawled by 'til I heard choppers in the distance. 4 of the Grunts stood up and charged through the grass, howling and screaming violently, with their weapons emptying on automatic. I thought that this only happened in the movies, I thought that Sergeant Stryker was dead and buried on Iwo Jima. Not so. The Marine Corps was still the Marine Corps. What goes around comes around.

I lay in the tall and quiet weedery thinking, maybe those hard chargers were nuts or drunk, or maybe they wanted to fight the war to end it immediately. Or maybe the point man was a close friend, bitten by Cong's metals. Never the less, I felt vanity impregnating my very being, as I witnessed comrades of few, decimate the enemy's stronghold and existence that morning.

The pacified area was now smoke bombed to mark the helicopter's LZ (Landing Zone). One landed to medevac 3, while another tore up the stage with its mini guns, being as sociable as a hungry eagle. Impersonal rockets also made the choppers unpopular with the NVA any time of the year.

And they left with our past Warriors, us in a large circle awaiting orders. We turned to slowly retreat to sumptuous Hill 22.

A light puff in the wind sometimes flashes me back to the day of non-restrained shockwaves from concussions of grenades that fanned out warnings and steel, not relief from heat.

The answer is blowin' in the wind.

Standing Orders, Rogers Rangers

1. DON'T FORGET NOTHING.
2. HAVE YOUR MUSKET CLEAN AS A WHISTLE, HATCHET SCOURED, SIXTY ROUNDS POWDER AND BALL, AND BE READY TO MARCH AT A MINUTE'S WARNING.
3. WHEN YOU'RE ON THE MARCH, ACT THE WAY YOU WOULD IF YOU WAS SNEAKING UP ON A DEER. SEE THE ENEMY FIRST.
4. TELL THE TRUTH ABOUT WHAT YOU SEE AND WHAT YOU DO. THERE IS AS ARMY DEPENDING ON US FOR CORRECT INFORMATION. YOU CAN LIE ALL YOU PLEASE WHEN YOU TELL OTHER FOLKS ABOUT THE RANGERS, BUT DON'T NEVER TELL A LIE TO A RANGER OR AN OFFICER.
5. DON'T NEVER TAKE A CHANCE YOU DON'T HAVE TO.
6. WHEN WE'RE ON THE MARCH WE MARCH SINGLE FILE, FAR ENOUGH APART SO ONE SHOT CAN'T GO THROUGH TWO MEN.
7. IF WE STRIKE SWAMPS, OR SOFT GROUND, WE SPREAD OUT ABREAST, SO IT'S HARD TO TRACK US.
8. WHEN WE MARCH, WE KEEP MOVING TILL DARK, SO AS TO GIVE THE ENEMY THE LEAST POSSIBLE CHANCE AT US.
9. WHEN WE CAMP, HALF A PARTY STAYS AWAKE WHILE THE OTHER HALF SLEEPS.
10. IF WE TAKE PRISONERS, WE KEEP 'EM SEPARATE TILL WE HAVE HAD TIME TO EXAMINE THEM, SO THEY CAN'T COOK UP A STORY BETWEEN 'EM.
11. DON'T EVER MARCH HOME THE SAME WAY. TAKE A DIFFERNET ROUTE SO YOU WON'T BE AMBUSED.

12. NO MATTER WHETHER WE TRAVEL IN BIG PARTIES OR LITTLE ONES, EACH PARTY HAS TO KEEP A SCOUT 20 YARDS AHEAD, TWENTY YARDS ON EACH FLANK AND TWENTY YARDS IN THE REAR, SO THE MAIN BODY CAN'T BE SURPRISED AND WIPED OUT.

13. EVERY NIGHT YOU'LL BE TOLD WHERE TO MEET IF SURROUNDED BY A SUPERIOR FORCE.

14. DON'T SIT DOWN TO EAT WITHOUT POSTING SENTRIES.

15. DON'T SLEEP BEYOND DAWN. DAWN'S WHEN THE FRENCH AND INDIANS ATTACK.

16. DON'T CROSS A RIVER BY A REGULAR FORD.

17. IF SOMEBODY'S TRAILING YOU, MAKE THE CIRCLE, COME BACK ONTO YOUR OWN TRACKS, AND AMBUSH THE FOLKS THAT AIM TO AMBUSH YOU.

18. DON'T STAND UP WHEN THE ENEMY'S COMING AGAINST YOU. KNEELDOWN, LIE DOWN, HIDE BEHIND A TREE.

19. LET THE ENEMY COME TIL HE'S ALMOST CLOSE ENOUGH TO TOUCH. THEN LET HIM HAVE IT AND JUMP OUT AND FINISH HIM UP WITH YOUR HATCHET.

MAJ ROBERT ROGERS 1759

I found these 'orders' given over 200 years ago from an officer to his troops. They hold true in any war, for successful completion bringing peace and victory. *Our* hatchets were sharp enough to still any quarrel, but we let 'em rust on our belts.

The long, thin country gave us another day to cope with, relentlessly hot. The 'walls' of our tent were tied up, exhibiting another poor excuse for air conditioning as insects violated our privacy. 24 hours a day, they searched over us, next to us, behind us, and if they could, they'd find a way inside of us, to chow down and leave behind a hatchling cavalcade.

It was May, of '67. I recall drought for the last few weeks, clutching all of us in it's dry fingers of feverish proportions, making most want to run AWOL, but where to?

The dirt of Hill 22 was loose with dust, a tan dust that showed hard, siphoning eyes, nose and throat at its leisure.

On vacations, tropical 'paradises' must be fitting, but in war or workplace, the climate proves indignant.

Pig Masters were scrubbing and polishing their green elephants while swearing, sweating, and shunning their place in the sun. I already had the radios checked out, then radio checked into Battalion. No mail arrived, and my rifle shined, so at 2 in the afternoon I was a free man, to do as I please. "Anybody for cards?" I asked the motley crews. All I got was an oily rag for my trouble, and a lousy pitch it was, at that.

"We're workin', you lazy J.O.! Get the fuck outta here!"

"Thanks, Sarge!" I walked back to my area, on the advice of Weave, and dug out some Detective Comics from my moldy footlocker.

Batman foiled his nemesis the Penguin, when a clamor began with the Grunts of 'H' (Hotel) Company. Delta Company left the hill weeks earlier, being 'war worn', and otherwise, under manned. Too many casualties in the field, and "22" made the Company inoperable to perform tasks the 100 man outpost required.

"We just spent 11 days out on those fuckin' Operations!" reminded the C.O. The history lesson didn't impress the Captain, with his reply. "Tomorrow is the start of ANOTHER op, so shut up! One more word, and you'll go on record!"

It wasn't the first display of mutiny we felt on the hill, but ultimately, cooler heads prevailed without a handshake. The bitterness and resentment of our involvement in South East Asia foamed over and onto the officers, full fledged, and never seemed to be governed by the individual. The most heated just said what they thought, whether talking to an officer or a water buffalo.

Luke was on his Pig when I climbed up to tell him the news. "We're hittin' the field again."

"WHA? Where? How go ya' know?"

"The Cap told his Company. I think it'll be tomorrow."

We were a support battalion, the Anti-Tanks, and we went were we were told to go. We might go with the Grunts, or stay on the hill, just like the time we left the hill to aid the South Vietnamese with their CAP or CAC units (Combined Action Platoons, Combined Action Company), while Delta Company remained on the hill with beer and pretzels. Sometimes I'd stay on the hill to maintain radio comm. while the Pigs would sight see, and other times I'd ride the 106's to call in results of contact to our Battalion Commander.

Sgt. Jame was quick to add, "We're going' somewhere with 'Hotel', and it'll be tomorrow. Real early. The Cap tol' me and Weave to ready the Pigs right away. He said we should bring as many rounds as we can take. Glad you reminded me, Ski, 'cause YOU can help carry 'em over. The 6 by set the crates behind our tent. See 'em?"

"No Sarge, the dust is hidin' 'em." I saw the wooden box, but enjoyed teasing the grease monkeys. Tex grabbed me by the belt and forced me to the job.

The sun beat its waves of heat like a set of bongo drums, never missing a beat, liking to laugh at us as we transferred 15 rounds to their appointed destination.

Luke looked inside the driver's pit. "That's enough! Where in hell am I supposed to sit? And what if I hit a mine?"

Weave chuckled. "You stupid shit! If you hit a mine, it wouldn't matter WHAT was in your compartment, now would it?"

It got quiet as Luke thought about it, with the others shaking their heads.

The 2030 sunset found the temps falling to the mid ninety's, as we sat on our racks dealing cards and talking about home.

"Ski's our radio HAM and our C-rat CAN! HEE HAW!"

Weaves humor was ill felt, with the loom of the field tying knots in our thinking. I'd written a letter to my parents, explaining my infrequent ties to them. There was very little to tell, other than facing disaster daily and catching morbid sights of men with guns and guts.

Jame reminded, "Guns GOTTA be clean! Make sure your ammo's clean, too."

Even the heat couldn't keep me from the limbo of sleep. Dozing was an ephemeral friend forever, which I'd hoped would last until my rotation date. The pleasant habit, however, was interrupted wickedly with the growling of the diesel's compressions, powering their exhaust to our breathing systems.

I laid in my rack as if in a drunken stupor, not knowing where I was and not caring about anything, but just desiring a drink of the good life which was hogged away from us 12,000 miles to our front.

I slept dreamless. It became a habit for my mind to be robbed of dreams since I met Vietnam. They're necessary for sanity, I've read, but how can a person trigger or avoid them at will? I suppose a psychologist can explain the theories, but I've never availed a Shrink for my own use. Sometimes dreams do re-occur, but never do they crowd me out. Just blessings for the mindful, I guess.

I thought of the operation and our unknown destination and cause. Would I carry the Prc-25 on my back or be a rifleman? Ride the Ontos or wallow through the mud? I wanted to stay in bed 'til noon.

Would there be an array of bombshells in the air or a mere, unopposed sweep that the press would configure a lose to the American public?

"'Yer stayin' with us," Sgt. Jame yelled out, over the noise of the C25. Choppers were lifting out some of Hotel's Warrior's, forming billowy tornadoes of the hill's top layer, clouding out the sun.

"George is driving, so hold on for 'yer life!" as the tracks flapped and crackled under us. All of the crewmembers were supposed to be able to drive, so George had to practice his stealth, even though we were leaving on what would be a life and death struggle.

Lines of Grunt were ahead of us on the twisting road I'd already traveled a hundred times. The main sweepers led the march, keeping a dirge-opponed rate of advance as they waved discs of discovery over the rock hard surface as our Ontos' tracks jumbled defiantly.

Weave's Pig crept a few hundred feet ahead. He stood on the ridge of the door's opening with radio helmet keeping comm. and arms wrapped around the .30 caliber machine gun, professing love for the steel Groupie.

I had my Prc-25 harnessed on one of the 106's, decidedly a better shoulder to lean on than mine. The 'sitting duck' Joker I became again, as my 9 foot high seat and a 'break neck' speed of 4 mph gave me cause to recall those I'd seen ripped and dragged from the jungle's teeth to a whirling escape with Choppers.

Dying was one thing, but suffering BEFORE the finale, well, *that* obstacle was the leap I wanted to avoid if the Grim Reaper swished his sickle. So, as the Pig rolled ever so plainly, I found my way to the pavement to hike Gruntily, less conspicuous in the multitude than a parakeet perched.

The procession stopped at a curve engineered to our right. Brown asphalt was stabbed for the presence of explosives they suspected. A 'charge' was set, and all went for cover. We were far enough from harm's way, so we sat and waited for the report. It was small enough, but my Mite-Mite and driver would have been torn to shreds with the mine's impact. I looked up at Luke. "Wanna go on a mail run, Pal?"

"Chuck YOU, Farley!" Luke didn't go for unexpected bomb routines.

We got to the hole in the road, which gapped around 3 feet deep, and about 10 feet wide. James' eyes bugged out. "It would've split up our tracks AND the driver! Just keep goin'. George." George's one front tooth, again, indented his bottom lip, as he accelerated to 7 mph.

My travel time to Battalion was 20 to 25 minutes, but it took the company 3 hours to defeat its gravel.

A misty drizzle began as we reached the straighter and more foliated byway dotted with small villages composed of native children with families behind them. They held their hands out, as they jogged next to our Pig for welfare throws of food or smoke. Their skin, darkened from sunrays, glittered with the mist's mis-proportion. I removed my helmet to accept the wetness while it was there. Doffing resembled a solemn respect for the ultimately under privileged of their country.

They're frozen in my mind, these refugees and down trodden, in their own land by a country that felt responsible for their prosperity, yet irresponsible for many actions. I still see the innocent, running barefoot under the palms, all dark haired, all under nourished, all in need of a savior sans shelling.

I'd throw a can of food to the ground for them, being careful not to aim it too close for fear of injuring one without a catcher's mitt. They'd scramble like dogs for the catch of a supper, pushing and shoving, exemplifying survival of the fittest. Those images will never disappear from my mind, therein my life.

"Stay up here, Ski!" ordered James. "One of those kids might drop a grenade down your pants." He said it jestingly, but I had to know it was the truth.

Hand signals ordered us to take a break, the Grunts heading for the roadsides. "Aren't we going to the side of the road, Sarge?"

"Yah, Ski! George, pull to the side and see if you can find a mine somebody forgot, okay?"
He expressed feelings with an extended middle finger.

"I didn't want to delay the little buses that came through here, Sarge!" They WERE little, only large enough to sit 8 or 10 small in stature Vietnamese, but usually another 8 or 10 of them would hang from the sides tensely for return or deposit. I saw 3 or 4 mine-wasted during my stay, twisted and turned sheet metal painted, with cadavers of inopportune travelers lying face down and pointing in rigor mortise as in accusation for the release of their souls.

All four of us lit a cigarette within a minute of each other. Just a bad habit, we all agreed quietly: something to do before we die.

Half finished with the smokes, our invasion lines re-ignited to advance to wherever. I jumped aboard, but stayed from the gun tops.

"Luke, YOU drive. George, sit on top of the guns and watch how far Luke stays from the Grunts ahead!"

Jame sounded unsettled with George's driving procedures. He was to leave at least 100 feet between the troops and the Ontos, but kept moving up impatiently, blaming the slow pace.

We rode another 10 minutes or so when small arms fire broke out near the lead jeep. I rolled off the Pig and clipped Luke on the back of his head with my knee, then thudded on the ground in front of the halted vehicle. I scuffled and kicked up dirt, finding a mud puddle to slip and fall in. The mist was hard enough to leave traces, but stopped too soon for lasting relief.

I called up to Jame. "See anything?" George had his back up against the rear of the Pig, lighting a Salem.

More small arms fire answered my question as Grunts ambled pack-heavy to the hidings in the plants on the roadside.

I set my rifle in the Pig's back door opening and went for the handset to listen for a sit rep. There were casualties, and it sounded like the V.C. hit a few of our officers.

"Hotel, this is Hotel Actual. Need Medevac, ASAP!"

"Actual, this is Hotel, I have received, and WILL comply ASAP!" The firing continued, and the deteriorated radio procedure meant mass hysteria in our weakening situation.

"Someone's been hit," I informed the crewmembers and the Grunts who began to gather behind our protection. Luke had his pistol drawn, showing a vexed look on wrinkle brow.

"Gimme the set, Ski!" He grabbed the handset from my reaching hand. "Hotel, this is Charlie 2-5. Need help up there?"

"YES!" demandingly.

Jame was at the .30 cal' commanding, "Drive up, Luke! You're too slow!"

I hopped into the Pig's compartment, hoping that the shooting would stop before our arrival. Luke floored the Ontos as Jame left short bursts out of the machine gun. George sat next to me, lighting another cigarette as he slid the barrel back on his 45 to lock and load. "It'll be okay, Ski. Nothin' ever happens" through his cigarette.

We rambled ¼ mile up the road where lead still flew. The Grunts continued to fire as we drove passed them.

"Jump out!" yelled Jame. My helmet made a distinct clump on the ground when I landed. We made it to the rice paddy side, for a buffer in our roll. My boots were toe first in the paddy water. "You okay, George?"

I saw no injuries, as he reached for another smoke. Our sleeveless elbows were bleeding from flopping on the hard turf.

"Were ya going'?" he yelled as I rolled away from him to spread us out.

"One grenade'll get you all, remember?"

"Oh, yah!"

Rounds ricocheted off of the Ontos, sounding thudded, like a washtub hit with many blunt instruments.

The firing slackened when some loud charges, maybe M-79's, thumped into the ground a few hundred feet from the Pig. We saw the Grunts in our peripherals crawling back to the road, so I felt it was time and motioned to George to inch along with the rest.

Energetic Choppers buzzed in as I got to the two Pigs and their crews. We were 100 feet or so from arms that were wrapped across each other on each man's chest, white gauze, crimsoning, and a chalky shade blemished their complexions. A man's cover lay on the ground, exposing his head with a flowing, red gash that awaited attending. More horror, a stomach wound; crying while barfing bloodied C-rations.

Some of the Grunts headed into the tree line to the left of the road and forward, shocking all in their view with automatics, M-79's, and hand grenades. We could hear crazy laughter, "Mama Efer's", and "C-Suckers" amidst crashes, booms, and rat a tat tats. The sounds resonated and pierced the village grounds, now making THIS the worst place in the world.

Some Grunts and platoon leaders were doing their best to wring out testimonies from the already terrified village people, slapping one elder in the face and grabbing another by the shirt in an attempt to choke the life out of him. Seeing this made me wonder who the hell is running the show? Can we expect to gain a following of Vietnamese by acting like street gangs from a ghetto in Jersey City?

Luke saw my puzzled stare. "These gooks KNEW about the ambush, and they saw us coming. They could've sent out SOME kind of warning, but NO! We're fighting for THEIR freedom, Ski'. We got ours, just waiting back home. See the guys on the ground and hear the helicopters?" He turned his head in the opposite direction because his eyes looked really teary when he looked at our wounded. Now, as before, confusion and frustration.

"Cover your eyes gentlemen, the chopper is landing," was redundant advice given by Weave as the medevac hovered, then landed. In a flash, the bodies were loaded and swished off to never, never again, land.

"We're movin'! Let's go. JUMP ON!" Jame seemed in a hurry, not gripping with the order from the front of the parade that continued to march us on.

"Luke! Let the Grunts pass, then fall in be- hind 'em."

"Yah, sure", frazzled and worn from the enemy contact, noise, bugs, danger, hatred, and the ever-angry sun.

The rest of the day turned dull, with Mother Nature offering her pests as our only opposition. Insect spray must have served as an intimidator, the suckers only sounding for reinforcements when the green can was passed from body to body. Called an ointment, it trans- formed sensitive skin into rash strips. I dwelt bug-thoughtful, as the night dropped in on us for 50 percent alert.

Finding a place to crash wasn't difficult to do. Any nook or cranny, and most square yards of surface looked the same. If it offered shelter and cover from the foe it became a fair den. But before I bedded down, I had to deal with the Sergeant named Weave.

"Herstowski, you get midnight to 6,NO SHUT EYE! Understand?"

"Yah, but I thought the duty was 12 to 4!" I became REALLY out of sorts. Being the junior 'prisoner' in our Mighty Few platoon of 7, I usually got stuck with the worst time for guard post. But 12 to 6? Pure torture!

"Feel discriminated? I just want you to pull a few hours off the crewmen's clocks. They been the ones driving 'YER ass around so you could stay off 'YER feet. And Jame and me are in command, so WE don't HAVE to pull ANY guard duty if we don't wanna. REMEMBER?"

I pointed to the area of rest I'd be at when midnight came around, and left it at that.

So when the clock struck 2355, George nudged my shoulder for another of my mornings of unconditional alert. Without a barbed wire defense, our vulnerability was easily calculated at 100%, and it made me wonder why we weren't at 100% alert.

I fled to the top of C25 for a bird's eye view of the river 300 feet to our front. I may as well have kept my eyes closed, or caught another 40 winks while I sat up there, because the night's purple cloak made the observer sight deaf like a Pennsylvania coalmine.

Go outside, far away from ALL lighting, with a cloud filled sky, and try to see ANYTHING! Impossible, you might conclude? RIGHT! It WAS impossible, and adding the 'Black Hole' element with an enemy who would fight to the death to run you out of their own back yard, made a Warrior cringe with intestinal *in*fortitude. They also fought with the element of surprise, which wasn't booked as a dirty tactic unless you were on the receiving end.

But that was only one of the rules of guerrilla warfare that Gunnery Sergeant Such never revealed to me when I enlisted for service at the Berwyn post office. I'd have joined up, no matter what, so it didn't matter WHAT he told me.

I also recalled my Dad writing, "Don't EVER volunteer!" The stink of the bug repellant on my hands rose to my nose with an invigorating effect. Almost like a 'No Doz' out of a chemical factory.

Hell, it must have been 60 degrees out, but I wore my shirt to keep warm in the surprising chill of the damp forest air.

0500 found darkness yet, as the clouds curtained any attempt the sun made to start the new day. I continued to stare at the nothingness presented to me, and began to hallucinate, with sounds of creatures becoming the enemy's sniper rounds.

Slapping myself repeatedly helped me stay awake, but not alert. I jumped from the Pig and did some motioning exercises to warm up, and then all hell broke loose on the riverbank. I fell to the ground tearing up my knuckles, glaring at tracers (Every fifth round in a string of bullets that sizzles as a flare to show the fire of direction) the M-60's were firing in retaliation. Explosions sounded demandingly, and their flashes unfriendly showed prone bodies of Marines destined for American History detention according to some of our Wire Services.

I was bare headed, as I began to empty my first magazine trained at the firing from across the river. My helmet was on the Pig, but no matter. The damn thing made a habit of tipping forward to misalign my usually fret-sweated glasses, distorting my field of vision anyhow.

On our side of the waterway, I could see L.A.W.'s (Light anti-tank weapons, disposable, replacing 3.5 mm rocket launchers) power unleashed by the Grunts, with screams and yells of irredentism that echoed cries of their processor's on Guadalcanal's beachheads.

C25 was in position, Jame trying to get the radio operational. "This handset's STILL not workin'!"

I got myself to the Prc-25, to find the radio still turned off. "I GOT IT", I yelled in his ear.

"Actual, this is C25. Sit rep. Over."

I gave the call twice, with no response. Slight breaks in the clouds showed Jame my shaking head. He snatched the handset from me and tried to make contact with our leader, twice, without success.

"Get the engine running!"

It started with the first turn.

"Now, GET OUT!"

Jumping into the cockpit, Jame turned the Ontos 90 degrees to the right, and while flicking the headlights on and off, found an opening in the tree line in which to fire flachette rounds at will. "George, find the C.O. and tell him that we're gonna stop the incoming RIGHT NOW! And HURRY BACK!"

The sun's light was welcome, but it barely helped our vision. I lay next to the Pig's tracks with handset pushed against my ear, waiting for a call and inevitable burst of flames from our cannons. George was returning, tripping over legs and broken tree limbs.

"Go ahead and shoot! We got the okay to do what we want!"

The firefight radiated on as Jame motioned for me to get down to the right. I fled with all of my equipment, slamming the radio down on the ground ahead of me, which made a rough LZ for my chest. I lay prone in the dirt while firing semi-automatic.

The first projectile caught me off guard. My left ear never came back to the world of hearing, but my right ear was semi-spared, covered by a handset in most clamorous of times.

The jungle was torn with darts distributed from the round's cone setting on its tip. It made the sound of the surf, 'swoosh', as it tore through the plants and flesh in the garden of un-Eden.

Another 106 took chase, seeming to explode as soon as it left the barrel of the rifle. The backlashes removed semblances of a tree behind the Pig, and the grass smoldered, protesting our actions, a propos mother earth.

Unnoticed by most of us, the sun cleared the clouds from its face, amplifying the smoke screen we created with our power show.

"I'm getting' SICK!" protested George, crouching list-fully from the layer of the self made dust from all of the guns that still wanted to fire.

And, incoming remained the same, kicking up the ground, and strewing bits of the bark splintered from the trees.

"Fire in the hole", the muffled voice of Luke announced. One more strafing on order plunged lower, and more directly on the beach.

Weave's crew had joined the fray earlier, and instead of the fight drawing to a close, booming's and rattles flowed on raucously, as if to dash out and reverberate their independence at a mock Fourth of July celebration minus the pop and beer, sack races on picnics, Mom's apple pie and homemade potato salad.

And I didn't even *think* about a parade.

A firefight, we were told, should only last about 30 seconds to a minute, so what we were attending must not have been a firefight, but a volcanic eruption. It would've lasted another day, if not for the Air Force. It came over the radio.

"Sarge, we gotta pull back!"

We saw the infantry on both sides trying to crawl backwards, still firing and reloading. Phantoms (Jet bombers) could be heard screeching to our call, with their shipment of fire and brimstone they'd drop as a calling card.

"Let's get the fuck outta here!" Jame yelled. I threw the radio on the Pig's top, even as Luke was maneuvering into escape position, and the rounds continued to pelt the trees and dirt, but none of us.

"C'mon, you Polish turtle!" they all seemed to scream at me in unison.

I came close to bashing out my front teeth on the platform the Ontos provided for me to land on, as I scrapped and clutched for dear life to the metal monster. Luke floored the already moving vehicle, with stragglers from Hotel Company lunging for a ride.

"Easy, Luke. Let 'em on!"

"I WANT OUTTA HERE!"

Trying to board a moving Ontos proved to be a near impossible task, with the sides of the vehicle's only 'chicken bars' being the 106 barrels, but they had to be reached up to, and the turning tracks below then offered only crushed toes and a one way ticket home, footless.

"Stop the Pig, Luke!"

When he stopped the rig, at least 10 Grunts crawled, climbed and otherwise, pulled each other up to the escape mode.

"Okay Luke, LET THE GOOD TIMES ROLL!"

We felt the terrible heat expanded behind us by gelatin mixed with gasoline by the ton. If the explosive fires didn't get them, the heat surely must have.

Luke pointed towards an assembly of scattered troops, with James' ok over the radio. He pulled the Pig next to Weaves', his cargo of riders fondly dropped off to return to their fire teams, myself loosening my flack jacket to drop to the ground. The inside was sloppy with sweat and dirt, so I traded it in for my jacket, which promptly transferred to the same condition in a few minutes.

"Actual this is Charlie 25. Sit rep. Over."

"Charlie 25 this is Actual. We had 6 WIA, 3 KIA. Presently waiting for orders to next destination. Over."

"Roger. Out."

I told Jame who looked at me with turned down lips. We both wondered how close we came to be on the same list, and at the same time, I wondered how many of the enemy wouldn't return home for campfires.

A conflict fought in my heart again, between right and wrong, yes and no, good and evil. Taught about communism in grade school, it was presented as an octopus, with all eight tentacles grasping and choking all who interfered with its commitments of supreme rule, with the State being the only shareholder. And God was unheard of under a commie regime, so the Catholic Church gave an unchallenged description of the horrors laced with a tangled government. In plain English, we were scared into belief of our own God, which was immeasurably better than getting squeezed to death by the arms of the spider's cousin.

Maybe the severe tongue lashing spit out by Monsignor Cummings at Epiphany gave me the force to fight communism in brutal fashion. His reverent impression of the importance of God without opposition was stamped on me forever, for in all of man's accomplishments there lay a fallibility with a deficit of a supreme being, who is God. And to even *think* that we are supreme or supreme beings at that is a monstrous joke.

Right or wrong, we fought the rule of communism while suffering in a climate of the damned. Sgt. Jame applied his humor, throwing a case of C-rates out of the back of the Pig. "Here's 'yer chow, Pukes. EAT!"

We looked at the cardboard chorus of crap, then scrambled for a meal box that didn't contain a portion of Ham and Lima beans; better than a starving alternative or a sharp stick in the eye.

"I want Bean's n' Franks!" said Weave, pushing his associates aside for first pick. "AND, I'll take the Ham n' Eggs for dessert."

We silently applauded as he took the meals to his Pig to chow down, solitarily.

"He's eating with all his friends, again," Jame exclaimed. "I feel sorry for him. He wasn't this bad when I first met him. Kind of a fun guy at first, this place really turned him around."

We were all changed or getting changed from the fighting and all else that coupled with the war. Generals and Presidents could babble on with their smarts that proved how we were the victors in small or large skirmishes, but there's never really a winner in a war. Both sides lose entirely or partially, lives, limbs, and most assuredly, minds.

I was spooning into the can of fruit cocktail that complimented a pressed pork persuasion when a call came in. I saved a can of fruitcake for any kid in any village, and then answered the call.

"Actual, this is Charlie 25."

"Charlie, this is Actual. Send your Actual to the front."

"Roger. Out."

I pointed to Sgt. Jame, then to the area for a meeting of the minds.

"Ski! Couldn't they just give the information over the radio?"

"I guess not, Sarge. Besides, you're getting fat! You need the exercise." It was refreshing, to be able to jest with someone of higher rank without worrying about getting reprimanded.

"You'll get 'yers", as he one-stepped over jungle debris of sticks and stones to reach our top commander.

The weird looking tree we used for shade creaked side to side with the slightest of breeze, sounding as though it was on its last limb. Orange powder decorated the ground that the roots anchored in to. Unknown to us, the Agent Orange was cancering the life out of the all plants, later on, people. We were cleaning our personal weapons, when Jame returned with the word. "We'll be movin' out in an hour an' I don't know where. Just follow the one in front of you, Luke."

We lined up parallel to the bubbling river, all 100 of us or more, awaiting the order to move out. The sun bleached and baked, prejudice to no one and nothing, with the diesel engine submitting heat from below. It surprised me that it wasn't over heating.

"Sarge" Luke warned, "shouldn't I shut the engine down? It's bakin' us!" Jame looked to the head of our convoy.

"Yah, go ahead. Looks like we'll be sitting here awhile yet."

Hurry up and wait came to mind. It was the same story in any branch of the service, any-where, anytime.

With half of the convection oven cooling, I jumped off to stretch my legs. Boredom was another faction war can't do without. I leaned against the side of the Pig and heard a round fired from across the river. The small arms projectile landed in the sand-like floor near a group of 5 Grunts who were standing around B. S.ing, pissing them off. "When the fuck are we gonna move?"

Laughter from associates.

A closer look at them showed them to be grubby, intimidated and forlorn, uncaring and bitter, ready to raze Vietnam. Their faces were unshaven and dirty, hair greasy and sweaty, green trousers of jungle style had flattened spots that were light browned from their bed stays in the clay. Shirts were browned to promote business suits, with lower pockets weighted down with hand grenades and hot cans of Coke Cola while top compartments held C-ration cigarettes. Crusted mud protected their forearms from the sun.

Then, I looked closer at myself. I was the same, on the outside to be sure. But on the inside, I began to wonder how my soul's replicate would show. Certainly not with a bright outlook on life as it used to view. More changes to come, I hoped not for the worse, but what was meant to be was meant to be, a gifted scholar once determined, probably of Shakespearean genre.

The prophecy occurred finally, with the commander's jeep moving at the lead, with infidels struggling behind with guns at the ready.

"We're startin' Luke. Let 'er rip!"

"When you gonna let me drive again Sarge?"

"When the war's over, George!"

A half hour passed when I jumped back on.

"Can't handle it, eh, wimp!"

A snapped forefinger against Luke's neck acknowledged his wise-ass remark.

Some Grunts became walk weary in the furnace heat, and deposited extra LAW's, grenades and whatever on the Pig to lighten their load. A few deposited *themselves* on the Pig, moaning and groaning from the aches and pain, induced from search and destroy.

"You guys REALLY got it made!" came from a machine gunner. "Why didn't *I* get a slacker's job like this? You guys never gotta walk! It's like a job in the office!"

Jame didn't like the last word. "OFFICE? Who the fuck 'ya think nailed that tree line this morning? 'Yer a REAL asshole! Keep talkin' that shit, and you'll be walkin' again!"

The Grunt didn't respond, but removed his helmet and laid his head back to rest.

Mental anguishes happened frequently, and tossing in the towel was the best resolution. Most quarrels were petty, but pride was diminished with each of them: pride of the Corps, pride of the Warrior's, pride of country.

The trail we made the first few hours was rough to blaze, obstacles of terrain density being the driver's most formidable foe. Jame jumped in front of the Pig to aid Luke a few times to 'thread the needle' of trees.

Large streams didn't bother C25, but the Grunts swore and slid in the waist deep water of the first one. As usual, the water's fragrance proved stomach turning.

"Smells like a garbage pit! What the hell is IN this stuff?" Luke was the closest one to the cesspool the Ontos was stirring up, getting the full gravity of the situation. "Sarge, can I be relieved of duty before I puke?"

"Son, you're doing a fine job. Keep it up!" Jame didn't feel like driving, and he surely didn't want to put George on the sticks.

We moved on, through this tropical rain forest that I marveled. Some views explained Paradise to a tee, with foliage joined and intertwined, forming nature's canopy of vine and branch. Our expedition passed under it, experiencing the cooler, dampening air a 100-foot long area concealed from the sun.

Flower's scented it, like incense brought forth from the earth, as if to entice the larger than average jungle bees. One of them looked big enough to carry a cherry tomato.

Swamps were ranker than the streams, with the stream's moving water helping to burn out viruses in the sun. They were tricky to wade through for men tied down with cementing weights.

Some held on to the side of C25 for balance, while some of them jumped on to clear some of the mosquito's maternity wards.

Fowls of the air flew in the trees freely and curiously. Some flew close, fanning beautifully hued plumes, as if to tell us that there are glorious and more spectacular things to do with our lives than what we're doing with them now. The gigantic trees they dwelt in looked to have been seedlings when Abraham Lincoln became the president of the United States. With a species of birds flying over them, scenes of the original King Kong reflected back to me. I forgot about the war temporarily, and asked myself what kind of animals lurked in the dark recesses of the adjacent jungles. I didn't remember any indoctrination from the Corps pertaining to animal life on the continent we were marooned upon. They did warn us of snakes, venomous enough to kill 10 with one bite and the insects, of course. "Take your malaria pill daily."

The signal was passed on to take a break. I jumped down to find a mud puddle with my name in it. The clothes that I had been wearing for three days were ready for the laundry anyway. I stripped, in front of God and everybody, to refresh my flesh with some clean rags.

"That looks mighty fine, "Luke complimented. "You goin' on a date?"

"When I yell 'Toilet paper', you come rollin' in!"

George lit up a cigarette then pointed to the sky, laughing, preaching, "It's a sinful man who goes to the bottle. Look what you done did to yoo'self!"

The scenery 30 years ago still elates to my memory in dreams, me walking through a haunting, melodramatic drama with my wife and children, coupling our hands in the ever Utopic Dawn of Time. Carefree without the fear of gunfire, I would reach for the fruit of a Papaya tree to divide with my wife and children of a new dawn. It was pleasant enough to watch my visions that presented an alternative to the war fields, beautification less bloodshed.

Luke looked at me curiously. "What's on your mind, Ski? Got the 'jungle jitter's? Or did 'ya get a 'Dear Ski' letter?"

"All of the above. I just wish I could go home for a while to patch up a few things. Ya know?"

"Yep." He was out of the cockpit, staring around at our tropical forest frame, looking inquisitively at the emerald belt waving in the wind on high. We had no comfort of a breeze the treetops experienced, but their boughs offered a haven from the sun.

"Hey, let's get the hell outta the sun." He pointed and navigated himself through the tallest of elephant grass to the glade in the shade. It screened out the sun, but also harbored scores of bugs of a hundred divisions. We sat on the grass shaded, swatting and slapping at teams that wouldn't succumb to our handball practice, minus wall or ball.

"Luke," I complained, "Your fantasy land isn't the answer". I stood up slapping, and walked back to the Pig in the sun.

He followed me in a pissed off ire that he seldom expressed. "Well, I tried!"

Jame was sitting in the rear port, sweating to beat the band. "Dear God in heaven, how did I wind up in hell? I was a God fearin' man 'till I got here. Do I deserve this?"

George leaned against the Ontos, near enough to his crew chief as if rendering his consolation to the man.

"Sarge, nothin' lasts forever, and you've been in these spots enough 'a times to know that everything's gonna work out okay." The only element missing was a pat on the shoulder.

"What's up?"

"Nothin" alerted George. "We're just talkin' about goin back home."

Luke and I both saw the anguish in James' eyes. Everyone from the fields showed the blank stare.

I got on the radio for our sit rep. at Jame's spiteful request. "Do you think that Mr. Ski can call for our next move?"

"We might stay here tonight. That's all they told me."

"Ain't this some shit? Another night in these stinkin' boonies?"

James got to the top of the Ontos to scream four letter words rivaling a drill instructor's argot. He pulled the slide back, re-chambering a round in the .30 cal., making him an enemy of all on the grounds. Luke and George pivoted to his side to lax and clear the machine gun.

"You goin' nuts, Sarge? What 'cha wanna do with the 30?" Luke yelled to his Leader who was re-balancing his thoughts.

"Nothin'! I'm just screwin' around, Luke. Just screwin' around." He stares into the trees.

This wasn't Sgt. Jame. It had to be the heat, for a starter.

It was my turn to consolidate us. "Sarge, sit down awhile and relax. The sun'll be setting soon, and it'll cool off." I handed him my canteen of hot, iodined water. He took a mouthful, and sprayed it in the air.

Luke took it with a grain of salt. "Why you rotten son of a …"

"Whoa!" George interrupted. "Easy now. If you wanna fight, stick 'yer heads up my ass and fight for air!"

Luke was on the rebound. "Let's play cards, you Twerp."

We had no cards, so we guarded for Jame's sanity. His yells were heard by nearby Grunts, who grinned and bared it. They saw flare-ups before and chalked it up as another casualty of war, with nothing else to do but laugh at it. But then after it all, the sergeant calmed down quickly enough to remove the red alert signal from our perimeter. His anger and trial of war composed his war cries.

I called in for another sit rep.

"…be advised that our perimeter will form at our present posit, 100% alert!"

"We're stayin' the night, Sarge."

Instead of another display like the last one, He gave a knowing smile and said, "Okay boys, you know what to do."

The last 2 of the crew looked at each other and shrugged their shoulders.

In the tone Jame gave, it sounded like he didn't care WHAT his boys did. Maybe his mind was still in the heat of the night, but his resignation to fulfill his commanding duty more than annoyed the three of us.

Luke told George that he was going to tell Weave about the misconduct. "'Yer nuts, George! Don't even bother telling that a--hole what happened.

He won't help out, anyhow. He might even report it to Battalion. Then what?"

"He'd need witnesses" I obliged. I was hoping that even Weave, being near the same age of Jame, would show his compassion with his war background showing.

"What the hell's goin' on down here, Jame?" It was Weave's way of introducing his entrance. "Got a cold 6 pack?"

"I ain't got nothin' here, Weave. What do 'ya want?" He spoke in a troubled, defensive voice. "I don't want nothin' from you, Hillbilly!"

He sat down next to Jame, acting con- siderably subtler than ever.

"Sarge, any problems I could ease away for 'ya?" He spoke in a whisper, so as not to let the tribe know that he was weakening to help a fellow man in need.

"Sgt. Weave, NO ONE can stop my problems here, and I don't have a cold ANYTHING, thank you!"

Sgt. Weave walked away with his lips pressed together hard. With his reputation of being a Rowdy, nobody wanted to fall to his sarcastic aid.

Bravo asked Luke what the problem was.

"No problems here, Bro. Jame just got some readjustments to make, that's all."

"Never noticed anything before, Luke. He seemed like a nice, laid back guy. Maybe you guy's been messin' with him too much?"

"Naw. He just needs some R&R, that's all. He'll feel better after he gets laid."

"I'm going back to my Pig."

The sky light shone its gloom for our only luminance. We were all ordered to trip the light fantastic until dawn prevailed for a break in the action, even after the last few, difficult days.

I resigned myself to another night of misery and misconception, hoping that no lost snake would venomize me or that a mad monkey would mistake my head for a coconut.

The darkened forest didn't permit shadows in its atmosphere, so I was allowed to stand, sight unseen, next to C25 while Luke sat in the driver's seat. Jame leaned against the 30, and George slowly walked around us on the turf.

"Christ, Ski, its only 10 o'clock!" Luke got quiet for a few counts. "If I was back in California now, I'd be at San Bernardino, sweatin' out beer by the surf with one of those Beach Bunnies on my lap. How about you, Ski?"

"I don't know, Luke. Maybe drivin' around, stoppin' for a hamburger. Or goin' to a Sox game. Or takin' a shower."

"A shower WOULD be nice, wouldn't it?"

George heard our wishful thinking, adding, "How about Kentucky Fried Chicken, or a foot long hot dog. How about a little ice in our water? HUH?"

His emphasis on the word, 'huh', gave proof of his bitterness, showing us unarguable with our own distaste for life at this time, being a personal descent to be dealt with alone.

I looked up and back to see Jame wrapped around the machine gun for his beauty sleep. I tapped Luke on the shoulder and pointed to our chief while I snickered through my nose. He looked back at me with a turned down smile.

"Don't bother the guy, Ski. Sleep'll help him lose the blues. Hey, did you find any cards?"

"Where? Did I miss a drug store on the way up?"

"Ski, you're a riot!" George stood in front of the Pig to gain our attention. "Yah, the drug store was on the left, 2 miles back. Wanna take a walk?"

"Right George. You take point, and I'll be right behind you, okay?"

He stared at the constellations in view, disregarded back in the big cities by clouds of pollution shoveled into the air by cars and unfiltered factories.

Little specks of glowing stones were visible often, falling to the earth for final landings.

"Guys, see those meteorites?" Luke advised.

"They're falling all over the place! I hope we don't get killed by one of them!"

"Your chance of getting KIA'd from a VC bullet is better than getting hit with one of those little stones, dip shit! I saw hundreds of them tonight, how about you guys?"

Neither of them answered. They just kept gazing at the haven bound stars that glittered and sparkled by the thousands without power of their own. "One star up there for each day I have left here." The 'twinkle, twinkle' blueprint continued.

"Hey, Ski," George whispered. "I'm goin' to sleep for a while. Wake me up if anything happens."

He lay down in the weeds next to the Pig. Snake bait.

"Ski, you tired?"

"Why? You need a rest?" His voice was rationed, as though he gulped 2 pitchers of beer in a pinch.

"I'm crashing, Ski. I can't hold my eyes open anymore."

"I'll yell before I shoot, Luke."

I was fully alert, that witching hour. One of four HAD to remain on the defense, Lord knowing how many fellow Spartans went to sleep in the woods for their own solitary cover.

Thinking on that order, I began to conclude that I might be the only one awake within 100 yards, so falling asleep was the least of my concerns.

The sandman did arrive at about 0300, invading my eyelids with grains of fatigue that burned my eyes and invited my lids to close.

I couldn't stand the inspiring monotony of another falling star, so cautiously I nudged Luke for his turn at guard.

"Wake up George. Jame is in the same position he started in. Maybe he got a sun stroke, or something."

"Go sleep somewhere, will 'ya? 3:30? Where does the time go?"

I climbed onto the Pig and laid under 3 of the guns, cradling my 14. Luke sat in the hole near my feet. "Luke you'd best get up and walk around to wake up. George is on the ground, next to the tracks somewhere. Wake him up to keep you company. You both got 3 and a half hours sleep, so you should be okay."

"Right, Ski. Shuddup and go to sleep!"

"Sorry. I just don't want to get awakened with a knife against my throat.

"Don't worry, Pal, with George here at my side, we could stay awake 'till doomsday."

We were passing time all night long, and we never saw a face we talked to. Shaded nocturnally, we became specters in the gloom- iness, pausing from talk only to marvel at the falling novas.

The few hours of sleep tried my body at its limit's. It was a tease, I thought, allowing a body to slumber at one third of its requirement, then drumming upon it with steel weights while
combustibles from the sky bake it inside and out to a golden turn.

My eyes opened to gray thickness. "No sun today? What did you guys do when I was gone?"

My attempt to start the day thinly jovial went over the crew heads as they polished 106 barrels. That's what James meant when he told them that they knew what to do.

I left them to their chores for mine. The battery was weak, and I had only one left, so the Operation must be coming to an end. I hoped.

"Actual this is Charlie-25. Radio check. Over."

Radio check with new power source was SOP (Standard Operating Procedure.)

"Charlie-25 this is Actual. I hear you loud and clear. Wait."

Jame was writing a letter home, maybe from where his problems stemmed. Feeling the lose of a loved one to death or an arrow misguided by cupid, may have been the reasoning behind his contempt. I wanted to find out, to help him regain his form, so I looked over his shoulder to read his 'newspaper'. It was blank except for the word, "Dear."

I turned away, asking him, "How's it going' Sarge? Get enough sleep last night? You looked bushed, so we took over your watch for you."

"Thanks, Ski. I don't feel so good. Worn out. Don't want to be in the fuckin' Marine Corps, anymore. Just too much on my mind."

"We're all like that Sarge. Just gotta keep pushin', that's all."

His look was one of death warmed over. Eyes half closed, starring incomprehensively, with a distorted to angry angle on his mouth completing his scowl, it personified a complete lack of interest and the morale imbalance of the foot soldier in this terrible guerrilla war.

"When did you eat last, Sarge? 'Ya know, 'ya gotta eat to stay alive!"

He didn't look up, but he mumbled. "I don't give a fuck anymore. Nothin's worth anything anymore. Nobody cares anymore. *I* don't care anymore."

Behind him, in the open compartment of C25, were crumpled and torn pages of a New York daily journal. I reached in for a sheet. It told of the protesting, the flag burning and name-calling. Photos deliberated images of signs held high, denoting us as warmongers and baby killers. Some of the photos showed police bloodying their nightsticks on skulls of the mis-lead. Some signs read, "Bring the Boys Home Now!"

I believed the strife and depression Jame suffered came from the war back home, not only the one we engaged for them here. I leaned back on the Pig and waited for the upcoming sit rep.

"Charlie-25 this is Actual. Radio check. Over."

"Actual this is Charlie 25. Loud and clear. Request sit rep. Over."

"Charlie this is Actual. We're movin' in 10. Over."

"Sarge, we're movin' in 10 minutes!"

His stare looked reverted to reality, as he ordered "Saddle up, you a ho's! GEORGE, DRIVE! LUKE, guide this boy outta here!"

I noticed both of the workers exerting smiles through their sweat, assuredly due to their astronaut in charge's re-admittance to earth's gravitational pull, plunking him down, both feet on the ground.

Weave turned his head around as he stood in position with the .30 cal. Their Pig grumbled 100 feet ahead, but in a glance I could see the 'thumbs up' signal he flashed as a peace offering to all on C25, or maybe he just pleasured with the fact that his chum was back in the world of the attentive.

The slopes worsened in our advance, as both Pigs found the soft, marshy floor comparable to a sand dune in Indiana. Take one step to fall back two.

Charlie 24 was frozen in the mud ahead of us, and pulling up next to it, we found Tex knee deep in a slough of despair, looking stupid as he attempted to push the 9 1/2 ton behemoth onto the shore of the ooze.

"Was never like this in Texas, you'd best believe!"

Bravo dragged on a Salem. "Pull the chain outta the back door, Cowboy. When I asked for 'help', I didn't mean for you to PUSH this damned thing!" Weave suppressed his anger for a change. "Jame! You gotta get around us to pull me out with 25. I can see dry ground on the sides." He pointed. "Go STRAIGHT to it. At 90 degrees! Get stuck, and I'll kill 'ya!"

Luke was already back on C25 standing next to me. We were both looking down at our supposed pathway for George, watching for flaws in the flora that might sink or hold us for a swamp's kill. For an instant, I returned to Pine Lake, kneeling at the front of the boat, observing the weeds in the upcoming brine to guide my Dad left or right so his Firestone outboard wouldn't be submitted to their thick treachery.

We hit pay dirt, and came around to rescue C24 and it's inhabitants, with C25 swaying, then hesitating like a ship in a mid Pacific mix.

The chain linked the twins for a pull to destiny, liking the pictures of slaves persuaded with whips, dragging great boulders to the scene of a forthcoming pyramid.

"Easy now, George! We just wanna tighten the chain slowly, then we can try to pull'er free." Jame was back in gear, reverently giving orders. "DON"T stand near those chains! If they snap you'll be dead as a doornail!"

The commotion got Weave insistent. "C'mon Charlie 2-5! Pull in the slack an' SAVE US!"

The slack in the chain gone, C25 began to show defiance in sound and heart, as it began to maneuver itself left or right in the mush it was churning in the soggy lowland. Diesel engines screamed, pleaded, roared for assistance as they propelled the Pigs tracks from near insurmountable dregs.

On the landing, Jame complimented George. "I couldn't 'a done better myself, Buddy! No broken chains, either! I DO believe you are hired!"

"Aw RIGHT!" yelled the new driver. He was sweating bullets in the cockpit, happy to have been promoted. "Do I get a raise?" His one tooth smile gave us all a laugh.

"You'll get one when you get home" intervened Weave.

Somehow, the word "home" was a part of every other sentence uttered in this country, just for the sake of it, just to disturb everyone's normalcy. Just to embellish those 'wishes upon a star'.

The many more pitfalls encountered on our expedition rivaled our pull from the swamp. Blockades of elderly timber had to be crossed in around about way, slowing our movement to a snails pace. Forceful streams knocked over equipment laden Grunts for afternoon baths, while ruining much of their supplies. Dense foliage itself proved near impracticable, as the point men passed a machete like a baton in the Olympics to rest wearied arms and catch breaths.

C24 was called to the front of the safari to see if the weight and tracks could assist burning the trail, but it joked, to the jungle. Slurping swamp was the only defense needed to offend us.

"Move back to your original posit, Weave. The Corps should shit can the Ontos!"

Weave was distraught with the Major's conclusion. He leaned on his machine gun while his beloved Pig sat idling, waiting for the troops to file by until it was time for his vehicle to fall back in. His head hung low, like he'd just lost his best friend.

We meandered through the warren of insecurity for a total of 3 or 4 days, with most opposition occurring during the first half. The thought staggered me, that in these decidedly perfect venues for ambush, few enemies were seen or heard. Was the terrain too rough for them? Reports said NO, that they were ready to fight anywhere, any time, any place. Did we bungle in the jungle, passed them? Hardly. We were noisy enough to wake the dead, with groaning engines, howling Gruntery and C-ration induced flatulence that could kill a monkey at ten paces.

Maybe the VC didn't want a scuffle, or they were low on ammo. Maybe this Garden our Advisors careened us into was the very end of the earth the enemy wanted to snarl at, not snare.

We were in somewhat of a hurry to reach the bunkers and trench lines of our hill numbered 22, *it* being a cut above the two inequities.

Reaching the inner gate, Luke and George warbled, "Be it even so crappy, there's no place like Hill 22!"

"Shut the fuck up" came from Jame, brusquely.

Our racks showed evidence of a hurricane visiting our tent grounds, sitting upside down and across each other like green snakes in heat. The dirt floor looked like it had been osterized for dinosaur bones, and the tent flaps were lowered, not half-mast, as we were accustomed.

"Who 'da hell went through our house?" screamed Weave, bellowingly "Some S.O.B. went through my SEABAG! DAMN!"

Jame went to the C.O.'s tent to report the incident, returning shortly with papers for us to fill out.

"Read the paper. It'll tell you what to write in the blank spaces."

After rearranging our 'furniture', we started with our paperwork. It took only a few minutes for Tex to ask, "What address do we put in, Weave?"

The Sergeant was amazed. "Dear Lord, PLEASE give me strength! Mr. Tex, what do you THINK your address be, while you're here in Charlie

Company, 1st Anti-tank Battalion, Republic of South Vietnam?" He yelled across the tent, to me. "Herstowski, you puttin' down Warsaw, Poland?"

"Ain't that where we're at?"

With radios, cameras, clothing, and other worthy materialisms stolen, no one felt like laughing.

"Jame!" Weave called, "Did the C.O. tell you what the hell happened here?"

"The rest of the tents look like they been emptied too, but I didn't ask him who did the mess. I told him we were robbed, and he pulled papers from a stack and handed 'em to me."

"Why didn't 'ya ask him who dunnit?

"Weave, I just didn't think of asking him, and it wouldn't help matters now anyhow."

The touchy matter was closed. We were all too tired to cry over spilt possessions.

"I'm goin' to the well."

All needing the mud washed off, we followed Bravo for the most recreation we'd had in a week: pail immersion.

Breaking all shower run speed records, we pedestrianed back to our billet, with guard orders for 50% alert given by a lance corporal we'd never seen before. It didn't phase our sleep-deprived minds in the least. We all crashed on our good old canvas racks, now reconsidered a luxury. True patriotism hates injustice in it's own land more than anywhere else.

Won't you look down upon me Jesus; won't you help me make a stand? I don't know whom I can depend upon.
My whole body's aching and my time is at hand...
I've seen fire and I've seen rain. I've seen sunny days that I thought would never end, I've had lonely times when I could not find a friend...sweet dreams and fine machines in pieces on the ground.

Fighting the summer, and *in* the summer of 1967 and taxed by the ever present heat, the super sun submitted it's smoldering properties scalding, with gut wrenching demonic strains of stress that everyone who toured in the field met with and housed like a permanent tenant. They were two of our silent enemies that were un- avoidable, making life even more complicated than it already was. Not that walking a patrol route is pleasant at 80 degrees, but it sure beat 110.

Choppers hovered day and night. Some days the sight and sound of the whirlybirds became totally repulsive to me, with the repetitive flapping of their rotor blades being constant reminders that the war continued and safety was at a premium. But with the stress factor being omni competent on our hill, as in the field, reminders of the war were better than getting shot in a war.

So one diversion was vaulting into the trenches for lazin' on a sunny afternoon, while the noisy mix masters emptied their rockets at known sniper positions until the incoming stopped.

And one of my most memorable plays in Hades was on one morning in August 1967. It started like most mornings, with me checking in to Battalion.

"Cantilever this is Cantilever Charlie. Radio check. Over."

"Cantilever Charlie this is Cantilever. I hear you loud, with static. How do you hear me? Over."

"…I hear you loud and clear. Break. Any mail come in, and what movie is at the club? Over."

"…You have mail. Break. The projector's broken. Over."

"…I'll be in later. Out."

"Ski, I got 10 days to go!" Luke studied his "Girly"calendar. "It's August 19th! 10 DAYS TO GOOOO!!! EHHH HAHHH!"

I was happy for him, but I had 6 months left myself, so reveling was a difficult harmony to tune. I faked a smile as I sat on my rack, hunched over with heat and depression that awoke me every morning. And hell, the nights of sleeping on the ground and on a steel bed of Ontos were taking its toll on my young frame. I ached all over.

The sun shone lustfully as the first round of incoming thudded deafeningly on the opposite side of the hill.

We all jumped straight up, out of our racks and out of the tent that had its roof ventilated with shrapnel.

"What the fuck's goin' on?" yelled Jinx, another kid from Chicago, who looked sweet 16. He got on Hill 22 only weeks earlier, and this was his first brush with death in the 'Nam'.

We saw the Grunts diving into the trenches. Some of them resembled Santa Claus, with half bearded faces of Burma-Shave, but belly-less. Another eruption much closer had us joining the fearful bunches in the already prepared graves that circled the compound.

The cries of 'incoming' ceased, being superfluous as another shell landed on our previously impassive setting.

A gunner down the line, wrapped in a green towel, opened fire indiscriminately with his M-60 into the trees, towards the 'friendly village' and anywhere he damn well pleased. He howled choruses of hatred in four-letter word fashion, and didn't stop shooting until his ammo belt was expired. His cursing continued for another minute, not being one to appreciate his morning shaving ritual being disturbed.

"Herstowski, get on the handset!" ordered our new Ontos Chief, SSgt. Hayne.

With the attack, I left to bring my radio in the tent. The dire emergency made me almost forget my name.

I did a low crawl 20 feet or so back to my rack to radio in our distress signal.

"Cantilever this is Cantilever Charlie. Be advised we're under attack." I'd make the call quick and to the point, not waiting for any acknowledgement.

Spitting small arms fire was everywhere minus explosives. It meant that no enemy troops were nearby to lob grenades at, but our sit rep was discernible enough to be considered clotted.

Back in the trench with the radio, I waited acknowledgement of my last transmission. Hayne crouched next to me, the only one wearing a helmet. With tranquility regained, I wondered about Sgt. Jame, who rotated a week earlier. I hoped the problems he developed here vanished, as we bumped against the dirt wall waiting for another salvo.

"Cantilever Charlie this is Cantilever. Radio check. Over."

Hayne heard the response buzz through the handset, and then grabbed it to give his opinion.

"Cantilever this is Cantilever Charlie. Be advised that we've been under a mortar attack, waiting for your acknowledgement. Do you have a problem with your radio? Over!"

Would it matter if they knew that we were getting shelled or not, except that we might have to ask for permission to fight for our lives? But Hayne was really pissed with our radio communications.

"This is Cantilever. We have no radio problems. We never got a sit rep. Over."

Haynes glared at me with fire in his eyes. "Didn't you call in the sit rep?"

"Sure I did, Sarge! Back in the tent!"

"Well, Battalion said that nothing was called in!" he turned away, glaring at the landscape ahead of us.

SSgt. Hayne wasn't a bad guy to be in command under, but sometimes it seemed that he was untrusting in his troop matters, skeptical with our answers. His 'high and tight' hair cuts reflected a deep dedication to the Corps.

Weave, another short timer, scurried low to Hayne, sweating bullets like me.

More staggering small arms fire.

"What's up? You call choppers in?" His eyes widened.

Hayne was on the radio doing just that on the Battalion net. He finished with the call, then almost grabbed Weave by the neck, growling, "Where's 'yer Pig? Why ain't you on the 30?" Weave's eyes showed us that he was ready to rotate, and that he had no intentions to play in an Audie Murphy role. Not to save his soul.

"I, I came over for our sit rep." His stuttering announced to us that his fear overwhelmed his bravery. Hayne turned away again to the open field, handling his 45.

Preposterous it was, to think of an attack on a Marine base in broad daylight. So it was labeled a preposterous attack, with us doing the bitchin' and sweating without a target to assume.

We took target practice from our positions, picking a branch or a rock to shoot at, helping to ward off more incoming while becoming more skillful in our trained endeavors.

"Herstowski, you got comm. with the sweep team?"

"Nope. Never did."

Haynes was extra observant. "I can see the trail of dust from their 6 by. They must be on the way back."

They heard the noise on the hill and cut their sweep short, but their return trip was detained when the truck stopped before our M-60 firing would cut it in two. We could see the contact from out box seats, one half mile to our right. The sweep team and its defenders hustled to the roadside cover of green to avoid the ambush, while our firing kept the enemy pinned sown.

With the aggressors seemingly subdued, the infantry re-mounted their bus to reach home base. They became our center of attention, since incoming on the hill stopped and the truck was in a vulnerable position.

The road took the vehicle further away from the hill, on radii engineered to avoid large natural inclines and rice paddy reaches. Its gravitational pull from the manmade ramps opposed and practically stopped the 6 by, forcing the driver's hand to beg 1st gear for help.

The fear I felt daily when routing my Mighty-Mite for Battalion visits met term with a surprise attack on the slowly moving truck on the final hill before our barbed wire entrance, a quarter mile down the road. I knew it would happen some day, to me, or to the 6 by now being destroyed, with 15 Marines dealing for their lives.

I'd mentioned to my superiors numerous times about the danger of that curve in the roadway. It turned a full 90 degrees, causing the driver of any vehicle to almost halt at approach. Following only yards away, was an incline of at least 25 more degrees, with walls of dirt adjacent, on either side, 15 feet high and covered with brush for a perfect zone to drop grenades or the kitchen sink.

But none of the Big Boys listened, so a dozen or more of the mine sweep team were now paying dues, for the government that ignored my pleas. Right in front of our very wide opened eyes.

Another incoming crash.

"Herstowski, get the P.C. (Personnel Carrier, seats 6), the place is up for grabs!"

'Grabs', indeed, closer to annihilation, as I shifted gears, racing to the turmoil that waited not far ahead. My M-14, worthless to me as a driver, bumped against my knee, like a dog pawing for a treat. The black and gray smoke billowed, engulfing the sky and shadowing the sun, as I slowed down a half a block before the collision, then stopped on the roadside.

"What the hell are you doin', Herstowski? Pull up!"

"Get to cover!" I yelled to him, ignoring his stupid order to become another, larger target with a truck. He imitated me on the other side of the road.

I lay in the tall weeds, firing at the top of the embankment that was smoking from Satan's coven, stopping because the Grunts rambling to that area were hurling grenades and vulgarisms.

The noise ended with birds hesitantly chirping through the smoke, so I ran to the P.C. broadcasting to Hayne, "NOW let's move up!" He scowled but jumped in, speechless.

We saw Grunts, prone and motionless on the side of the road. I stopped next to one of them who needed help, bleeding from the neck down, ruining his business suit and the turf bed. I tried to ignore blasphemes coursing from his mouth and from two other wounded who bloodied my pants and shirtless upper torso. One I couldn't ignore was a black Marine, screaming for his head to be held up and that he couldn't breath. He was bleeding terribly, and I mean, ALL OVER! I've dreamt about the poor guy and this incident, wondering if he survived.

A 6 by with corpsmen and reinforcements rambled to a stop to aid the wounded and recon the area with tools of their trade, so I sped back to our hill with the wounded.

Medevac choppers were settling when I pulled in, the Marine in my passenger's seat chuckling lowly and pointing to the whirlybirds with a hand with two fingers missing. The blood didn't seem to bother him too much. He exclaimed, "I'm goin' HOME, brother! FUCK this place!"

He opened his door and ran for the helicopter for his one-way ticket home, never looking back.

A Grunt ran to my truck to help unload the others. Both of the wounded were quiet and stationary, maybe in a death grip. I assumed they were dead, leaving another haunting, horrible cenotaph.

The other 6 by returned with its unsavory cargo, including Hayne. The choppers disappeared, leaving only pallbearers to carry out the diplomatic mission we were brought to RVN country to perform, which started with just staying alive.

"You okay, Ski?" Now Hayne was being diplomatic, dropping Herstow.

"Yah, sure. How about you?"

"I'm fine. Where's the Prc-25? I'm gonna call in a report on this occurrence. Maybe we'll get something outta this."

He talked with Battalion for a while but never heard anything about the 'Courage Under Fire' episode we presumably carried out for the Corps and our countrymen who lay dead and bleeding in the road that one morning in August 1967. No commendation.

Heavy raindrops started to inspect the hill, and I stood there wearing only skivvies, to cleanse my body, and hopefully, at least part of my soul.

The barbed odor of burned machinery still clung in the air from the smoke of the deranged 6 by.

For what avail the plough or sail, or land or life, if freedom fail?

Author

Wouldn't you like to ride, in my beautiful balloon...we could float among the stars together, you and I. We could fly!

Two or four bodies, or a hundred bodies were found after the morning scuffle. I don't remember how many, but I felt beaten again. There was nothing left to live for. Atop lose of life, there wasn't a Donna waiting for me back in Illinois and I'd be a hero for myself and no one else. I was my parents pride and joy, but even the most glorified heroes reflected most glaringly in their eyes, so I sat down to write them courage, and that I'd come back home the same idiotic kid that I was before I left for the war. Parents, after all is said and done, are the creators of our haphazard universe. They work, they slave, they raise, they discipline. All for the common good for themselves and posterity, for a common valor, usually with nothing in return save a college graduate or a warrior's homecoming.

So I plunged onto the paper with pen to lie to Mom and Dad about our opposition, weather forecasts, housing, and our standard of living. I entered that I'd stay an extra 6 months if needed.

Don't believe the newspapers B.S. It's really not as bad as they show it.

Your Loving Son,
Bill

P.S. Don't send pistachios. They rot before they get here! '4 days, and a hook!'

4 days until I'd board a plane to Bangkok, Thailand.

With another patrol completed, I flopped on my rack, not even thinking of the next day's glamour and intrigue in another foreign country. I didn't know anything, I confess now. There was no this or that, no girl, no car; just me, and me, and me not even trying to see a future.

"Got your bags ready for R & R, Ski?" SSgt. Hayne was kicking me in a boot that I hung over the end of my rack. "You got your orders, didn't you?"

"Yah, I got 'em."

"Bangkok, right?"

He slid his feet across our dirt floor until he got to the rest of the platoon to tell them the next order of the day.

I rested my eyes, but could hear his words. "Tomorrow, we'll patrol the villages, then…"

His voice flowed into the darkness as I fell into a restless slumber.

I was a deserter, my dream flashed to me. How could I leave for Rest and Recreation at a time like this?

'Men are not supernatural beings, and it is imperative the you remove yourself from the rigorous toils of war to perform gainfully at later hours', was the answer from my inner being.

The hot sweat that awakened me wasn't unusual, but I felt that it wasn't the omni-potent heat but from my soul, telling me to cool off inside, and for me not to regard the war in a personal essay. Take it as it comes, a part of your own life and no one else's. Live your life to the fullest, feigning those from the shadows.

Luke drove me down to the air base in DaNang. We didn't have much to talk about, our minds closed to the living after the attack we'd suffered only days earlier. He would leave Vietnam while I was in Thailand, so we shook hands mightily as conquering heroes, vowing to recreate our friendship some day in the not so distant future.

"Don't forget that Black Jack money you owe me", I concluded, for a guy who fought in a war and was returning home victorious.

Jinx jumped to the front seat, asking, "You two Lovers gonna break up, or what?" The cramped back seat could hardly hold his 6'3" frame, so he was glad to see me go.

Luke jumped into the driver's seat. "Chuck you, Farley" with finger waving replacing a salute. He got one back as he drove away.

Air conditioning in the jet was enough to knock 'yer socks off, and seeing the curvy stewardess' in mini-skirts was enough to knock 'yer *pants* off. It had been over 7 months since cool air or round-eyed women, so my flight was one of turbulence inside and out of the plane.

I laid my head back to doze in the comfort of secure surroundings, and the seemingly short flight had me wanting to stay aboard for more dry air and views of America's most wanted.

As the attendants pushed us off board, I started to wonder. Where the hell was I going? I had no idea, so I looked at the other passengers and tapped the closest shoulder to ask direct- ions. The fellow Marine named Bob, said that he was lost too, but we could get a cab and ask the driver where the 'hot spots' were around town.

My diary enclosed the name of the Marakat Hotel as our drop off point. I would never have remembered it on my own.

The first self-indulgent order was to splash in the bath until excruciatingly wrinkled. It was heaven sent, the clean sheets and cool air. I jumped into the bed and passed out for hours until Bob knocked me back into submission by pounding on the door.

"HEY, SKI! Let's go out and see the town!"

I got up to let him in, dragging the sheet behind me, half asleep. "C'mon in."

Our bellboy Charlie walked in behind Bob, asking, "You want numba one girl?"

In my daze, I thought I was back in Vietnam when I saw him. Their cultures may differ, but faces remain the same.

"YAH!" Bob chortled. "Number one girls!"

He gave Bob the name of a bar in exchange for some American currency. Charlie bowed and disappeared through the doorway.

"WOW, Ski, look at this!" he showed me the names on the paper. "The Boston Bar!" he cried out. "I can't believe it! I'M from Boston!" I reminded him that it was just a bar, not really Boston, Mass. He gave me a snide look. Dressed in civies for the first time in 8 months felt weird and great. No longer in green, we both felt like prisoners out on parole, ready to do the world at it's own expense. And no burdening jungle boots!

The cab driver took us to the bar as if there was no tomorrow. Talk about maniacs, these were those. They changed lanes quicker than a Bobby Hull slap shot, going 50 in a 25, nearly hitting pedestrians on the way. When the driver stopped in front of the bar I jumped out in jest and for life.

Bob paid the cab fare, and I opened the door, appreciating his generosity. "Thanks, Chum. You can get us back."

We sat down at the bar, which looked more like a lounge back home decorated with palm trees and flora that took me right back to the jungle. "Hill 22. What a magnifif---in'cent landscape!"

"Huh?" puzzled Bob.

"Nothing'. Tender, rum 'n coke, please."

"Make that two!"

"Like your rum, Bob?"

"When I drink, that's what I like."

I gulped mine while gazing at companion seeking girls at small tables. Each blouse was embroidered with number tags.

"Bob, are those numbers for what I think they're for, or is this a dance hall?" 'Hee, hee's' answered my question.

He called the bartender over. "How much for number 20?"

The tender spoke broken, but comprehensible English. "They $18.00 each. Stay all night. Which you like?"

"I like 20, How about you Ski?"

"Number 18 looks friendly enough." It felt wrong for me to pay for a girl's company, but if God were willing to forgive me for killing in the fields, He'd surely forgive me for paying for the accommodation of a woman. Besides that, He might be waiting for me around the next corner on my mail run.

I found myself staring at the drink in my hand, thinking about that road and the guys I carried to the choppers. Then a hand touched my shoulder and I jumped. HHH, I sorry sir. You okay? My name is Toy. You like me?"

"Hi. How can you like someone you just met? Can you like me?"

"Shoo. I like you." She walked between Bob and me. "What you name?" smiling.

"I'm Ski and that's Bob."

Her smile and long black hair sold me. I edged a twenty towards the bartender. "Keep the change."

Bob was busy getting acquainted with his future border Koko, at the table near the door while Toy asked me about the war, America, cars, baseball, money and other subjects proving in cohesive to me. Rum helped ease the pain of a near boring conversation with a complete stranger: beautiful, but transparent.

But the night wore on until the call of the untamed was sounded for retreat.

"Ski, let's go back to Maraket or Karamer, or wherever we came from." His gait was impotent and eyes only semi-visible.

"Okay Dude, let's cab away!"

I too was abbreviated in thinking and walking at the same time, and the both of us grinned too much to be recent war veterans.   The condition proved to be a boon though, as I snoozed through hair-raising cabby obstacle courses, arriving slightly rested.

Showering without a bucket was ecstasy. Standing in leech-free water and drying off with a clean smelling towel finished off the transition for slumber well earned in a pre-heated bed.

All's fair in love and war. The morning found us meeting in the lobby. "Hi Koko. Sleep well, Bob? I crashed good, I'm here to tell 'ya!"

"Me too. The 'Nam' wore me out Bro. I could use a YEAR of this place!"

"Toy tells me that Thai boxing in the scene."

"Sounds good to me."

Cabs were lined up outside the entrance and Toy picked one out. I think she knew the driver as they spoke in Thai. Or is it Siamese?   "Hey Ski, did you get any beer sent to your room? I got one in a big, brown bottle that said 18%! And it FEELS like it!"

"YAH! There ought a be a law."

We sat in the 5th or 6th row, and the fighters were already kicking, punching, head butting and whatever else they could do under their own power. Bouts didn't last much longer than a round or two, with the loser usually carried off over someone's shoulder or on a stretcher. I think that bets were taken in corners of the building, but I never questioned legalities. If girls wearing number tags weren't questioned, why would the government worry about bahts (Thai currency) being bartered on bouts?

The following day found us on a tourist train rolling over one of the Death Bridges built over the Kwai River. I saw the academy award winning film, and now we rolled over the real thing.

The train stopped and we got out to walk around. Toy pointed to the cemetery lined up with thousands of crosses, and a monument honoring the men who built the railway bridges.

An inscription read:

In Honored Remembrance of the Fortitude and Sacrifice of that Valiant Company who perished while building the Railway from Thailand to Burma during their long captivity.

Those who have no known grave are commemorated by name at Rangoon Singapore and Hong Kong and their Comrades rest in three war Cemeteries of Kanchonaburi Chungkai and Thanbyuzayat.

I WILL MAKE YOU A NAME AND A PRAISE
AMONG ALL PEOPLE OF THE EARTH WHEN
I TURN BACK YOUR CAPTIVITY BEFORE YOUR EYES
WITH THE LORD

I read the inscription and gazed at the cemetery, with a tear, thinking of so many lives lost in the name of freedom for the world. Such sacrifices, such pain, such tragedy. Does it matter now? Does anyone care? How many know about the plight of those brave souls?

We boarded the train for a quick return trip, through a tangled multitudinous garden quick to be called the hot house of Asia.

"Ski, it looks thicker than 'Nam's bush!"

I agreed, but didn't say so. I just looked into the jungle to see if there were any eyes watching back at us. I practiced for the morrow.

Cobras were the main attractions at the zoo we visited, captive in glass cages bordering the patron's walkway.

Bob had to tease the snakes to see if they were real. One snap on the glass with his finger, and the resting serpent erected with its head flaps open to take a bite out of the glass. It angered the girls.

"Dummy, why you do? You baboy baba!"

And a crocodile pit. We were lucky enough to walk in on their supper, lumps of raw meat.

Lastly was the boa constrictor, which could easily ingest a chicken with one gulp. My notes didn't tell its length, but it tipped the scales at over 200 pounds. Falling out of a tree would have been enough to kill its victim, so one this size didn't need to use the coiling method.

"I'm tired of the jungle and all of its circus animals! Let's go get a drink!"

"Ski, I'm right behind 'ya. C'mon girls, lets go to town!"

It was our last night of freedom and civvies, of mattresses, and fine food w/females. "Girls, take us to the best restaurant in town!"

Luminance from the neon signs was beautiful, if not blinding.

"'Ya bring 'yer sunglasses, Ski? Sure is bright, for 10 at night!"

"No, I didn't. I left 'em in my footlocker." My eyes were changed already from the sun's insistence in 'Nam'. I have found that I need to wear sunglasses for comfort, even on mostly cloudy days.

KoKo said something to the driver and he pulled to the curb in front of a ritzy looking eatery.

"I hope we can afford this joint, Bob. I'm almost out of money. How about you?"

"I think I can handle it. But let's go! I'm starved!"

Seated with Carte du Joure, Toy asking if I liked noodles. "I love 'em." The bowl she ordered for me was out of this world, garnished with spices not hot but tasty, and the large portion nearly filled me up.

Snake meat and shark completed the servings, excellent in every way.

A bottle of wine sat on the table, so in traditional fashion we filled the glasses and toasted ourselves to good luck and a quick journey home.

"All in one piece, right Ski?"

All four glasses clinked. "Right, Bob."

The girls both wished us a safe trip and for the war to end soon, as we exited the Marakat for points known. We walked passed a jewelry store on our way to the cabstand, and a ring in the window caught my eye. It was a black star sapphire, with diamond chips studded in the gold in an 'L' shape. It cost about $40.00, however, the keepsake is gone forever, due to a petty thief's hand in a Cicero apartment, soon after my wedding.

On the flight back to DaNang, I removed the string of flowers that were placed around my neck by Toy and looked for a place to discard it. "Want these flowers, Bob?"

"Nope. 'Ya want these? I won't need 'em where I'm goin!"

"Me either."

We left the fragrant bouquets on the plane and "un-feathered" the big bird to find rides back to the bush. Bob was returning to someplace up north called Hue (Pronounced way) City. "Never heard of it, Bob. Good luck!"

"And good luck to you Ski."

We shook hands, parting with good memories as we boarded our buses to flack jackets and ammo. Jinx was driving. "Any thing happen while I was gone?"

"Nothin' real big, Ski. Some sniper rounds. A big rainstorm. We got ELECTRIC on the hill now! Can ya' beat that?"

After I gave no response, "How were the ladies, Ski?"

I told him everything was just fantastic, as the Mite slid down the muddy road with my scowl returning in cinemascope. "Electric on the hill?"

And they who for their country die
Shall fill an honored grave
For glory lights the soldier's tomb
And beauty weeps the brave.

To live, you must nearly die.

It was 1800 when we got back to Hill 22. Jinx added more sit reps for me on our drive home, including the 100 percent alert we were to perform.

SSgt. Hayne was cleaning his 45 as he sat on his rack.

"Did Luke rotate?"

"Yes, Bravo did, too. How was Bangkok? Get enough of the women?"

"It was a different world there Sarge, but about as hot a this hole."

I threw my summer uniform on the dirt floor resentfully then donned my jungle pants. What the hell are we ruining lives for? Does anybody know what's going on here? A glance at any newspaper from back home showed the world still turned with the same revolutions. Woolworth's still sold baby turtles and hula-hoops. People drove to work the usual way, weekends were still filled with fun and frolic and double-headers. And it just didn't seem to matter what happened on this continent, to the multitude of the U.S. of A. I just did too much thinking. Remember the soul searching, I asked myself again.

Loud explosions blew me out of my trance. They were far enough away to keep us from vaulting to the trenches, but the look Hayne gave showed deep concern.

"NOW WHAT?" he bellowed. It sounded as though he didn't expect explosive conduct in this war, like some teen blasting an M-80 in the street, down the block.

He walked into the baking, fading sun to ask the Cap if he knew where the bomb exploded. I just lay in my rack to read another chapter of Batman's adventures.

He returned shortly with news of a bridge being destroyed near another outpost, Hill 55. A new man, big enough to play on the line for the New York Giants, followed in his footsteps. "Ski, Butler is Luke's replacement."

The giant of a black Marine had such a wide smile that I had to smile back. "Hi, I'm Ski".

"Please to meet cha', my name is James Butler!"

"Butler. Find a good rack and set yourself up here." Hayne pointed to an open area near the center, on my side of the tent.

Dropping his gear, expelling "Hot damn! 'Dis tent sure got 'da hots!'", he exposed his pearly whites again, now with a wrinkled brow.

"I hate to tell you Butler, but September is a hot month too. The D.J. said so, anyhow."

"D. J? You got TV here?"

Hayne stepped in. "Are you kiddin'? Lucky to have AIR! There's no electric, no running water. The toilets have to be burned everyday and our shower is usually a cold water well!"

Butler was amazed to find 1967 to be like this. "I DO smells 'da outhouse!"

After a few days, I realized Butler to be a man born with a smile. It deepened as he loaded inhumanity into the hungry breeches of the Pig's 6 barrels.

"Get some rest while you can" I recommended Butler. "We're on 100% alert tonight."

"That means we ALL stay up?"

"ALL of us!" informed Hayne. "No sleeping for anyone, and don't take it lightly. Everyone knows that I'll write up anybody who's found sleeping on guard! It might gain brig time."

Butler looked at me, prone and half asleep, nodding his compliance with the extreme of things.

At nightfall, Tex yanked me from a bridge that encircled a cemetery. It was a quiet dream, without a river.

"I'm an extra hand here these days. Weave went out on an Op with an officer and a new driver. C25's the only pig on the hill, Ski! I sure hope the VC's got enough respect for only one Ontos and they leave us alone."

Agreeing, I threw my shirt over my shoulders and tripped out the flap-way, blaming R&R for laxness on lopsided flooring. Fog had already rolled into many of the low
spots in our field of vision, with lunar reflection highlighting a Scottish moor theme.

Hayne, being a staff N.C.O., pulled guard duty rarely, but he decided to stay with us for the greater number of our 12-hour shifts.

"Battalion Command reports enemy activities are heavy in these mountain ranges so be alert to your fullest, gentlemen. When the VC blew up that bridge, a Marine was killed and two were injured. I wouldn't doubt that they're ready to hit every outpost within 20 miles of here. The Captain has coffee brewed for the long night, so fill up on the caffeine."

"I hates caffeine".

"Butler, just stay awake!" Hayne left to walk along the trench line to reacquaint with its surrounding pitfalls.

We three just stared at the landscape, stars, moon, and whatever. I thought about Donna again, reassuring myself that she'd still be my girl and we would get married and live happily ever after.

"Where ya' from, Butler! I'm from Smallville, Texas."

With the moon we could see the reflection of Butler's teeth. He gave out a big, deep, convincing laugh. "HAA, HAAA, HAAA!"

I couldn't figure out why.

"I'm from the south of South Carolina, boys. An' I feels great just thinkin' about going' back there. I been here only 2 days, and I miss home like crazy!" He was just another refugee from the heart. I guess some of us here didn't really miss their homes, but I hadn't met one yet.

"Hayne told me you's from Chicago, Ski. Miss it?"

"Yah, sure." I lay prone on the top of C25, hoping not to see movement, hoping to awaken in February 1968.

Haynes completed a round of the trenches and bunkers to find the compliment fully awake and at their ready.

"It's almost midnight. Is everybody still awake?"

"We're okay Sarge. What's the good word? Anything new?"

"The Vietnamese have some kind of elections going on, so the VC blew up the bridge as a show of power. They don't want anybody out voting."

There was a parallel with any bridge in any war. They get blown up here as they were destroyed in WW II, always to break the links for troops and supplies. The Death Bridges in Thailand were no different than these in Vietnam.   I questioned the policies our Intelligence engaged to keep our defense at its peak.   "Sarge, shouldn't we have been more on the alert? I mean, the guys running this war must've known about the elections coming up, and that the Viet Cong want to disrupt any democratic process in the making."

"We're not running the show, Herstowski. We just do what we're told. Just be on alert. Tex! Claymores up?"

"Yup." He held up the small housing wired to the antipersonnel mine on the downgrade ahead of us. "I'm all ready, willing and able."

I couldn't believe that I was eating shark fin soup and toasting a glass of wine with beautiful women 24 hours earlier. What an insane world we ruled.

It was about 0200 and the fog thickened to pea soup consistency when we had a few rounds of small arms fire zip through the air around C25. Hayne jumped to the .30 cal. while Tex and I fell to the ground ready to return fire. We were afraid to shoot without Haynes' approval, so we lay in the dirt waiting for his okay, or death, or a bus to Madison Street. He was on the phone, talking to our hill commander.

The halo from the moon glowed our movements enough for a good sniper to see us and pick us off, so I rolled and crawled to the slight shadow offered from the side of the Pig. Then I thought about the prospect of an enemy rocket or grenade unearthing the ever-conspicuous target we caressed, like children clinging to their Mother's apron strings.

We knew that the friendly village shouldn't be fired into, and that was exactly where the muzzle flashes were from.

"Start the engine, Tex, just in case we gotta move!"

Ninety degrees from our posit, firing flowed back and forth. That being from a free-fire zone, no permission to retaliate was needed. We saw flashes that imitated strings of firecrackers spent on any Forth of July, long strings that smoked and cracked in the night.

Hayne told Butler, shivering next to me, to be ready to load flachettes if a wave of enemy was seen in close proximity. I viewed ahead, and seeing some probable enemy movement, or maybe water buffalo, I told Hayne.

"Ski, I TOLD YOU that we can't shoot in that direction! There are FRIENDLIES down there!"

Rounds ricocheted off C25. Heartburn blazed.

Exchanges continued next to us, maybe 100 feet away when we heard choppers winging to our aid. I feared the dark to mislead their target, and we'd be listed killed by friendly fire.

Grunts had 3 searchlights mounted on tripods in front of their positions, turned on when the onslaught started, but proved to be somewhat of a hindrance with the fog reflecting and magnifying the light beams glaringly. Just like the fog's reflection off the bright beam when traveling on the Wisconsin roads back home. Back home.

Then I realized that the pilots would recognize the lighting as a signal from their allies as a finger pointing to the chopper's objective. My wish came true.

Humming from their mini-guns bugled the Grunts to loosen their loads of ammo, bar none, making the smoke produced levy with fog as a more blinding inhibitor than before.

But exposing the enemy didn't matter at that point, because the developed smog blinded attacker and attack-ee. The 79's continued to pop their grenades and 3.5's rocketed rounds, with the small arms pinging until the 'cease fire' removed the marksmen from their appointed 'roundings'.

The choppers fluttered back to the 'rear', leaving their impressive toll below our hill: brush fires and a body count to total when the sun re-ignited.

With a calm before the storm, Hayne squat-ran around to the bunkers where the fighting was the heaviest. We lit up our favorite brands to enjoy the lull in our action, having only to receive more harassment from a different location.

"Jesus "CHRIST!" I cried in the moonlight. "What the fuck are we gonna do?"

Hayne, already on his way back to C25, heard me and doubled timed to pound on the ground next to me.

"What's your problem?" He spoke, muffling his voice, as though the VC didn't know where we were. As though we were hidden in a palm tree. "You wanna get yourself killed?"

I looked in the direction of his whispers. "Oh, I suppose that Charlie out there can't see us, right? And we're supposed to just sit around smoking cigarettes and wait until we get killed or crippled. Right?"

"Calm yourself down, Herstowski. We're all in this together, remember?"

"You just got here. I got 7 months in country, and I seen ENOUGH! The a-holes sitting in the air-conditioned offices never even see the jungle, and the operations they send us on depend on where their darts stick in a map on the wall! They don't know how to fight this war and they don't know what they're doing about ANY- THING! OVER!" (Radio operators in 'Nam would occasionally end a sentence sarcastically with the word 'over'.)

I surprised myself, verbally attacking a senior Staff N.C.O. like I did. He looked at me like a worried father would, wondering if I was right and if I could perform my duties up to snuff. I thought that I might get a court-martial because of my big mouth.

"I'm sorry, Sergeant Hayne."

He looked away towards the battleground, then duck-walked without a word. He knew I wasn't sorry for what I said, and that all of it was quite true. A short time ago Hayne and I raced down the road to possibly physical danger or death, to aid our comrades who were ambushed and mutilated from a position that was known to hold a strategic ambush danger for our enemy. Now we're enemies to each other.

Tex and Butler were B.S.ing when Hayne returned. Insubordination on my record, I predicted. The sun was starting to show, as he knelt down on one knee next to me.

"Ski, I'm going to forget your little outburst. I saw that kind of crap before, and writin' you up will do nobody any good. On my last tour, I saw Grunts cracking up and fighting with their own friends that they spent months out in the field with, so I'll forget this little incident ever happened."

NOW, I find out the Boot looking E-6 was on his second tour! I felt like a REAL you know what, and wanted to re-apologize to the man.

I wasn't aiming accusations at him, he just happened to be the audience of my opinion. I apologized again, and he seemed to think nothing of it, and I'm sure that it bothered me more than it did him.

Funny, but when the sun came over the mountains, we walked upright again, not like a hunched over ape. Aren't we still in Charlie's free-fire zone anymore? Was a truce signed? It just didn't sound right to me. Walk tall in the daylight hours when a target can be seen for miles, but in the dark, squat and crawl like more things that go bump in the night. Go figure.

Most of the Grunts took to patrol for enemy kill. A few of them looked like they were ready to do more battle. Some of them looked like they were young enough to be playing G.I. Joe in front of their houses with grade school chums. I stretched out on the ground to watch them enter the tree line a few blocks away, and heard the rattle of machine guns, exploding grenades with war whoops.

Hayne said they're harassing the forest, trying to flush out any 'rabbits' that might be left from last night.

The firing led on for a minute, then the Grunts ambled back towards our hill, slowly. We were *all* tired.

When they got near the entrance, a few could be seen dragging ponchos in the dirt, weighted down enemy carcasses.

The Captain stood at the gate. "We got 5 of 'em, Sir, and nobody here even got a scratch!

"Good hunting, Marine! Good job!"

His words made me wonder about the civilized world.

My daily register at Battalion complete, I turned in for a few hours rest.

"Herstowski, get back by the Pig and stand watch 'till noon, then you might have to drive in for the mail." Hayne was returning the favor for my rebellion.

And I had all I could do to sit up and scratch my boots on the C25. Tex was already in the sack, and Butler waited for relief.

"Well, Mr. Ski. He sent YOU here? I thought radio men weren't put in with us Grunts." He bellowed his coarse laugh, not at me, but just at our situation

"Are you kidding me? I've been with *you* Grunts for 7 months now. YOU get outta here and go to bed."

"Good night, Ski."

He walked off, his contagious laughter echoing, giving me a fake smile and a fake outlook. How the hell could he be laughing like that after last night? It was for him to know and for me to find out.

I almost fell asleep in the sun before Hayne came to pull me off of the Pig. He was smirking.

"Had enough?"

"Huh? Is this a torture?"

He laughed. "Ski, this is a war, and no, I don't torture anybody, they usually just torture themselves. Anyways, call Battalion. If there's no mail, you can sleep in."

I walked back to the tent, hoping against hope that the mail planes didn't make it in for a few more days.

The coin I dropped into the well never hit bottom. The mail HAD arrived. I told Hayne that I needed somebody to ride shotgun, preferably 2 or 3, with local upheavals enduring.

"One will do. If you had 6 shotguns in that jeep, do you think you'd be safe? I'll go, to show my confidence in you and our security in the valley."

SECURITY? This country had as much security as an open cell door.

We plummeted down the road with our helmets bouncing as bobble headed baseball player statues did on front and back dashboards in cars back home. Back Home.

"Do you always drive this fast. Ski?"

I felt more at ease, being called by my nickname by a man I irrationally labeled as a Boot to the Nam, when in reality he was dodging bullets while I was in high school.

"No Sarge, I usually drive faster!" I shifted into second gear to motion quicker over the upcoming ascent. The dirt-paved maze provided a decidedly more menacing landscape of fern and palm adjacent, and I concluded that the only to go was to imagine it a raceway. Specifically, just a raceway with no pitfalls of ambush or land mines, just a clocked expressway for the mail to go through.

I had to forget about the ambushed mine sweep team, at least until the day came when I had to no longer sweat down the flow of suicide road.

Being completely exhausted, we picked up the mail and turned to get back to our hill for the racks. Hayne sensed my hurried state.

"The main P.X. is only 5 minutes up the road, Ski. Need anything? I'd like to stop there."

I didn't want anything but my rack, but hesitated to disapprove with him, since discretion was always the better of valor. "Okay, Sarge, but let's make it a QUICK stop, please."

Fans were circulating the stagnant air, hardly keeping the chocolate bars from turning to an ice cream topping until they reached the sunlight.

"I need some shaving cream."

We reached the magazines for elation of the day. Hayne was the first to notice.

"SUPERMAN! THE OCTOBER ISSUE!" Hayne was over 30 years old! So unforeseen in my teenage mind, a man of his caliber (no pun intended) was moved by, with, and to, the brushwork of Jerry Siegel and Joe Schuster.

"How many copies are there? I usually get some Batman, House of Mystery…"

"You read comics too, Ski?" He sounded like a kid looking for a friend, and that he'd just found one.

"All the time. I have boxes of 'em back home." Back home.

With the cover prices at 12¢ and our price dropped to a thin dime, we could experience the joys of the free world, and the priceless, excited state of boyhood again.

Our frenzy controlled, we sped off for the highway to nowhere. Even near the P.X, the brush was thick and cumbersome, and my fear of ambush had me near to close my eyes. As a cabbie, the prospects were fair to meddling for a man to reach retirement age.

"Damn!" Hayne exclaimed rejection to the fullest at the drenching downpour from our dry spot in the road. It was hot and sunny until the shower, a few hundred feet ahead, blanketing the road, met us full force as in proverbial buckets. Twenty M.P.H. became too fast.

"Are the monsoons early this year?"

"Keep BOTH hands on the wheel!" Hayne was petrified.

It took just a minute's worth of rain to make my speedway quite irreverent to even 4 wheel drive, making the sloshing noise of the tires challenge the flapping sound of the windshield wipers.

"You'd best get new wipers, Ski. How can you see through the rain with those crappy things?"

They were as bad as he said and only three weeks old. The sun bleached them 15 hours a day to a cracked consistence.

"Sarge, with this heavy of a downpour, new wipers wouldn't matter, would they?"

Our door-less carriage's front tires were good for throwing mud pies onto our front floor, pin holes on our convertible roof dripped water, and the headlights flickered on and off, all adding convulsion to an already unattractive cruise with abuse. But ahead showed a refuge of sunlight, no clouds. The rain's heavy contest stopped abruptly.

When we started reaching outskirts, our desiccated driveway remained dusty and rutted. I slowed down near some of the grass huts that housed Vietnamese who I'd come familiar and friendly with. Children hustled through the doorways, reminding me of the little kids back home, except that these had no candy stores to offer goodies for a nickel after their long, strenuous day behind the inkwell.

Whenever I slowed down in their neighborhood, I HAD to stop. The little beggars would encircle the vehicle as a team. Slowly, deliberately, they would confront a driver by edging in front of the moving jeep, eventually causing a halt. Their outstretched paws always had me digging for treats, hoping to make them realize that our mission was one of friendship, not war. It made me think that maybe I was still alive because I was good to the people in the poor grass houses. Maybe they stopped my enemy from planting mines for jeep discovery. Sugar draws more flies than vinegar.

Little hands slapping the jeep's hood made Hayne rest his hand on his holster, but I assured him that I knew this group to be friendly, if not starving, students of mine.

I think that the only words I taught them were 'candy' and 'chocolate'. At least they were usually the only words I could recognize in their screeching.

"Ski, Ski!" they'd shout. Sometimes I'd find it repulsing, especially after days of gunfire and mortar shells that invaded our hill.

"Hiya, Guys!" I rationed bits of chocolate to as many as I could, trying not to leave any of the kids without melted chocolate on their hands and faces. "It would be nice if our government would spend some money on shoes, Sarge."

My 'girlfriend', name forgotten, came out to say hello. Her long black hair reached down almost to her knees, and she smiled all the time as Butler did, only she was more pleasant to see.

"Hiya, Ski." She pointed to Hayne. "Who he? You friend?"

"Of course. Everybody is my friend."

The rain followed to the vil, and the gigantic leaves of the palm tree's overhead had trouble holding it back from our hiding place.

Turning my head left to see if the road was clear, my cheek bumped against a wide-eyed water buffalo's nose that was ridden by an 8-year-old local. Both of us in green nearly crapped in our pants, but the mob of youngsters got a charge out of it, as they 'dee dee maued' (Run away) to their dirt floored hooch's to escape the waterfall.

"See 'yas later". I jammed our Roadrunner into gear for the last leg of our journey. Looking at my rear view mirror gave me a laugh, seeing the rain on the road making the previously dry segments soaked and black, like Mother Nature's hand wiping off her tablecloth with a wet rag.

We passed more hamlets, all deserted look- ing because of the scheduled weather. Vietnamese seemed to have built in barometers
indicating whether rain was to fall or clouds were to pass.

We drove pass citizens who braved the cloud's circumstances, still riding or leading their water boo's down the road and through the brush.

I reached hairpin turns, still racing the wind and rain without abandon. Some of the buffalo on the curves waved their horns at the jeep or us, ostensibly in rage, perhaps in intimidation to start a ruckus with the jeep. I'd wager on the buffalo. They probably
weighed more than the jeep.

We were near our turnoff for 'suicide', when we came to a traffic jam. A *real* traffic jam, the first I encountered on the road. It filed about a block long, comprised of mostly mini buses that transported people from DaNang to wherever, but one was ripened for the junkyard by a well-placed land mine.

Rain pour turned to misting, so Hayne and I left our sand bag

laden transport to look up the road voyeuristically. A crowd gathered around the misshapen vehicle, pointing, shaking heads, grimacing at bodies and parts of unidentifiable travelers.

I fell back into my driver's compartment, sight wavering. The view of the dead wasn't appealing to more sensitive viewers, but lack of sleep contributed to my condition.

The truck in front of us began to move up slowly, as though less speed would help eliminate concussions that killed when explosives were detonated under one's seat. I gave it 50 feet or so and then I crept up with the convoy.

Helicopters hovered over the roadside near the stoppage, as if to expect a VC with a sign, reading, "*I* did it! Please shoot me!"

We edged past the torn bus. Its sides were shredded and rolled up like sheets of aluminum. I turned away, to leave it as I saw it.

An infantry unit of Marines was helping to pick up pieces, and cameramen were there for the Noon News, not a traffic report. Smoke was freeing from the wreck as the camera crew made their living off of conflict.

We cruised again, with Hayne admitting "You know, Ski, if we hadn't stopped at the P.X. for comic books, we may have been the ones to trigger the mine."

"Thank God for Superman!"

Resubmitting to Hill 22, I gave Tex the handful of mail to throw out to the rest of our platoon. I set the letter from my parents on my footlocker and then fell into immediate rest, not sleep, hearing the rustling of the letters being opened and read in silence and heat, imagining my Mighty-Mite being in wingless flight from the exhaust of a 250-pound block of TNT ignited under the sand bag. But the jeep wasn't blown apart. It was merely catapulted through the air to land next to my rack, depositing me where I laid. It was like a comic book cartoon.

After a few hours rest, heavy pitter-patter on our canvas roof awakened me, sweating and cussing as usual. It blanketed me with the thought of 100 percent alert, no firing without permission, rations, and our daily standard of living. I read clearly now, that I was becoming excessively contemptuous of war and Marine Corps tradition.

I believed that if *I* sacrificed like this, *all* men could, and should. It was a mortgage to pay for tenancy in a free land, I gathered, and if you're physically fit, grab a gun and get your ass in gear and join us. Join us and lose your true identity forever.

On the positive side, I walked prouder within and without, from hard hitting ideas making me more obedient to command.

Also, participating in a war paid a man's 'blood taxes' for a freer ride through life, with complimentary tokens to aid the trolley ride of ups and downs. But the unparalleled assumption turned out to be just that. Facing future rigors in life found little if any governmental assistance evident. It was spun together in the ribbons of already misused red tape. I can also claim the war as a propellant to my psyche.

Pills to stay alive? They are *not* without charge. Hines Veteran's Hospital in Illinois demands $7 for each prescription I need to stay alive after a heart attack in 2001.

I search deeper for the merriment to be enjoyed in every waking moment, fun around every bend: war consequences life to be a calmer, if not a duller escapade, making some times flooded with whiskey…

Daily awakenings by the clock radio now make me rebellious, as it insists, "Get up, go to the same job you've been undertaking for 27 years. It's Monday and you have 5 more days until your insufficient pay arrives. If you work Saturday, it still leaves Sunday for time to you to repent. Then, next Monday …"

But, anything beat Vietnam. ANYTHING.

You gain strength, courage, and confidence by every great experience in which you really stop to look fear in the face. You are able to say to yourself, "I lived through this horror. I can take the next thing that comes along." You must do the thing you cannot do.

...let me go home, why don't you let me go home? This is the worse trip I've ever been on!

September started unconcernedly, monotonously delivered as another hot 30 days and daily patrols, same as the rest.

Radio checks, mail runs, muddy days and dusty days, the same as the rest.

Our insect supply became inconsistent with the previous months, doubling weekly. Mosquito nets over our racks saved our days and nights from their unscrupulous and perpetual stalking for human blood. It became common for any of us to blare out "M.F.in' little bastards…" while swatting violently at the airborne predators.

"Ski, we're goin' to the CAC unit a digging exercise, so check out the radio on Charlie 21." Hayne had his helmet on, so I knew he was in a hurry.

C21 replaced C24, Weave's Pig that took him and his crew on an Operation a few weeks earlier. I wondered where they'd been for so long of a period, and then remembered that he was short and may have rotated back to the states already. What happened to the Ontos remained to be seen.

C25 was in repair back in DaNang, so that left us in support of the Grunts with only one Ontos again when the platoon was supposed to be comprised of 5.

But I felt glad to be rid of that particular Sergeant and his blistering attitude, so I positioned myself on the 106's barrels once more, 1 percent happier.

Tex drove us down 'suicide', unescorted, the Marine Corps seeming to notch the vehicle infallible, a complete hindrance to aggression. I'd heard of stories of Ontos' that hit land mines, getting torn to bits, but never being ambushed. They DID carry an element of recoil.

Tex was less experienced than Luke to taxi us smoothly to the CAC unit, but he sounded amused doing it. Shattering the stillness with "YAAAHOOO!"'s and "EEEHAWWW!"'s in his metallic rocking horse, he roused villagers young and old from siestas, leapfrogging to see their friendly neighborhood Ontos click by.

I recognized some of the people and waved, but on that day, none were returned. What went on? Did we do something wrong? Could we expect an attack on the hill? I yelled my story to Hayne. His eyebrows gave a wrinkled reply of nonchalance.

"Is this your family out here? Maybe they just had a bad hair day."

I resented his response, opinionated that we should make a closer relationship with the Vietnamese people, not treat them like cattle. Talk to them more. Try to make them closer friends. Visit them occasionally. I thought that was how we were trained and what we were supposed to do.

The CAC unit used a one-story schoolhouse for a union hall, concertina wire surrounding it for protection of about 30 youngsters, 4 Marines and 10 Vietnamese soldiers. Kids done being tutored ran after each other in the playground, just like back home. Entering, Tex made a close right turn and busted off part of the gate that completed our barbed wire  defense. He was tapped on the head with "Stop the train!"

He jumped out to look at damage done. With fists on hips, "Tex, how long you been driving Pigs?"

I jumped off laughing at George and Tex, both smiling with teeth missing and Butler's dentures making up for the both of them.

"I been drivin' about 9 months, Sarge. Off and on, 'ya know?"

"It looks like you just STARTED driving! Park the damned thing over there, and don't hit any kids!" He pointed to a corner of the building.

"C'mon, Tex. I'll guide you over." I backed to the corner behind me, waving my arms to the left and right to clear the kids out of the way. They jumped up and down in front of the sputtering vehicle, hoping that their schoolhouse would get crushed.

"De de mau" broke spirits, and one fell and scraped his leg pretty badly. A few of his friends ran to his aid to mimic struggling G.I.s dragging a wounded comrade out of the range of fire. But they were laughing.

Haynes came over to us to point out next stop. "Tex, you and George stay here and keep an eye on things. BE ALERT! Butler and Ski, grab some the E-Tools, and follow me."

We walked a hundred feet or so to a grove that resembled a graveyard. Command suspected that the VC hid ammo and guns in the area, so Hayne volunteered us to excavate spots on the grounds. 2' mounds of dirt identified them as graves.

"I picked you two because of your size. George and Tex couldn't handle the heat. Butler weighs more than the both of them put together."

Butler's eyes met mine in disbelief. I wondered what the M.O.S. of a mortician was.

We were instructed to dig in two areas of freshly set earth, thinking to myself that maybe the napalm carried too far into the village.

Butler cringed. "There's dead people here, Sarge! What if I hits one of 'em?"

"They won't feel a thing." Hayne turned away with his eyes looking for more fresh mounds, and then lit up the first cigarette I saw him smoke since I met him.

I shoveled shallowly when my worst fears were confirmed. The soft thud of my E-Tool reported a chunk of meat. It stuck on the point of the shovel resembling a side of whitish hued pork sitting in the butcher's refrigerator for retail.

"Sarge, I got something"!" One glance at it was all I needed, so I turned my head away from the view and the smell to let Hayne diagnose my findings.

"It's covered with dirt, Ski. Try to shake some of it off."

I rattled the shovel, and the 5" portion of meat fell back to the dead.

"You're digging too deep. Just scratch the surface." He yelled the same to Butler, but too late.

"I got somthin', too! Awww, Gawd!"

The graves were shallow, so whoever buried the bodies must've been in a hurry to do the job. The part he cut loose was full of hair, like maybe he cracked a skull. Butler spat repeatedly to keep from loosing his lunch, mostly from the smell he said, of the dead.

Mined
Civilian Bus

We never did find enemy supplies hidden in the cemetery, but now I remember my reason for not wanting to dig worms out of the victory garden.

We headed back to Hill 22 a little sicker and a little more tired. I waved to the folks in the vils, still with none in return. Was there a fly in the ointment?

It was around 1900 when we pulled next to our tent for a rest before guard duty, so I thought cards might be in order. "Hey Butler, you know how to play Black Jack?"

I expected a big belly laugh, but all we got was, "Black WHAT?" His eyes were blank. From the graveyard, I guess.

"You know, 'ya gotta get 21, or close to it. Tex, teach him the game."

"Not me, Ski. 'Yer liable to take him like you took Luke."

The game of chance was postponed when Hayne began edging with the sundown, his cue for us to 'line' as sentinels. He confessed his weariness, and that he'd come back in 3 or 4 hours or whenever his mind allowed him to, so George powered his portable radio to help us make it through the night. It wasn't allowed, but the volume was low enough so we could still hear any 'creepings' in the wire. Also, Claymores gave extra confidence.

A particular show called "The Young Sound" was aired in the later part of evenings with instrumental versions of the top rock and roll songs circa '67. Some songs brought me melancholy seizures; reminders of Donna and home once again, so vivid and deeply depressing that I felt that the hazing, white moon was afire, and that even if I went home in one piece, without Donna there was little sense in returning.

The next rendition came on the radio with no one noticing but me. Teammates kept whispering jokes, bartering laughter, so I considered the words of "The Impossible Dream", alone.

To fight the unbeatable foe…
To bear, with unbearable sorrow…
To run were the brave dare not go…
To right the unrightable wrong…
To be better far than you are…
To try when your arms are too weary…
To be willing to give, when there's no more
to give…

To be willing to die, so that honor and justice
may live…
To be willing to march into hell, for a
heavenly cause!
And I know if I'd only be true to this glorious quest, that my heart will lie
peaceful and calm, when I'm laid to my rest…

Those lyrics always inspired me, like a personal anthem composed for the Gallant who offered their heart and soul for justice. If not for them, we might be under the hand of Hitler and his allies.

Hoping not to sound too corny or boastful, if not outdated, it's just the way I was and still am, a flag waver with desire for the strong and the brave to rally.

Guarding our perimeter was quiet that night. No enemy contact, just bleeding hearts and mosquito bites.

And most of September was without major tragedy, unless you were one of the few medevac'd with a sniper round imbedded somewhere in his self.

Rain became less intermittent, bigger drops causing the usual complications; buoyanting, without cement gutters or just plain old drainage systems.

Trenches acted fine as reservoirs and defense, but layers of loosened mud and clay darkened rainwater to a golden hue. Rifles and other weapons were not made to sit in mud, so hang 'em high, was the rule of thumb.

"Our new hill commander wants the trenches to meet, so we have some digging to do", Hayne dug into us, one dark, drizzly morning. This being my sixth month on 22, I was a self-proclaimed salt of the earth, with no one matching my time in the neighborhood. My estimation told Hayne that we were content with our present count of trench-line. We never brushed elbows with each other in it. There was always enough room, so why dig further?

"Because the Captain said so!" He became unsettled when his orders were questioned. Just do what you're told was the military's unending philosophy.

"Grab the shovels, and let's go!"

And we dug in the dirt and the mist, with Hayne at the whip.

"Isn't the rain softening the dirt?"

"Clay is always hard!" sweated out George.

We were pissed off, as usual, the mood the Marine Corps loved to see us in so we were always at the 'natural killer' echelon. We were doing what seemed an unnecessary job in an uncontrollable environment.

Hayne cut us loose after a few hours of slipping and swearing, hating the world we lived in as the rain began to pour, washing mud and crud from our clothing.

We got back to our areas in the tent, soaked with rainwater, shivering, filthy with clay, worse than miserable. The tent flaps were down to hold any heat we might trap, while blocking the wind that never blessed us when the mercury hit 115 degrees. Despondency was another intangible of war, and it never loosened its grasp on Hill 22's cellmates.

At 2000, Hayne reminded us that 100 percent alert was still in effect. I sat on the end of my rack with my face pushed into my hands, wondering if this nightmare would ever end. I knew it would end physically, but I didn't dream that the memory bank would keep the deposit forever.

"Slants are all around, so you'd best be awake, or die." Hayne had his own way of preparing us for the worst.

We sat guard that night and many others like it, sweating under ponchos and helmets, seeing nothing through the rain, hearing nothing but the drenching on leaves and lizards.

This would be my last close encounter on Hill 22. In bucketing rain it happened, blinding and near to everyone. It was most fatal to a grunt that must've felt secure in the rain, falling into his final sleep in the next dimension because he fell asleep in this one. An enemy soldier crawled through the wire and turned a claymore opposite, towards our compound. Incoming small arms fire, hardly audible through nature's noise, gave Grunt a retaliative need to trigger the mine in front of him, consequently removing his face and life. We never heard the snipping, just the terrible thrash of the detonated claymore.

Then again, the jungle hid the enemy to our right, making me scream inside that the bay of trees should've been eliminated months ago. It harbored death for us on 22. Without it, our compound would have been much less accessible to the enemy.

Commanded by the Captain, Hayne ran to us explicating, "We gotta turn right, and shoot into the tree line! Rev up, Tex. Butler, load flachettes, FAST!"

Lightning flashed and crashed into the trees where the enemy was hiding, giving our scene a haunting melody that could have been ended with a VC escaping on a broom with an AK-47 (rifle) replacing a cat.

Tex drove ever so slowly to the point of elimination, with rounds chambered for dissipation of cowards who shot in the dark.

I stayed nearer the Pig's groundwork, and felt the draft of the recoilless rifle's dart round committing its load to the dark. Thunder rivaled the Ontos in the now hell fired cloak of darkness, with the 106's finishing a close second in the competition. The orange blazes from the firing looked like colossal cigarette lighters, giving sight to our front momentarily, only to be left blind after extruding.

Weapons crackled and 'kaboomed' with uncontainable stamina. Fierce, unrelenting, loving the crescendos striving from their toys, the Grunts were toxic in their free fire zone and would explode the mountains in the background if so ordered.

I fancied in my mind the eyes of we youngsters in our most dire of brittleness, reflecting Satan even in the ebony, begging the foe to show full frontal their limb and trunk disassembly. Brows pointing to their open mouths, grinding teeth in the midst of unshaven chin and cheeks, Hell hath no fury…

I finally bent my glasses to my shirt pocket. No eyeglasses *can* give sight to the blind.

"HERSTOWSKI! ON THE RADIO!" Hayne screamed next to C21 in the muddied water. He was panic-stricken as most of us were. But not the Grunts. If they had lost control it didn't show, war whooping as in drunken fits while lobbing frags like immense Cherry Bombs on Fourth of Julys back home.

I had no contact with Battalion but kept trying. I assured Hayne that the battery was new, and to quit putting the blame on me for lose of contact with our Command.

I flung my face in the mud when Butler announced quietly, "Far in 'da ho'!"

Hayne and I were next to the Pig when it erupted previously. I dropped the handset and my weapon in the water that inched over the clay. The plastic bag that the battery came in was wrapped around the handset for obvious effectiveness against the rain, and with the skirmish complete, I called Battalion thrice with no response, finally giving the handset to Hayne to let him give it a try. I sloshed to the tent, tripping only once over a steadfast rope to the mud. With a migraine headache from blasts and stress, I sat in the mud nest of a rack to try my own Prc-25. I fumbled for the handset in the dark then used my Zippo for a quick spark to show me the way. Still, no one was at the post for response. I was mentally worn from the communist aggression, and wanted to roll to the rack behind me to forget the radio, explosions, and life in general. Instead, I oozed my footlocker out from underneath my rack to try to find my list of variable frequencies. I draped my plastic rain jacket over the footlocker and re-lit my Zippo, finding the precious information on the shelf. The limited heat from the burning lighter felt good to my water wrinkled body, but I was anxious to see if the radio was in working order so I turned to and found it positive.

"Charlie, gotcha' loud and clear. You guys get hit? Over."

I didn't get his call sign, so I just answered "Yah. Out", and returned through mud.

"I didn't even know you left. And you got through? I'll have plenty to report tomorrow!"

Tomorrow?

The choppers hovered again, dropping flares and zipping patchy fire below them. The rain had stopped, so they braved anew, as wind and rain were fury they didn't want to contend with, much less hails of bullets.

The rest of the night found us with no opposition except the buggery that must've been melted, smelted and spilled over all inhabitants of Southeast Asia.

Fog was emulsifying in the wind free air and sun. It sat like globs of whipped cream on a very large conglomeration of green and yellow lettuce leaves, with bits of tomato and crab meat contrived with human flesh. Smorgasbord complete, our shipment of meat left on the whirlybirds. I didn't want to watch the loading. It was 'run of the mill', a circumstance of everyday life on this Hill called 22.

I took to washing under the freezing water that our makeshift shower offered. It hardly cleaned the skin, but it removed a layer of mud. My eyes looked bleeding, Butler laughed to me, from soap and sleep deprivation.

"I'm just a Grunt radio man, Jim, not a Hollywood star. And by the way, eat shit and bark at the moon."

Grunts went out to search and destroy any movement in the leftover tossed salad. Most fog dispersed by the sun made the parts of radishes easier to find with the hunt and peck method (stab at possible survivors with bayonets, chuck grenades, riddle with bullets).

Maybe if everyone including senators, congressmen, princes, kings and their sons in college were put to the test of war, wars would end. Useless bloodletting might stop because the most of them would be too sick to continue. Let *them* handle the guns, let *them* squeeze the triggers. Let *them* do the killing, later to watch their Flag burn on a collage campus.

I *did* get a glimpse of the man who got killed with his own claymore. While the corpse was loaded into the chopper, a prop's squall blew open the contained poncho. Imagine leaving a shower, seeing at a corpse with no face. Not clean, but juicy and lumpy, black red in the sunlight. He headed for his closed coffin funeral. Others were crowded next to his body, some moving, some lifeless.

September left me in complete horror-shock. I thought of the previous August as the low light in my life, but the recent mayhem was making me question my ability to hold on to my sanity. It was just too morbid for my mind to perceive much further on.

Letters from my parents came in a couple of times a week, telling me not to volunteer for anything, keep your head down, the Cubs lost another double header. All words from another world, all making me hate Vietnam and the Corps even more. My duties remained the same, no matter what was sent to me through the mail.

They'd ask me if I was in the Front? There WAS no real Front, I told them over again. The newspapers told them that, the T.V. told them that. The last time they asked that in a letter, I wrote "Yes!" and they never asked again.

But it was unfair to take my frustrations out on them, my loving parents. I made my own crib and I was sobbing in it. And I gave another excuse for our fighting to the death. We're the only animals on this planet known to kill for reasons other than to eat for survival. We're less than cavemen, I told Jim, George and Tex, all in their racks. Jim answered in agreement, but the other two snored in dreamland.

"I believe in the Lord, Ski. Do you?"

"'Course I do. We aren't the only ones around. We sure ain't the best, either."

Thoughts of my upbringing with God at my grade school level still didn't focus with my joining the killingest organization in the world. 'Thou shall not kill' haunted and haunts me, but I never thought to be at odds with breaking *that* commandment. I guess I never thought of anything at all while enlisting on the dotted line.

Jim kicked Tex's rack and laughed when he jumped to the floor, ready to fight. Jim got up and wrapped his arms around the appreciably smaller frame to laugh even louder, "I's sorry Tex! I's just jokin'!"

The 40-watt light bulbs we were blessed with showed the two scuffling on our mucky floor. Tex was having an uncontrolled fit of extreme anger controlled by Jim's massive arms, and Jim was having a laughing fit, almost to the point of loosening his hold on his wrestling chum.

"If I get loose, I'll KILL 'ya, 'ya big, dumb shit OX!"

Jim laughed in reply.

Hayne came in growling. "If you have so much energy, maybe we should dig more trenches, HUH?"

Jim let Tex loose, but kept laughing. They separated and went to their corners swiftly.

Ironically, fighting with comrades broke Marine Corps rule, and court martial was the penalty.

"We might be on full alert for another week, so I'd advise as much rest for the wicked as can be gotten. And I don't see any more Ontos coming here for reinforcement, so we gotta make sure that our Pig is good and ready."

Well, C21 *was* ready throughout the early autumn and October days and cold, wet nights. Sparingly, we were allowed nights in the tent for all night sleepovers after Phantom jets were ordered to destroy the tree line that covered our enemy. If they had done that before, many of our casualties wouldn't have happened, and our minds would have held fewer images of the grisly to bear.

Non-critical events confronted me:

Returning from a mail run, I drove over a piece of metal in the road, causing a ruptured flywheel, making me drive 5 or 6 miles back to Hill 22 without a clutch. Tense.

I got chewed out once because of a dirty battery.

Ortiz and Harden a concussion and broke a leg after flipping a P.C. over on the muddy roads of Quang Nai.

I had 2 flat tires.

Wednesday, October 18, "G" Co. 2nd Battalion, 7th Mar Div, reportedly got overrun, 5 miles from us.

Saturday, November 4th, a hairy day to be sure. On that particular afternoon, I drove a mortar team to an outpost for coordinates for night illumination. Not an unusual run, until we were on return to 22 in the near dark of 1800 hours. I knew the road well enough if we scampered in no better than with second gear, but the Lieutenant who shot gunned next to me insisted on more light and speed. We knew it would be self destructive to run with headlights beaming the way, so he called back to the outpost we just left for illumination from the 81's (81mm mortars).

They lit up the sky, but it was surprising to see that they weren't very bright in the driver's aspect because seconds after they ignited brightly, the fluorescence burnt to a lower candle power, leaving a softer glow and night blind eyes especially for quick curves.

"Jesus Christ! Uh, uh, where 'ya going?" The officer questioned my driving, *and* he forgot my name.

I told him that the lighting was terrible, and that if he were ready to drive, I'd sit aside.

Of course, he didn't take the wheel to challenge the coarse, course.

...and you don't know what you got 'til it's gone.

Thursday, November thirtieth, 1967:

"HEY GUYS! GUESS WHAT! WE'RE LEAVIN'! Pack up!"

"JINX! You're kiddin', right?" After spending over a half year of my life in these badlands, I couldn't imagine someone pulling a prank like this on me.

"You DID hear me right! SADDLE UP! We're LEAVING!"

I HOWLED.

In a few hours, Hill 22's metamorphosis was complete. Tents and their stays were packed with everything else on 6 bys that seemed to smile as they were driven down suicide road. I perched upon the Pig, and would, later in life, recall that day while watching one of the most poetic television productions aired; sit-comical series, M*A*S*H*.

Set in the Korean war years on a remote hill, it entangled doctors with their own conflict, showing grief and dismay against the toll the war charged to the best of America's youth and productivity. Captain Pierce, an M.D. who found humor in practically every situation, was losing, mentally. Patching up kids and sending them back to the front from operating room tables made Hawkeye more sullen, rebellious, and broken. Sunken eyes showed lack of sleep being part of his problem, confusing his dreams with reality.

The finale of the series showed the tents being lowered and removed with all restricted and personal articles loaded on 6 bys to leave the hill as it was before the war started, as though nothing had happened, as though no lives were lost or saved, as though no minds were touched or changed.

The final scene was shot from a helicopter, showing the hill vacated and bare, with worn pathways to the mess hall and latrine being the only evidence that it was inhabited.

It fell in place, with my nightmarish hill, 22 feet above sea level. I saw people and Companies come and go from Her, Him, It. Hell, in 6 or 7 months, a person HAD to see a lot happen on the block.

And funny enough, I remember the hill being about one block square.

But we left for higher ground without ceremony or pageantry. We just left. No fanfare, no banner waving, as the mine sweep team led the way for "The Green Machine" to evacuate the premises. I could imagine Hill 22 looking like the forbidden hill of Korean War infamy: dusty, worn, gasping for air.

It didn't mean much to me back then, other than just to get the hell out of the boondocks to a safer billet. But the final episode of M*A*S*H put it in a different perspective. It *was* my home for a very long time, be It ever so humbled with a grand view of the war.

Explosions on the road indicated the sweep team detonating their finds; the enemy had the inkling that this move was to take place.

Yes, I was finally leaving my home, and I looked back from my perch on the 106's and there they were! Memorials left on the hill for the communists to love and cherish, straight from the United States Marine Corps; our piss tubes.

Thanks for the memories.

Hill 22

I have seen him in the watch fires of a hundred circling camps, they have builded him an altar in the evening dews and damps...

Hill 55 was closer to DaNang than was Hill 22, with more incoming and other treachery. We piled in like lost relatives, expecting free food and housing waiting for us with open arms. Not the case. We had to pitch the cumbersome tents and retrace our steps to find the racks that were thrown in under much of the other equipment on the 6 bys. It took most of the day, and lucky we were to have the rain sporadic at best. The terracotta was wet enough, as it made footing difficult when we tried lugging the canvas to another god-awful area, without puddles. Tents manufactured olive drab were now pitched with light brown stains of clay, giving them a more camouflaged appearance missing an artist's touch.

With our temporary estate assembled, we sat on racks, thinking and discussing possibilities of the truce ending conflict and butchery. We heard about it over AFRVN, but none of our commanders visited out compounds with good news or heartening verbalism to make us believe that an end was near. It was only 1967.

"Jenkins, pull 21 next to 24, and keep 'em together while we're on this hill."

Jinx had been on Hill 55 a week or two waiting for the Pig's repairs to be finished. He told me that it ran better, but not as good as it used to. I told him that *none* of us ran better than we used to.

We were near Marble Mountain, and that's all we were told. I guess that we were on the other side of DaNang, with the mountain range separating us from the big city. The Higher Ups got word that the NVA had a rocket attack in the making, so we were going to act as a support unit for the Battalion officers that relaxed through most of the war; baubles in their jewelry box.

The next day we disembarked for a strategic position in the mountains while tens of choppers menaced in the skyline, aching to find souls for their baptism of fire. Fluttering from the opposite side of our position on the mountain, their base refueled them as a pit stop crew would at Daytona. For not perfect formation, they'd resemble a small group of bulky but streamlined dragonflies.

We did a high crawl on the road to our campground, with a ledge on one side displaying a view of the road we'd just grabbed over, the other side thick with brush with few trees for monkeys to climb.

Reaching a flat near the mountain's zenith, Hayne slowed us down.

"Follow me!" He walked ahead then motioned us to stop. After looking around, he called us forward.

"This should work out okay. You guys see anything I might be missing?"

"Where's the toilet?" smiled Jim.

"Okay gents. There are only six of us up here, all fair game. We must help each other. 'Gung Ho', and no foolin' around!" Staring down at the valley, "We're in a free fire zone!"

I was serious, but the others needed coaxing to realize the dilemma that could surprise us in the night. Maybe the 'free fire zone' got to them.

It started to rain, so we tied up a tent to a side of C21 and one to the rear of it, using 292 poles for tent stays to hold up the other side of the tent. Trouble was, dirt floors turned to mud.

It was only 1800 hours, but the blue was already darkening with a cloud covering. Hayne called us to issue frags and pop flares.

"I hope we don't need to use the 'em, but if you need flares, we have plenty of 'em to go around."

There was a wooden case of grenades in the Pig, so I didn't see why we had to be rationed only 3 apiece. The slope was made for frags to roll down at the enemy. It had some brush, but it wasn't heavy and they grew about 10 feet from each other.

Looking around, I noticed a change made on the Pig. The corner 106's were replaced with two .50 caliber machine guns! Jim noticed the change, too. "Sarge, how do those new guns work?"

Jinx answered, "I know how to shoot 'em, Jim. Buttons are inside here."

It still had the .30 cal. so the best we could do at close range down the slope was use every- thing but the 106's. They couldn't turn the guns down at a steep enough angle to hit anything advancing at 45 degrees.

The .50 cal. were in the experimental stage, non-pivot able, unlike the 30 mounted on pods. I was beginning to realize how useless the Ontos could be under certain anxieties. No wonder they were Army rejects.

We looked down at the valley called "Happy". Hundreds of campfires burned in scattered villages below us, some vils being about 2 miles away, some further in the distance. The light rain obstructed some of our view of the farther sights, but I didn't find any reason for us to be concerned with objects that far away.

There was still enough light to see people riding their water buffalo home after a grueling day at the paddy. And we could see tracers being fired in the faraway landscape where I guessed Hill 22 to be near. Choppers still buzzed overhead, to and from their base camp as Hayne told me to be a part of C21's crew. I stood on the back ledge of the Pig by the .30 cal., it giving a shielded, unobstructed view of what was to take place in the morning hours.

C24 was about 100 feet to our left, with joking laughter emitted from its crew, as Hayne tried to stifle their noises so the NVA didn't think that we enjoyed their playing field. Their noise was smothered when the first rocket was launched in our direction, a few miles down below. I jumped from the Pig, yelling and pointing, "THERE, THERE!"

Hayne wondered, "What the hell was it?"

I was dumbfounded, and pointed down in the valley to show him what I saw, as flames could be seen erupting behind the missile to propel it over our heads, over the peak behind us, crashing somewhere in DaNang or on our airbase.

The sound was unlike any I heard before in my life, almost non-explosive. Simply, a big crash on impact, like metal crunching metal.

"Get with Battalion, Ski! Tell 'em we see where the rockets are takin' off! BUTLER, JENKINS, H&I to the ready!"

Pigs didn't travel with rounds chambered due to miss-fires, but they should've been loaded when we reached the plateau.

I got through with my first try, with a response, "WE KNOW, CHARLEY ONE. WE'RE GETTING HIT!" without an "out."

Jinx tried firing the 50's, but after a half minute, the button stopped functioning the anti-aircraft weapons, so he vaulted to the 30.

Hayne was anxious as we saw slowly ascending rockets leave their pads, so close, yet so far away. "You guys FIRE WHEN READY! MOVE IT! SKI! GET THE FUCK AWAY!"

He couldn't see me in the dark, but I knew the Pigs were ready to fire, so I sat to the side of C21, compressing my ears with my fingers, watching another rocket take flight from the same locale.

Both Ontos' left loose almost in unison, with me drawling closer to the ground, flinching from the explosions. The tracer like rounds drilled loudly through the rain and impacted fiercely, missing the launching zone.

"Were we close, Sarge?"

Just then, another rocket started its ascent.

"I see that one", cried George. "I'm turnin', Butler!"

Small arms tracers added to the display in the catastrophic chasm.

"OKAY!" Jim jumped off from behind the Pig. "SHOOT IT! SHOOT THE GODDAMNED THING!"

The rounds tore through the air, landing and destroying ground in a second, as the rocket that was launched before that was just now roaring blue and orange flames a few hundred feet over our heads.

Yet another rocket was slowly leaving its base. It's ascent started slowly enough, and if we were closer, we could have probably shot it out of the sky like a clay duck at a skeet shoot. It elevated that slowly. But we were hardly at that range, so we had to just sit back and take it. Bizarre box seats with our hands tied as at a crucial ball game with home team losing. There was nothing to do, but watch and wait.

Tex expressed his emotions for all of us. "YOU ROTTEN, NO GOOD, MAMA FATHERIN', SON'S 'O' BITCHIN COWARDS! 'YER A BUNCH 'O' CHEATIN' BASTARDS!"

Hayne asked him quietly as he went to the other Pig, "You through?"

Tex got out of the drivers hatch, popped a flare, lay down in the mud, and threw a grenade down the hill. "Fire in the hole."

We were all hiding from the glare when Hayne came back.

"Jinx! Who threw the grenade?"

"Tex, down there!" He pointed down, in front of the Pig, where Tex lay prone in the mud.

"Did you see anything, Tex?"

"I thought I did. No sense takin' any chances, right?"

"Next time, call me over first."

"'Ya mean, if I see somebody down there, I gotta call YOU over first?"

"If you're definite that the enemy is there, go ahead and shoot. If you have any doubts, call me over."

The moon peaked through to show a speck of Tex's eye looking at Hayne, as if to tell him to go to hell, and that this is a war and he wasn't going to waste time asking for permission to stop a VC.

0200 hours and air ships passed us to circle the air over the valley for coordinates reported as probable enemy strongholds.

"If those are the planes I think they are, they're gonna stop the gooks right now."

Nicknamed Spooky or Puff the Magic Dragon, they were either curious children's playmates or airships with machine guns that fired thousands of rounds per minute. With one of every 5 rounds lighting a path for the gunner, fire flowed from the barrel with a ray gun effect. Impressive, the power and might of the ship's humming machine gun sound, not rat tat tatting. Their pellets shredded forests and people alike with humming coupled with the rays of tracers forcing me to believe that it was an alien saucer of unparalleled power, not a United States airplane that had to beg for permission to fire like the rest of us war weary, on their ground below.

"Cantilever this is Cantilever Charlie One. Radio check. Over."

"Charlie One this is Cantilever. I hear you loud with static. How do you hear me? Break. We have WIA's call me later. Over."

"This is Charley. Hear you loud and clear. Roger. Out."

As it turned out, we in the field escaped injury during the attack and the office boys got the worst of it. C'est la guerre.

Puff continued flaring and killing below in our field of vision. With Puff's guns and flares, artillery, and small arms fire in front of us, it reminded me of what could have been the most spectacular firework extravaganza ever assembled, but terrible.

The morning left us to our own thoughts again as we rolled back to our new home-hill. I thought about the busted up packages from my Mom and her never-ending letters of hope and faith with God to bring me back unharmed. Contemporarily thinking, I had another bigger thought and decision in my mind.

Enlisted in the Marines Corps for a 4 year obligation to my country was all well and good, but in December 1967, I had only served 21 months of my 48-month hitch. If I served my 13 months tour and left in February of '68, I was almost assured to get orders to return me to 'Nam' for another full 13-month tour, since I would still have 24 months left on my regular enlistment to serve.

Talking to some Gunnery Sgt. straightened me out for a fast 'solution'. He told me to extend my tour here for 6-month battalion duty, with a 30 day leave off the books, and all travel expenses paid, round trip. By doing that, I wouldn't have enough time left for another tour.

It was the best way out, so I signed on the dotted line.

...I was there when the General drank, while the Blitzkrieg raged and the bodies stank...

To everything, there is a season...a time for love a time for hate, a time for war a time for peace...

I was at Battalion Headquarters in DaNang, sent to one of their permanently based 'tents' until my next set of orders read 'San Francisco, FPO'. I just wanted OUT of country! At least for a free month leave plus about 6 days travel time.

At Battalion level, a different world was shown. The living quarters were much cleaner, starting with the wooden floor of plywood that was elevated a few feet off of the ground for less dampness and less insect invasions. More conveniently, the walls had screen, allowing light in and bugs out. And real screen doors on real hinges with springs that slammed them tight behind any drunken Marine's ass.

I looked around the personal area in the 'house'. Most of them had fans mounted on 2X4's that held up the roof, and plywood boards were walls between each area. Some even had ammo crates nailed together for shelving to display their reel-to-reel, 8-track Sony's.

During rainfall, the only dismay I could offer was the noise the metal roof made diverting it, because I was dry for the first time in weeks.

I was still in my muddied jungle utilities when I found my way to the office for directions to the nearest shower. A Corporal Sutton was sitting at his desk, typing and trying to look "Marinely" at the same time.

"Need anything, Lance?" I could tell that this Marine hadn't spent one day out in the bush.

"Yah. I'm new here, and I need a shower. Is there one close by?"

He looked at me, up and down. "Yah, you sure DO need a shower!"

He walked me outside of the office and pointed out the shower and the head. "The laundry's down there too", he added. "They charge 50¢ for a bag full. And the massage parlor's down a way's."

I went back to my new billet, stripped and rushed to shower, thinking. Massage parlor? After getting wet, I stood there and let the water run on me. I didn't need to take a 'Navy' shower. That is, wetting down and shutting the water off while lathering up. No, I soaped up while the water ran, and ran, and ran. The water still had it's own perfume of the wilds, but not as bad as the water on Hill 22. And electric lights led me to believe the shower was opened 24 hours a day, not just to be run in the light of the sun. And it was warm water. Not hot, just right.

I got back to my bunk, still under the spell of this Shangri La, wondering if these guys had women issued to them under dire circumstance.

With a clean set of utilities that smelled like the field I just left, I awakened to the nose, threw my loads of dirty clothes together and ran them to the neighborhood laundry.

On my way there, I passed a Captain who was alarmed when I didn't salute his double bars. Officers weren't saluted in the field for the obvious reason of signaling the foe to kill our ever-important commanders. My simple explanation seemed to elude the man, but he excused my rudeness when I gave the hand salute.

I got my laundry chit, and then returned to my area to rest and recall, lying down thinking of my friends and family that I would see upon my reincarnation to the world. Some of my cousins were like brothers and sisters to me, chasing me through the narrow gangways of Chicago's south west side, unnerving my younger mind with threats of dismemberment if they ever caught me.

They were hardly that tough with me, but branded with an 'only child' title, I was also labeled with a 'Momma's boy' moniker that tailed me to my 18th birthday when I left my own room in Berwyn that had toys stacked to its ceiling for parts known only to the Marine Corps.

Maybe it was Rich but mostly Butch, who convinced me to reach for heights of the best, to show my true gift in a fashion that none of the other Herstowski's showed before on our family tree. It surely was no fault of my own, that I was free of natural brothers and sisters, but I was treated like it was.

So in the end, I think those few that I loved and love, forced me into the pages of American History to do what I may have done on my won anyhow.

Uncles, you were quiet in the corners with your glasses of Blatz. I thank you for that.

Aunts, some of you still refer to me as a Mama's boy, but it doesn't bother me anymore, because you as women only knew the true horrors of war from the newspapers and film clips; you'll never feel the real meanings so keep talking, I'm listening.

Nancy was a kinder cousin to me. She would walk with me to Barton's corner grocery store to share a sky blue Popsicle, if I found 6 cents my Dad might have forgotten on our kitchen table. Also, she said that I bit her on the back once, but that I don't remember.

I fell to my most restful sleep in months, in the new area, awakened by Battalion radiomen whose prime concern was about what film was playing at the E-Club that evening. They had no concern about war or patrols. I lay there thinking about how unfair it was for the Grunts to suffer as they did, while an area like this was developed for in-country R&R during entire certain 13-month tours. Hell, I felt like I was cheating on my combatants by taking a real shower then sitting under a truly protective roof. C'est la vie again.

1700 hours found me hungry, so I forced myself to introduce myself to roommates so I could follow them in a friendlier fashion to a mess hall that I hadn't yet seen. The food was real, but still came out of cans, larger than the ones out of the cardboard boxes. And second helpings were allowed for everything but servings of meat, unless you had friends behind the counter.

I was asked where I came from, how long I had been in country, and where I was off to next, as though spinsters had the new kid on the block crowded in their kitchen for questioning. Their eyes widened when I told them of my 6-month extension and my thoroughly valid reason for doing it.

"You been in the field for 11 months and still want 6 more months of it? Hard core, baby!" one belched out, as I gulped down real powered milk.

"I don't want another MINUTE of it! I'll be at battalion level. Says it right on the contract."

We gathered our mess kits together to wash and rinse in 55-gallon drums outside the back door. The tray, silver ware and canteen were strung together to be dipped and brushed off in soapy, near boiling water in the first drum, then rinsed off and disinfected in the last two. Near the end of serving time, water in the drums would graduate with fat and diced carrots.

We walked back to our billet with our weapons clanking against our mess kits. I had no where to lock up my M-14, so I carried mine with to the chow hall, but I found that it was their order of the day to *always* carry their weapons with them no matter where they went, but unloaded.

I was inquisitive. "You guys get much incoming around here?"

"A few days ago. Rockets came over the mountains and blew up the air base. We got 100 percent alert then! It was horrible!"

I didn't feel like going over my side of the story, so I dropped the subject like the proverbial hot potato.

Getting back to my area, I dragged out my foot locker to look through my stack of letters for the phone number that would connect me with the real world and a high school girl who was nice enough to take the time to write a stranger in the fields of Vietnam.

I got a few letters from high school juniors and seniors, not thinking much of them, but I wanted a girl, a friend, who might listen to my problems for a while. It was an interesting aspect added to my life, which was really becoming necessary.

I finally found the letter, from a Miss Bonnie Fischer. The name Bonnie was feminine enough, and soothing to my ringing ears, so I wrote down her phone number for future reference. Donna forgot me, so making contact with this 'Bonnie' girl became a goal for me to score before the clock ran out on my leave.

She had red hair and blue eyes topping 5'2", and weighing 98 pounds, I was hooked into at least meeting this lassie.

Fate stepped into her Family Psychology class as an 85-year-old professor would, expressing his need for the students to be more attentive and studious, for them to succeed at anything in their future lives. In it's simplest form, she drew my name from a hat filled with names of servicemen tending the fires of Vietnam, truly at random.

And she sounded dedicated enough to wish me the best of luck, hoping to see me when I came home. It was written on November 13, 5 days before her 18th birthday and 11 before mine, and she sounded somewhat elated with an upcoming visit to Great Lakes Naval Hospital for gift giving and caroling for the wounded boys recovering there. I felt like I knew her already or that I wanted to. She was willing to give some of her time to the youth who were bleeding for their countrymen. Bonnie Fischer was a true American Patriot.

And she wrote further that she planned to write and keep writing to at least one guy who was great enough to be out fighting for his country. I stopped reading her message to wipe my eyes.

Continuing, she confessed opposition to any war, but if it had to be she would praise the guys who were out there fighting.

She ended with the news of their great gasoline strike, with buses dry and the city paralyzed. At that, I refolded the letter and stuffed it into my duffel bag to read again on my flight back to the world.

The billet closed in on me over the next few days. Writing letters and reading stories about the man from Krypton in my all too plentiful leisure bogged me down, waiting for the word to come through that my flight to Chicago was ready and that I had to double time it to get to the airport.

Nothing changed in the great outdoors. The rain stayed pitilessly at the tin roof, humidity still stepped up the ladder of discomfort, and our aircraft continued to bludgeon the grasslands to encourage an armistice in the Armageddon.

I could hear the explosions and firefights in the distance coming from over Marble Mountain, having me to think of Hayne and Butler, Tex and Jim and the other hundreds of souls that I met but never caught their names. We struggled together in the blasting heat and under our invader's persistence, sitting on Hill 22 minding our own beeswax, wanting to just bide our time until our tours expired.

How I sat in the 99 and 99/100th % safety of Battalion's rear perimeter, feeling extra remorse with my choice of tour annexation for my own satisfaction while the guns blared and mortified in the fields I just left, is still beyond me.

My depression was soon to push deeper, when a Sgt. Jones walked to my three-sided cubicle.

"Herstowski, right? We need you to pull guard duty tonight." He sat down next to me on the rack.

"We don't get much action around here, but you still have to wear your combat gear. There's alotta crap goin' on in the valley, so we're on 100% alert. We usually sit two in each bunker, and Sutton will be your company. Go to the armory with him for some ammo. How come you got an M-14? Radio men get issued 45's."

"It was issued to me when I got here. It got heavy, but I felt more thorough with it. More staying power, 'ya know."

"Okay. The truck leaves for the bunker line at 1800. Be ready."

Sutton was in his rack a few cubes down from me, appreciating his mail from home, chuckling, "Hey Ski!" he yelled without removing his gaze. "You been on guard duty before? I'll show you the tricks around here. First off, he sat up and put the letter down, "We'll take turns sleeping. We never get hit around here, so it's safe."

"You sure of that? Mistakes need to happen only once and BAM! You're in a body bag!"

"Out in the bush, yah. But here, nothin' ever happens. Hey, c'mon with me."

We walked around the back where a Pig lay, destroyed.

Rocketed Ontos

"What the hell happened, Sutton?" I walked to the front of the machine. "I hear that a rocket hit it. Guess the whole crew got killed. Nothin' much left to this one."

B24 was stenciled on a remaining front bumper. Weave didn't make it. His rowdiness didn't mean a thing anymore. He was gone forever.

6 o'clock entered quite readily as my collaborator, me and about 20 other office pogue mounted a 6 by for a ride to the mountain and its bunkers. It was on the side of the rise that the two Pigs and me sat on for the pyrotechnics a few days earlier.

The truck stopped to leave us at our posts.

"Follow me, Ski."

Sutton was a carefree type of enlistee, smiling, telling grade school level jokes and needing orthodontics for a missing front tooth, adding to my list of dentist's delights that I'd met in the 'Nam'.

He led into our bunker, smacking his helmet against the low hanging 2X4 that helped hold up the roof of sandbags. "Watch 'yer head, Ski! Low bridge!"

I walked down the 4 steps and felt around on the wooden plank with my foot. "Any sudden drops here?"

"Heh, heh, 'yer a card Ski."

The view was okay. There was about 3 feet of space between the roof and a deck of sandbags that served as an elbow rest, and the uprights at each corner did little to obstruct our vision. Shockingly, I saw the flat the Pigs were parked on during the rocket attack.

I pointed to the area of the rocket launches. "That's where they were shooting the rockets from, Sut. And that's where I was at when I saw 'em take off." I pointed to the Pig positions.

"You were down THERE? Couldn't 'ya shoot at 'em? You were with the Ontos, right? I saw your records in the office."

"The guys shot 6 or 7, 106's. .30 cal., .50 cal.! EVERYTHING WE HAD, SUTTON!" I started to burn.

"Easy, Ski. I think your Ontos guys would blow up this whole country if they'd let 'ya."

He was right.

I can't remember what state he came from, but we jawed 'til early morning about good times to be had back home. It was a favorite leisure passing of mine, reminiscing and pray the good times roll on soon.

"I can't sleep, Sut. Go ahead and rest awhile." He was already propped against his corner of the bunker, dozed away. The space we were in was roomy enough for 3 or 4, 6 footers, so I could stretch my arms and legs easily without disturbing his slumber.

The drizzle turned to rain, then to flow. Periodic thunder and lightening turned immense, broadcasting to its audience a link to a Halloween dance with Beelzebub conducting a symphony for the devil.

I never saw the flashes of light insist with such long intervals before. The entire valley seemed to blanched silvery for 10 to 15 seconds, much to the chagrin of creeping, would be slayers. Mother Nature was in charge, making Her effort known to quell and snuff out man's inhumanity to man.

The storming did comfort me because, who the hell would brave this unceasing torrent of water just to kill the enemy?

Thunder rocked the clouds and earth heavier than 175mm's, almost to the point of me expecting the earth's annihilation. Then, more lightening, a flash that alarmed me to a movement peripheral. I awaited another course of light and stared in the direction I realized the motion to precede. Leaning closer to the sand bag upright, I strained my eyes for better scrutiny.

The next crack of light gave me an up-close, eye-to-eye portrait of a giant centipede, crawling slowly between the sand bags and their wooden platform.

I read most of Edgar Allen Poe's works, but the chills my body focused to my brain when I saw this poisonous hundred-legger beat his thrillers, crawling still. The creature must have been 1" in diameter, and if they grew a foot long, this was one of them.

I couldn't take my eyes off of it as it manipulated itself vertically between the bags, then fell to the floorboards.

I stomped in a frenzy until I heard, and felt a crunch and a smoosh, and a, "What the hell you doin', Ski?"

The crunch ordered a ceasefire to my feet. I told Sutton that I was ambushed, but didn't need reinforcements because the situation was well in hand. Or foot.

The following morning, "Herstowski, report to the office. The Gunny's got some papers for you to sign." Sutton's one fang smile told me that my orders for home had come through.

"13DEC67. DRAWN ON TRANS WORLD AIRLINES FOR JET COACH CLASS AIR FARE FROM LOS ANGELES, CALIF. TO CHICAGO, ILL. AND RETURN TO SFO VIA…"

It was my flight to destiny, from DaNang to Okinawa, to L.A. to Chicago, to Lyons, to Bonnie…

California dreaming, on such a winter's day.

"I want you to want me. I need you so badly, I can't think of anyone but you...well, I think I'm goin' outta my head."

The trip took a few days, anxiety peaking as my jet set down at O'Hare on December 16th, 1967. It was like a fresh spring breeze after a long, desolate winter, this reawakening to the world.

Anticipations lifted my spirits over the crisp coldness of the Windy City's winter tide, as I trudged down the ramps to see my parent's smiles and a few more gray hairs.

We hugged understandably. Mom sobbed and Dad winced at my sunburned, more thought explained face, as we strolled to the parking lot with me in a slight hurry to resume unfinished business.

Mom was squeezing my hand. "How is it there, Billy? Look at your face! Gawd, It must be hot!"

I really didn't feel like saying much about Vietnam. I didn't want to talk at all. It was just great to be home.

"It was a long trip, Ma. Let me rest for a few days huh?" Her big smiles made me feel good, but Dad's 'I told you not to join' scowl reminded me of my misdeed. But we all fell into their new Galaxy 500 temporarily relieved, zipping out of the airport's hold to the inbound Eisenhower Expressway.

I sat in the back seat, stretching out, "Cubs didn't do too good, huh, Dad?"

"Ahhh! They NEVER do! The Blackhawks are doing okay, though." Mom interrupted quietly. "Did you hear from Donna or Marilyn?"

"Marilyn wrote, but I told her that she's too young for me." Short pause. "Donna didn't write." I wasn't sure, but something I wrote must have rubbed her the wrong way. Just one letter changed our lives forever, and now, I can't remember what I wrote wrong.

"Nothing? Nothing at all?"

"Nothing, Mom."

I could see Dad look at me in the rear view mirror.

"Don't worry. You're young, you'll adjust."

I forced a difficult smile to him.

"I DID get a letter from a girl in Lyons, wherever that is."

"It's somewhere south. Near Harlem and Ogden, I think."

"You hungry, Honey?" Without waiting for an answer, "Phil, lets go to Seneca's! Billy, you have to start eating better. How much do you weight?"

"160."

"Kay, will you leave the kid alone?"

I laughed to myself in the back seat. If they knew the crap I saw over there, they wouldn't call me 'kid'. But I suppose they would, no matter what, me being their only child.

We finally touched home base about 9 that evening. I left my sea bag outside the basement door and got to my bedroom, never before realizing how welcome the mattress could look. I fell into it with my uniform pants still on, and half asleep, I heard Mom come in to cover me with a new blanket she got from Sears. So thoughtful she was, *always*.

I slept, or lay in bed the next two days. No ambition, no energy, no nothing.

Sitting at the supper table, my parents showed disagreement towards my sullen expression.

"Oh, Peaches, Things aren't THAT bad. Why don't you smile more for us?"

I would tell them that I was just tired. I didn't tell them my first love was gone, and that I went through a year in a war without as much as a letter from a girlfriend. It meant much more to a warrior to get correspondence from female lovers than a mother could understand.

My mind was still messed up from the combat occurrences and I had no one to turn to for help. I told my parents and they insisted that I forget about the whole damn thing. After that, they worried more than ever, and I put them though enough already. It was my own inner battle to be won on my own.

My mind was so despondent, that I forgot about all the girls I was despondent over. The war did its part, sure, but the girls? Well, they were girls I wanted to be a hero for, and I didn't even hear from them after I left home.

I drove passed Donna's house the first week, too unnerved to stop. I just passed it by. I parked in front of her home once too, but just drove away. I

165

thought that if our love was strong, she would have written to me, so I considered it abated, and left it at that for the present.

Then there was the little red head in Lyons. She wrote that her friendship with some guy named John was dissolved, so I was sure that they were together again and proud parents of twins. But I said to myself, stop the self-pity, blockhead! Go home and call her up! She's waiting for you!

A woman answered the phone. "Hello."

"Hello. Can I talk to Bonnie, please?"

She set the phone down. "Bonnie, phone!"

Shortly, "Hello?"

"Hi. I was thinking about calling you, but I've been kind of busy lately. This IS Bonnie Fischer, isn't it?"

"Yes?"

"And you live at 4409 Elm, in Lyons, right?"

"Uh, yes, I do."

"Well, I'm glad I called the right Bonnie, at least. Do you want me to come over?"

"WHO IS THIS?"

With disrupted mind, I forgot an introduction.

"OH brother! I'm sorry. This is Bill. You wrote me a letter when I was in Vietnam."

"Bill! OHHH! How are you? I didn't know it was YOU! YAH, c'mon over!"

She gave directions to her house, and on an unseasonably warm winter afternoon, I drove over to meet her. Ron Britain's teenage humor spiced up his AM radio program, as I veered to the right off of Harlem Avenue, through the forest preserve, passed the Desplaines River to turn left on Elm. It was the first time I'd ever entered this enchanted labyrinth, and it looked nice enough to revisit.

4409 was glassed on the front door. I parked in front and looked up and down the street. It looked great to me. Hardly a car but mine stood in the way of the view of America's dream houses. The area looked calm and clean, inviting. I felt almost ready, so I got out of Mom's Ford and reached the 7 wooden steps that led to the porch and front door. Then I thought, what if things don't mesh? What if she's a monster?

It couldn't be worse than 'Nam', so I rang the doorbell. The door opened in a microsecond, and seeing her, I held my breath. Her smile was the best thing I'd seen in over a year, bigger than Ol' Sol on an August afternoon, appreciating it as a welcome home from Vietnam.

I stuttered "B-Bonnie?" admiring her bright, red hair.

"Bill? Hi! C'mon in, it's cold outside!"

Any model knows that to be more beautiful, they have to smile their best, so I pictured her as a cover girl supreme.

I tried to keep the conversation going. "Yah, it sure IS cold outside."

Her mother sat in a living room chair doing a crossword puzzle. "This is my mom, Loretto. Mom, this is Bill, uh, what was your last name, again?"

"Hello Loretto. My last name is Herstowski."

Bonnie's smile ascended to laughter. "HERSTOWSKI! Now I remember." We exchanged smiles. "My Dad won't be home 'till 6. Let's go sit in the kitchen." She led the way. "Want some coffee, Billy?"

"Okay." I was relaxed already, and I didn't remember how nice it could be to be called Billy, instead of that stupid Polish de-breviation I answered to since enlistment.

Coffee and words mixed, starting our relationship. Brightness in the kitchen helped keep me relaxed, with the sunlight's rays teeming through two high-set windows.

"Bonnie says that you have to go return to Vietnam?"

I told them my reasoning, and they agreed, but asked, "Are you SURE that you'd be sent back for a full tour if you didn't extend now?"

"Well, I believe so. The Marine Corps is good for only one thing and it's happening there right now."

"How is it there?"

"It's hot, Bonnie, very hot. I'll tell you the whole story sometime, but not now. I have to get going. Thanks for the coffee and your time. It's been nice."

Her mother stayed in the kitchen while Bonnie walked me to the door. I thanked her for the coffee again, and turned to see her smiling. "Well, take care of yourself, Billy. If I don't see you again, wish everybody over there good luck, too."

"I will, thanks." I wasn't really in a hurry, but I got uncomfortable when we started talking about the war.

Secondly, I hadn't been so close to a real girl for so long, I forgot how to act. And what did they think of me? A killer? A lunatic?

But Bonnie was very nice. She was petite, pretty, a quiet type but talkative.

"Uh, Bonnie? Can I call you again?"

Her smile lengthened. "Oh, yes. I'd like that", almost squealing.

My heart jumped to my throat. I reached out to shake her hand, and her light grasp meant that she could be a friend of mine for a long time to come. I liked it.

"Talk to 'ya later. Bye!' I saw myself doing a tap dance down her front steps in James Cagney style, light of heart and strength of character. Coordination unchallenged.

I sat in the car for a while and thought, 'Her EYES! That's what I was falling for! Not just her smiling lips! Her smiling eyes completed the painting like an artist's masterpiece!

I looked out of the window to see her holding the front drapes aside to wave to me. I waved back and started the car, and remembered the war again. Just like that, my mind left a pretty little girl for a glimpse of a trench line flooded with water.

The first stop at the corner found me pounding my head on the steering wheel. "Why did I extend over there?" I had my eyes closed for a half minute, until a driver behind me sounded his horn to awaken me from my seizure.

Route 66 at the end of the next block, I asked myself if I should bring Bonnie into my turmoil by calling her again. She didn't have my phone number, so it would be simple enough to just leave her with her youth and happiness, not to mar it with the likes of the Vietnam conflict.

I went home for more penance to serve in my room. Two days later, I was starving for Bonnie's company. Lying in bed, staring at the ceiling was no way to enjoy life. Dad walked in to see contemplation. "Bothered with the war, Bill? 'Ya gotta take it as it comes. Try to forget about it, because everything always works out."

"I know, Dad. Thanks." He knew of WWII and what I was thinking about.

"I got 2 tickets for the Hawks game tonight. Want to go?"

"Well, uh I was supposed to call Bonnie up, Dad. Maybe some other time?"

"Yah, sure. Next time." He set the tickets on the bed and went into the kitchen. It was to be my first date with Bonnie, and it turned out that the game my Dad got tickets for him and I went to his son and his date. I thought nothing of the brush off I gave him then, but since, I've felt like a first class heel. God, I wish I could turn back the clock. Even though he didn't love hockey, he got the tickets for him and me, and I ignorantly turned my back on him for the love of a girl.

"Hello?" She sounded anxious, and waiting for my call. "Hi, Bonnie? This is Bill. Would you like to go to the show or something?"

"Yah. Sure! I was waiting for your call. Did something happen?"

"No, I was just mediating." She laughed, thinking it was a joke. "I'll pick you up around 6, Okay?"

"I'll be ready. G'bye!"

I had one appointment I had to adhere to. Donna still had a hold on me, and in one of her few letters, she asked if we could still be friends while telling me about her new boyfriend. But I had to see her once more, so I traveled to the romantic West Side of Chicago to complete the self-appointed meeting she knew nothing about. I hoped that her father was at work, because I didn't really feel like talking to him. Tony was the strictest of the strict, allowing not a minute tardy to go unpunished. A 5-minute late return of his oldest daughter meant a 10-minute speech with grounding principles. We'd be separated for 2 weeks whenever we were too late for our own good, or so he'd imply. It was barbaric, his reins on his children, and in recalling his censorship, I found him to be my last obstacle to jump from Donna's arms into the net of the Marine Corps. It was a deep love her and I staged, and I was about to make my last appearance.

I rang the doorbell, surprising young Winnie to yell "BILLY IS HERE!" as she ran up the staircase.

"I'll wait here, Sis."

My Old Flame came down the steps. Seeing her made it impossible for me not to break a smile because she looked lovelier than ever, her long hair and blue eyes easily holding my heart again. She had a smile confused with a frown, and stretching out her arms to greet me, "How've you been, Bill? Didn't you get my letters?"

Now she had me thinking that U.S Post Office had something to do with the demise of our love affair. I didn't answer, but gazed into her eyes musingly, returning home in my Dad's GTO after a Saturday at Riverview Park for some wild roller coaster rides. "Do you have a new boyfriend?" I didn't know what to hope for.

"Yah. John is really nice to me, Bill. Maybe we can get together some time?"

"We'll see when I get back. Okay?" I knew I couldn't force us to love again. I was willing, but she, well, I never found out what she had in her mind. Then, a short goodbye kiss, with my heart torn to pieces as from a claymore.

And when I walked away from her forever, I prayed that it wasn't a mistake, and that she knew that I still loved her completely. I guess that she thought that I just up and left her.

Guessing again, I did.

My drive to Lyons took me much longer than it should have. I was ready for asylum custody, with more grief than most 20 year olds can scarce imagine. I cruised down 26th Street, passing my old neighborhood on Komensky Avenue, driving on side streets to get lost in the crowds. It was wintertime, so most people were inside, or out doing their last minute Christmas shopping. Me, I was shopping for my soul, and didn't know where to start.

Riding by ghetto type buildings, I came to see that I wasn't alone with troubles and heartbreak, and feeling remorseful was the last apt way to save my cranium from discombobulation. My solution may be in Lyons I reasoned, so I got back on the right track and left those heartbreak hotels. I vowed myself never to go back, as I hit Harlem Avenue south for points west. Swirling snow made me feel as though the medevac choppers had followed me 12,000 miles to billow white dust in my eyes and face, melting on impact instead of burning and smarting like brown salt crystals.

"Halloo!" Bonnie called out, almost before she had the front door open to me. "C'mon! Get out of the snow!"

She had the door open enough for me to squeeze through; impossible to walk passed her without rubbing up against her pixie like frame, with a closer look into her eyes. I wanted to kiss, but instead, we just shook hands.

"Hi. The snow is really coming down! I'm not used to driving in this! Mud, yes. Snow, no!"

I still had my coat on, and she nearly ripped it off of my shoulders. "You can meet my Dad now, then we can go out somewhere."

I followed her into the kitchen, where the man sat with a cup of coffee and a newspaper. He displayed the spectacle of a wrestler retired from the ring. 5'10" and about 220 pounds, with a voice deep as the Grand Canyon, he bellowed "HIII! Bill, is it?"

"Bill, this is my Dad, Art."

I reached out for a handshake, and his rough hands were proof he worked for his meals. "Hello, sir. Glad to meet you."

I sat down in a kitchen chair, nervous as usual. He offered "Coffee or beer?"

"Maybe just a little coffee, thanks."

The above kitchen lights reflected their glow off of his nearly completely bald head. I guessed his age to be around 60. "What kind of work do you do, Mr. Fischer?"

"Mostly oil burners. Side jobs keep me on the go, too. And call me Art."

He looked kind of uneasy stirring the sugar in his coffee. "What's it like over there?" in a quiet tone.

"Bill has to go back, Dad", Bonnie intruded sadly. I felt needed but also felt like I was already interrupting her life.

"See any action there?" staring at me as if to look deeper into my spirit to see of I was still human, or a Spartan ready for another kill. "I don't think we should be there, Bill. Those people have to fight themselves, right?"

"They haven't the means to fight for themselves yet. We're supposed to be just helping them." I took a sip of my coffee. Looking up, I saw the clock on the wall reading 6:00. It was time for us to depart with the end of war discussion. I looked at Bonnie. "Uh, I have some tickets for a play. It starts at 7:30, so I think we should take off."

I was waiting for Art to say something like, "Bill, you'd better leave, and never come back. And don't touch my daughter!" Instead, "You kids have a good time. And be careful driving with the snow, Bill!"

My spirits weren't that high since I met my folks at O'Hare. So far, I was accepted. We all went to the living room. Bonnie went for my coat, and I asked her father how the Blackhawks were doing.

"I watch the Cubs, but not too much hockey. Lemme go get the paper."

Bonnie was back with our coats. "Dad, we can look LATER!" She was in her rush mode, and I loved it.

"Oh, sure. You kids run along. Talk to you later, Bill."

"Nice meeting you, Mr. Fischer. G'bye, Mrs. Fischer."

Her Mom walked from her bedroom, just to say goodbye. Later, I asked Bonnie if her Mom was sick or something, being in bed so early in the evening.

"Uh", she hesitated. "It's more like 'something'."

I opened the car door and nearly slammed it on her leg as the ice crystals pelted my brown face. The jungle climate unaccustomed me to the winds of Chicago, the Hawk becoming insistent during Christmas tide. I jumped into the car, shivering noticeably.

"Freezing, isn't it?"

Nodding, I started the engine. "So you're going to Morton West. I graduated from there in '65." I got another chill.

"Yah. I graduate next June, finally!"

"I was sad when I graduated. Not that I'd miss school, but that my friends and I would be going all different ways. No one seemed to know where they were going to end up."

Our conversation briefed, as we slipped ahead to the Stadium. I thought about the grand days I experienced with my school chums when we'd pile in any car for bashes unmatched on Madison Street. Bobby Hull and Stan Mikita took to the ice against the Montreal Canadians, Boston Bruins, or any other of the 6 teams contained in the National Hockey League. Standing room only tickets were sold before each game @ $3.50, and unless you held a season pass, it was the only way to get in. Seating at the Chicago Stadium was 16,666, with the S.R.O. crowd total over 20,000, making the roar deafening and inspiring to the players.

Bonnie broke through my nostalgic cloud. "Is it real bad over there? We see terrible things on T.V."

I nodded, and quickly asked a question I already knew the answer for. "How did you get my name?" She told me, smiling at her random pick.

"Oh! Was Mr. Megro there in 1965?"

I answered her with a fulfilling laugh. "HA! Yah, he was there! A real pain, too."

Megro was chief of the hall guards, using an imaginary cat 'o' nine tails to keep the students under control as they strolled between classes.

I turned onto the Eisenhower Expressway, heading towards the heart of the Windy City's downtown light show.

"OHHH! We're going downtown to see the play? I NEVER get down town!"

"We're going to see a lot of plays, but we're not going all the way downtown."

We traveled in the dark, so Bonnie was really baffled and lost. Before reaching the Damen Avenue exit, the Stadium came into view. I pointed to our left. "See that big building a few blocks away?"

She looked back and forth. "Yah, I think so."

"Don't you know where we're at? It's Chicago Stadium!"

"OHHH! The circus is in town? I haven't seen a circus since I was little! This should be FUN!"

I was hoping that I wasn't bursting her bubble when I handed her the tickets.

"WHAAAT? A HOCKEY GAME? THAT'S GREAT!" I was relieved to see her enthralled with the outset of our first date.

We entered through the doors to the warmth and festivity of the Stadium. Frozen but smiling anxiously, we dusted off snow gathered on our shoulders from the endless walk through the parking lot. The giant organ rumbled 'Jingle Bells' to keep in tune with the season's chorus of love and brotherhood. But it hardly kept my mind from sweating in the jungle where my comrades kept the candle burning for my return. It just wouldn't go away.

Bonnie showed me the ticket stubs. "Where's Second Balcony at?"

"Hold my hand and I'll show you."

Second Balcony seats were wickedly elevated, taking 5 minutes of stair climbing to reach, even for the most physically fit.

'Jingle Bell Rock' was being played as we finally opened our eyes to the grandeur of the ice a hundred feet below which was also breathtaking, as we both leaned up against the brick walls to catch our breath.

Puffing away, "There's the beer vendor. Are you getting one?"

"Ha. I'm only 20, Bonnie." I couldn't vote yet, either. "Let's go find our seats."

Easy to find, they gave a splendid view of the player's pre-game warm up. I wouldn't trade these seats for the world, I thought. The view of the game and Bonnie were all I needed to keep me flying right. I put my arm around her and she turned to smile back at me, giving me foresight while making me believe that she was one to be trusted to hold my heart until I was back home forever. Of course it was way too soon to tell, but I'd find out before January 16th.

"This looks exciting, Bill. Where did the players go?"

"They just finished their warm ups, and they went back to the locker rooms. You'll know when they're on their way back."

She looked at me puzzled, but soon found out when the thunder of the crowd announced their approval of the goalie, Glenn Hall, admitting to the ice from behind the Blackhawk's net. The roar rumbled through the mountaintops and rambled in the dell, peaking when Bobby Hull's first blade scratched the ice.

I looked and laughed at Bonnie wincing, holding her ears shut to prevent hearing damage. She looked back with her eyes brows forming a 'V'. "They're all NUTS!" she screamed.

"YAH!" I screamed back to her.

Then the crowd was asked to rise for the playing of our National Anthem. I was reluctant to hear it, being on leave from a war that I had to go back to, and it was the first time I would hear it played since I was forced to wear combat gear and shoot guns for freedom. But now I felt that the song was being played in honor of all men and women who were involved in tragedies accrued from war.

I think the manufacture's name was Hammond. Whatever, when it started piping the Anthem, the organ rose slowly under a hydraulic lift, a few feet or so, then gave ground back to it's former position as the last stanza of the song was undertaken with another roar from the crowd.

So I had all I could do to keep the tears from falling from my eyes. I thought about anything imaginable, from an Ernie Banks home run to firecrackers. I don't think that Bonnie saw me wipe my eyes on my flannel shirtsleeves, but I know that the shirt *did* hide my chest swelling with pride.

I don't remember which goal produced it, but I stole a kiss at that moment, unchallenged. It was one of a multitude.

I think the hawks beat the Boston Bruins that night 3 to 2, but it didn't matter much. My new friend and I had a great time, and the snow waiting for us after the game didn't matter either. In fact, walking into a snowstorm after a hockey game was fitting and welcomed by most hockey fans.

But before we reached the street, mixed with the crowd on the stairway, the customary dirge from the organ could be heard. After a loss or a win, the sad restraints marked the end of another exhibition, with chords reaching out to the spectators as if to tell them to be sad that the game was over.

I never found out then name of the slow march, but it was part of the history of the old Chicago Stadium as much as were the Bobby Hulls and Stan Mikitas and the fans that roared there on most Wednesday and Sunday nights in the dead of winter.

We were stuck in traffic, but it gave us time to acquaint ourselves more and talk about the finer things in life. It was 10:30, the usual time the hockey games ended, so I was hardly ready to call it a day.

"Hey! Is 'Big Boy's' still around? I haven't had one of their burgers in ages! Or maybe you have to go home?" I was ready to steal her away, even If she said that she had to go home.

"Yah, it's still there. I can stay out while yet."

It wasn't far from her house, so I drove into the drive-in's parking lot knowing we had time to spare. I prayed that Bonnie's Dad wasn't like Donna's Dad, with the curfew bit.

The lot wasn't as crowded as in the summer, but Super Cars could still be seen. Goats, X's, Roadrunners, Chevy SS's and others sat waiting to race on a bet, slipping onto Ogden Avenue for $10.00 and up. Some drivers came around just to nit-pick or ogle carhops taking orders. It was a great hangout for kids from Berwyn, Cicero, Lyons and Brookfield.

"It used to be a lot noisier a few years ago before the law clamped down for stronger mufflers. No straight exhaust anymore. My buddy Bill had a nice, white '63 Plymouth we'd drive through once in awhile. Those were the days! Now, look at all of the stop signs they put up here!" I took it as a joke until I saw Berwyn Police cars waiting on the corner for a velocity induced youngster to leave the starting gate.

In an effort to kill the racing bug, this pit stop had 2 extra stop signs installed for speed control, 15 feet apart, only to add more fuel to the fire as the racers became more apprehensive with the final stop sign's delay another 20 feet up the road, releasing them to 30 mph speed limit.

"Here comes a car hop! What should we get? I don't remember their menu! HELP!"

"I like you, Billy. You're silly."

"I like you too, Bonnie."

The Hop interrupted us, "Hi, welcome to Big Boys. What can I get you?"

We ordered, and continued to talk.

"So how long is your leave?"

"I have to get back to DaNang by January 17th, but I have to leave here around the 15th." I stopped for a second, then "When can I see you again? Or do you have a boy friend?"

It just came out. I didn't even know if she WANTED to see me again.

"Yes. I *would* like to go out with you again!"

"Great! I like you a lot, and I'm glad I found someone so soon to help me spend my leave with. It gets lonely sitting around at home. My parents both work."

"School is closed for Christmas, so we'll have more time to spend together before you have to go back. Maybe we can go to the museums, or a show, or another PLAY?"

We laughed at the insinuated PLAY dribbling.

"I used to go to museums and the Shedd Aquarium with my Dad. Its nice and quiet there."

"Roll your window down, Bill. Here come your TWO Big Boys!"

Sliding to our car on the snow, the blond set the adjustable tray on the window ledge and propped it up to stay. She smiled as she said, "YOU gonna eat BOTH of these ½ pounders?"

Bonnie leaned against me to get a cleaner view of the blonde. "Bill is in from Vietnam and they don't get this good stuff over there." She acted like the carhop was trying to move in on her territory. I subdued a laugh.

Blondie expressed "OHHH!" in a surprised sort of way, rolling her eyes with her smile cut.

I stared ahead through the windshield and Bonnie got quiet. She must've thought that mentioning Vietnam wasn't a good idea, but she didn't start the war there.

I shoveled down the 2 meal sized burgers in the time it took Bonnie to eliminate one 'Kid's Burger'. We were both amazed. "Gimme two more!"

She laughed. "You MUST be kidding!"

"Yah! I'm tired of this place! Let's go to the White Castle across the street!" Her company with me made me jest and jovial prone.

"UGH! Those things are murder on my stomach. You're kidding again, right?"

"Yah, we can go home." The 'Slider' Sanctuary of White Castle boasted the smallest of burgers @ 12¢, but only the brave or adventurous would dare fill up on the onion en-graved patties.

The 2-block stretch of forest preserve gave us a fantastic screening of tree limbs burdened with the falling snow. I snapped the bright lights on for a view of flurry not unlike a ship flying through outer space on a Star Trek episode.

"Bill, I'm getting dizzy!"

I turned left on Elm with the regular beams leading the way. "You okay?"

"Yah, I was just kidding."

I walked her up the steps, excusing my arm around her to be for better balance. She didn't mind.

The lamp was lit in front window, so we wandered for me to greet her parents once again, but found the living room empty.

"They're both asleep. It's 12:30, 'ya know."

"It's THAT LATE? I hope we're not in trouble!"

"NOOO! My parents trust me."

I was relieved. We walked to the door to say good night. "I hope you had a good time, Bonnie. I sure did."

"Of course I did. I'll always remember it."

Her cute smile forced me to bend down and kiss her, almost stopping like a batter holding back from a curve ball. But I followed though, and found a hard set of lips pushing back, with a Frosh like giggle signaling a HI-FI compliment.

I said nothing about that goodnight kiss until a future date, because her smile told me once again that we were becoming close friends.

My conflict with the Conflict bothered me enough to almost forget that the holiday was upon us, so my phone remained on the hook. I wanted to be alone, even shunning the company of my parents and almost enjoying long stretches of silence. Watching T.V. sitting next to my folks, not expressing my opinion of any news specials, laughing with repression at Laugh In's comedic splendor and hardly appreciating Elliot Ness and his Untouchables indicated that I was still way out of the norm, with my best relaxation being in bed, not thinking.

I did watch some newsreels shown about the war's situations. They did show dirty, the war, more or less 'dirt' than World Wars I and II, but those wars didn't show the supper eating public dirt like the Vietnam War did. They didn't have T.V. at all. I'm sure if they did, the films would have outraged the public to burning more flags than could be manufactured because of atrocities they'd be witnessing.

My parents and I visited some Aunts and Uncles before and after the Christmas break, but on Christmas Day, my parents and I reminisced a little about Fritzi, our savage when he wanted to be, but lovable Toy Terrier. He left scars on my hands and arms from his playful surprise attacks becoming overly aggressive, causing my downfall. May the Devil Dog rest in peace.

Talking about our old neighborhood on Komensky also helped ease pressure. Candy stores cornering and centering many blocks, traded cones of fresh popcorn for a nickel and 3 inch cardboard cylinders of peanuts for 10 cents that offered a possible winning coin inside, up to a quarter. Illuminating my memory were the glass hard plates of bubblegum found in every pack of Topp's Baseball cards and conserved fireworks brought out of the dresser each Forth of July.

"Billy, do you remember the cherry bomb your father shot and I got some of it stuck in my leg?"

I sure did, and Dad never heard the end of it.

And I love Independence Day, reverently. From the Little League Parades to the soft ball games to the back yard barbecues, our country exhibits hunger for freedom and fun, even with fireworks excepted. I've read, that if the potato salad gets *iffy,* people over indulge and flies die from happiness, they haven't overeaten. It is patriotism.

Another day passed Christmas, and I fought the urge to call Bonnie for the last time.

The phone rang 6 times and I was ready to hang up, then the phone was answered.

"Hi, Bonnie. This is Bill. Merry Christmas."

"Hi, Billy. Christmas was three days ago, but Merry Christmas to you, too. How is everything?"

"Okay, Okay." I was cheery again. We made plans to go downtown for a movie, and her asking me to wear my uniform sat a little negative with me.

"We haven't seen you in it yet. My parents want to see how it looks."

She meant that SHE wanted to see me in it.

I broke down to her demands, and picked her up wearing my dress greens.

"Pretty snazzy, Bill. No arm patches?"

"No, Mr. Fischer. I'm in the Marines, remember? The Army wears patches."

We had a beer in the kitchen, then his daughter and I took off for the Oriental Theater. Parking seemed a mile from the show, but the snow held up and the walk and talk brought us closer still.

The lobby was roomy to sat the least, its ornate and dated construction took one back to the 1800's.

"This is a beautiful theater. It looks like an opera house! And we're here to see "The Good, the Bad and the Ugly"? What'll they think of next?", with her big, blue-eyed smile.

"Bonnie, it was *your* choice."

Walking up the balcony stairs, "Just like a Blackhawk game, huh?" She changed the subject halfway up the stairs.

"I wish you'd have called me for Christmas, Bill. My parents wanted to see you, and my Uncle Henry was over and relatives from my Mom's side of the family came by. We had a turkey all ready for you."

I felt really bad I didn't at least call her. "I'm sorry, Bonnie, but I didn't think that we were that close. I mean I'm REALLY sorry!"

"Don't feel too bad. I just wanted some company my own age to talk to. You know."

"Well, I couldn't leave my parents alone, either." I thought that she was really mad. She left the 'Y' out of my name.

"They could have come with you. We don't bite!"

She had me boxed in a corner.

"The movie didn't start. I'm going to have a cigarette. Do you smoke?"

"Once I had a pack of Newports in my purse for 3 weeks. I ended up throwing it out, they got so stale."

I finished the smoke and the coming attractions came on. "Let's go. It's time for the face off!"

The film was an award winner starring Clint Eastwood and Eli Wallach, but it was extremely long. Long enough for an intermission.

"Let's get a soda. I'll buy."

We went to the snack bar, then back to the balcony for another smoke. We stood there sharing the popcorn when 3 thug types came towards us. Bonnie saw them first.

"Uh, Bill…?"

I saw her eyes look passed my shoulder in an unsettled manner then I turned to see their approach.

"That's why I said I'd feel uncomfortable wearing this uniform, Bonnie. There's too much protesting and s--- goin' on for a serviceman to cope with." I didn't want to fight, but I'd take all three of them down with me if they started something, for Bonnie.

"Hey, you in the Marines?" one of them asked in a gruff tone.

"Yes, I am."

Another of them asked if I was in Vietnam and said that he had a brother there. The third one said that we should kick gook ass.

Then they all shook my hand, gave luck, and walked away.

Bonnie and I looked at each other, breathing a sigh of relief.

"Feel okay, Billy?"

"Yah. I didn't want to get their blood all over their leather jackets. You okay?"

We hugged, and in my arms she said, "I'm fine." I was "Billy", again.

The second half of the movie depicted the Civil War with its gruesome toll. Eli Wallach ran through a mile long necropolis with thousands of graves surrounding him, encircling me to realize that I would forever relate scenes like this with the Vietnam War. I just have to cope quietly, in my own world.

Leaving her home that night I was left with a more feminine kiss, and, "Next time you come over, come through the back. Ma had the rugs washed for the holidays."

"You're a very romantic girl, Bonnie. Are there any more at home like you?" With that and another kiss and hug, I left for home.

The gates at the 31st and Harlem train station were down for the passing freight train. I'd spend 8 hours of my special leave waiting for the gates to rise, cursing, wishing some C4 plastic explosive to fall from the sky to obliterate every set of train tracks in a 10-mile radius.

On New Year's Eve's Eve, my parents and I went to visit the Fischer's residence. It ended more sociable than I hoped it would be, and discovering their Faith to be the same as ours seemed to bring the Mom's to a closer under- standing of each other, while Pater fishing infatuation adhered *their* conversation.

We found out that we all spent parts of summers in the great north woods of Wisconsin, our vacation roots holding fast in Hiles while the Fischer's family considerations were further north in Land 'O' Lakes.

"My brother Joe is a trapper up there. He left Chicago in the early '50's and never came back. His wife, Edna and him would rather get snowed in, and I mean SNOWED IN! They have to make sure they have enough of a food supply 'cause sometimes they can't get down their road for weeks at a time. I love it in the summer up there, but they can keep winter."

Snowmobile sledding was unheard of, in the old days.

My Dad was quick to add, "I agree, Art. The winters are really bad up there, but the summers? I'd like to retire up there someday. My friend Fritzi has a bar in that sneeze town, and he doesn't recommend anyone to come up in December!"

I felt as far away from the war as I could get, not even a thought of it reached me. The families comparing their loves and wants made me feel like a part of both of them, and after all, that's what life is all about: Family.

Bonnie pulled me towards the kitchen sink. "Billy, what's a 'sneeze town'?"

I laughed. "'Ya mean you never heard of a 'sneeze town'? Ha, ha. It's a town so small, that if you're driving through it and you sneeze, you'll miss it!"

She laughed and then tugged me to their basement. "Dad's working to make it a rec room, so it's a little messed up."

We played an electronic pastime, influential to saloons and arcades even today.

"Wow! A bowling machine!"

"Dad's still trying to get it working right, but we can still play it."

We slid the steel puck awhile, embraced automatically, and then returned to the family base in the front room. They were discussing the world and the weather and where the next meal would come from.

"Bonnie, you and Billy can go to Brown's Chicken for our supper." Her Mom handed her some money and we dashed out the door. On the way to the chickenry, Bonnie slide next to me in the car, having me favor bench seats to the sporty bucket type.

Our side dish of corn fritters completed, my parents bid the Fischer's a happy holiday season, and left telling me not to be too late coming home.

Bonnie and I made plans for the morrow's New Year's celebration, with no objective in mind. "I'll call you tomorrow. Maybe we'll think of something to do by then." We were both under 21, so choices were limited.

New Year's Eve late afternoon found us together in the Berwyn kitchen, with the suggestion of tagging along to the party of their friends Hank and Helen, falling on deaf ears.

"We might stop there later, Dad. Maybe Bonnie and I will take in a show first."

We embraced and they left for their gathering. "Well Bonnie, I STILL don't know what we can do. Any suggestions?"

"Let's take a ride and maybe we'll find a place to stop at."

So we rode around the western suburbs and found nothing to our liking that would fit in with the revelry of a bash for the likes of us.

"Let's go back to my house. I can call some of my friends to see what they're doing. WHY didn't I think of that before?"

"You tell me and we'll both know!"

I called Bill, Bob, and Roger. "No one's home!" I alarmed. "What are we going to do?"

Her answer was a smile. With my next suggestion, she proceeded to the front room.

The street light in front of the house lit up the light snow falling, and looking through stained glass windows gave us a romantic setting that asked us to linger awhile.

Next move: "Want to stay here, Bonnie?" I mean, we can watch T.V. and have a drink. If you think it'll be okay."

I didn't want to push my luck to have her thinking that I wanted to take advantage of her. We stood next to each other looking out the window as I waited for the answer.

"We'll be okay here. It's too cold out there for me, anyhow."

"So we'll welcome in 1968 right here in my home. It could be worse! Uh, what would you like to drink? My Dad has a bar in the basement, so name 'yer poison!"

Bonnie laughed. "No poison for me, thanks. I think a weak rum and Coke would be good, though. What do you like?"

"Sounds good. I'll have the same" as we tiptoed down the basement steps.

"Ohh! It's all padded and cushiony!" as she sat on the high bar chair, we face to face.

Just the dull bar light exhibiting two drunkards leaning on a street light pole gave away our positions in the innocent Berwyn subterranean vault, and the clock ticked on.

"It's getting late, Hon. Make us some drinks, already!"

I laughed at her innocence, then blended the drinks to start celebrating in the worst/best year of my life. As I poured the rum, my mixed emotions were as confusing as the war, with an uncertain future hovering like a Huey looking for a safe LZ, and my future now possibly with a girl I hardly knew.

I poured myself a double, drank it down and mixed another.

"Penney for your thoughts." She gave me another big, bright smile, so without a word, I was told I'd make no mistake in asking her to wait for my to return from 'Nam'.

"Want another?"

Although I had never read "War and Peace", I believed the story of Bonnie and I to strike a parallel with the classical masterpiece painting the picture of a Warrior and his Princess back home.

"The lime tastes good. This is really tasty, Billy. Maybe you should be a bartender."

We had another drink then applied the next in the more comfortable setting of the lounge upstairs. Snow was still falling.

"Think it'll ever stop?"

"I don't know." I didn't care. "What should we watch?" I tuned to channel 7 then sat on her lap in the La-Z-Boy.

"UGH! Get off me, you moose!"

We switched places and embraced, rum loosened enough to tip the chair to the floor, nearly breaking it.

Her laugh was so deep and boisterous that I considered her a different girl in the dark. She laughed harder when I asked, "'Moe', 'Larry', or 'Curley'?"

We missed the noisemakers, shot gun blasts and firecrackers accompanying the arrival of 1968, while holding each other never wanting to let go. Channel 7 was our only onlooker.

Bonnie jumped up. "Billy! We missed midnight!"

"We did? So what? Are you happy?"

She knelt down next to me. "Yes I am, Billy", almost in a whisper.

We kissed again, and it was my turn to jump, shaking. Somebody celebrated with a cherry bomb blast in our gangway.

"Oh, you're shaking!" She nestled my head to her shoulder. "Must be bad over there, huh. Let's watch T.V."

After calming down, I excused myself to the bar for another double and came back to watch reruns of W.C. Fields. Bored with the movie, and a little high from rum abuse, I cradled Bonnie with an arm and gave her another kiss for a test, then proposed.

"Bonnie, will you marry me?" I wasn't drunk so I had no excuse for my conduct.

She cried and giggled simultaneously, and after carefully considering the good to outweigh the bad, 5 seconds passed and she accepted my proposal with a bubbling nose. "Yes, Billy!"

"Are you sure, Bonnie? I mean, we hardly know each other! We won't get married very soon anyway, so let's just think about it for now. If you can help me though this next year or so, we'll know more about each other, right?"

"I'll wait for you, Billy, if that's what you want to hear."

I was completely hers now. "Thank you. I needed to hear that without asking."

The proposal at midnight wasn't really on solid ground, and on New Year's afternoon, she asked, "Did you really mean your proposal last night or were you drunk?"

"Were YOU drunk when you said accepted?"

She knew we weren't drunk. Light headed for sure, but vigilant enough to know what we were saying.

My stomach turned when I reminded her of my next tour lasting until September. "I have to go back for 9 more months, Bonnie, so if you change your mind now, I'll understand."

We sat in the living room and could hear "Strangers in the Night" playing on the radio. I think that song helped seal our promises to each other.

"Billy, last night I got to know you better than you think. So if you want me to wait for you, I definitely will. Do you really care for me that much?"

My kiss answered her question then we edged towards the windows to look at the snow.

"It doesn't snow there, does it?"

She turned away with her quivering voice telling me that I had gotten her involved with my life already, too soon. I never saw this soap opera coming when I was in the jungle.

She turned back, clamping her arms around me with her 98-pound death grip. I didn't cry with her because of the insensitivity the war left in me, but I was very, very sad.

"Don't cry, Bonnie. I'll be back forever at the end of the summer. Then we can make plans and live life, with a future!"

"See you, in September?" She glanced a wet smile at me without a hint of throwing in the towel. But how was I going to return to Vietnam now? My life was complicated enough without bringing a high school student into it, so all I had done was ruin another life.

"You'll make it back okay, Billy. I'm sure of it. Our time together now won't be wasted, and when you get back we'll look back at this war knowing that it was meant to be for us!"

I left her early that night, not partying because of my hangover. That was my feeble excuse, though the war was my hidden reason to run and hide. It came closer with each sunset. And I didn't want to lead her on to the truth, not wanting to worry the innocent teen. Any time I left her early, I lied with a pitiable excuse just to keep her off guard from my real problem.

But I enjoyed my leave until the very end, valuing all four of our parent's company with Bonnie at my side to make me forget about my anticipated damnation. Being together daily brought on a cascade of love and friendship that I never before had an acquaintanceship assemble. I felt that Vietnam was meant to be, because it was a necessary stepping stone that led me to Bonnie, and without Vietnam, we surely would never have met. My name wouldn't have been in the hat for her to accept. And accept me she did, as I slid my golden Marine Corp ring on her finger.

"It's not our official engagement ring Hon, but it'll do for now. Okay?"

The symbol of the Marine Corps, the eagle, globe and anchor, embellished the halo around her finger.

She cried. "It's beautiful, Billy. Thank you so very much. I'll cherish it forever."

She thanked me the rest of the night.

On my last day, all of us sat around their kitchen table to discuss another losing year the Cubs gave their fans. Between arguments, Bonnie called me to front room where she hid. Her eyes were slightly wet when she whispered, "I told Ma that you asked me to marry you, okay?"

I should have known what I was in for with this red head. 'Okay' She asked? I acted calmly.

"I thought we said it was like a 'trial' proposal, Bon! Are you SURE that you should've told her that?"

She stared at me suspiciously sad, and I thought I broke her heart on the spot. Then her eyes got wider with sorrow.

"Please don't be mad Billy! We said we loved each other and I promised to wait for you, so why shouldn't I tell my Mom our plans?" We're proud of you. I'M proud of you, you big jerk!"

I pondered the situation, impressing myself with my unarguable testimony; war is the worst possible situation man can compete in. Nothing can compare to it. Nothing.

So with that in mind, I told my Sweetheart not to give it another thought. "It's okay. I don't care who knows our plans."

"That's GOOD, Mr. Herstowski, because I'm going to tell Vicki and Sharon and Joey when I see them at school! Then they'll tell the rest of the school that my Marine and I are going to get married! How's THAT?"

"What can I say?"

We were sitting close together when my Mom came into the front room. "Hey! We wondered where you two went."

Both in a sort of a daze, we stood up to greet her to our inner sanctum. "We were just talkin', Mom. C'mon and watch T.V. with us."

"Well, it's not even turned on!" she laughed.

She caught us. Bonnie turned the set on, but we continued to talk.

"Do you have everything packed, Bill? Daddy said we have to be going soon."

Everything was ready but me. I had a nest of butterflies hatching, metamorphosing inside me everywhere, not just the stomach. So with the hour of truth well nigh, I went to the kitchen to try to rush the inevitable farewell to my newfound family. Art was talking about their new garage door opener and my Dad remarked on how necessary it was because of the weight. I leaned on the back of the chair he sat on, watching a squirrel dodging snowflakes.

"Well, Yan-chee-banch, we'd best take off. The snow'll slow us down."

I caught myself sighing and sighing again. Bonnie's folks tried to console me.

"We'll pray for you every day, Bill." Her eyes were red.

"Thanks, Mrs. Fischer."

"Good luck, Bill. Be tough."

Walking from the kitchen to the front room encouraged more tears from the three women in my life. Moms went to Dads. Girl went to boy.

I reminded them that my next address would be at Battalion level in the rear, no shooting.

"But Billy, you'll be so far away." I thought Mom was going to get hysterical: another condition of war.

Art held my arm. "Don't worry, Bill. I'll take care of the Brat for 'ya." He called her Brat until his final reward. "She'll be here when you get back."

Jim and his wife Lynn were just getting up the snow filled steps when we opened the door.

"Boy, what a brother! Just in time to wish my fiancé luck!" Bonnie was being sarcastic, but wasn't.

"The snow is TERRIBLE! Sorry Bill. I see you're on your way. Best of luck, Buddy."

Long farewells are unkind but necessary and customary. We finally found our way to the highway, with snow in full command of driver's decisions.

"There's still plenty of time Hon. I made a lunch for you to take on the plane."

"Thanks Mom, but I have enough to carry already." I had no room inside for food. My mind wouldn't allow it.

"You can carry it for him, Phil."

"KATHERINE! He doesn't want it!"

Mom's concern for my lunch turned the car into a silent vault. Anyhow, there was little else to say.

We reached the airport quicker than I really wanted, with intercom announcements of arrivals and departures arresting my mind from wandering deeper onto mountains and into crevices. Dragging my sea bag over the slick tile floors also kept my mind in Chicago.

"Don't they have taxis or buses here?"

I checked in for my San Francisco flight then walked back to my trio personifying a funeral wake. I flirted with a smile and "No more jungle or mountains, no more ops or patrols! Don't worry!"

But all I got was the saddest of looks, like puppy dogs not accepted. They just could not believe that war could be so secure.

"Last call for boarding flight…"

Time was up. "G'bye Mom. Gotta go." We hugged like there was no tomorrow. For all we knew…

"We'll take in a Hawks game when I get back, Dad. Thanks for everything."

We shook hands, and unfair to them, they fell behind in the array when I moved to say goodbye to Bonnie. Her face was as a window drenched with rain. The most we promised each other was conclusive love, piously.

"I'm sorry I brought you into this, Bonnie. It was selfish of me."

"You're NUTS, 'ya know that?" She cried fiercely, breathlessly.

I had to pry loose of her hold, almost with an unfeeling shove. "The plane'll leave without me and I'll be AWOL, Hon! I must go! I love you Bonnie! Write!"

"Goodbye Billy. I love you too" with all heart and tears.

I walked then, up the ramp towards the big bird, got mixed with other passengers and stopped for a final sight of the closest three I was going back to fight in war for. My stopping caused a small boarding jam, but I needed to see them a last time: my folks standing at attention close behind my fiancée, her holding a handkerchief with one hand with the other standing tall in the air, joining my parent's hands in a final salute.

How terrible war is to a family, even minus physical casualties.

Mind churned, I walked down the aisle to my seat. I tried not to think of the many people who'd be mentally scarred forever, even without losing a son to combat.

I strived to look out of the window so graciously allowed by United Airlines. Huge picture windows in the terminal gave me no relief of a photo contrived of my threesome I denounced by departing, so I turned my gaze to the back of the seat in front of me, thinking of my wonderful Bonnie, and still wondering about Donna.

After reaching the taxiing speed of 125 mph or so, the jet catapulted me westward as I sobbed for a minute, intensely hating the war ax to be ground but excused it to the heavens because it was prerequisite for a "Bonnieing Degree."

"Flying at blah, blah, blah…" came over the intercom from the pilot, rustling passengers out of their seat belts for head calls. I sat on my throne and took a newspaper offered by a stewardess. Bad mistake. Reading the headlines fell far short of an asset to my cognizance, even though my orders sent me to the security of Battalion level near DaNang.

"U.S. FORCES IN VIETNAM BRACE FOR HUMAN WAVES AS NEW YEAR'S TET MAY REACH HIGHEST ENEMY OFFENSIVE YET! All U.S. bases expecting to be under attack…"

Tet was about a week away. Jesus, I prayed that no one back home heard about the bastard's onslaught. The whole damn country was about to bleed and spit guts, and I was going in for their New Year's festivities. I almost bit off my bottom lip in anger, at the fire and brimstone the government wouldn't let us use to end the war.

Flight attendant drops off Rolaids.

Catnap to landing.

Delays here and holdovers there had me in Okie for extra days of rum and coke with slot machine chasers.

After that, a rude awakening.

It certainly must have been a relief for the women to realize that one could be a woman and a lady and yet be thoroughly patriotic.
Pearl S. Buck

Wreck havoc and unleash these dogs of war.

My address became 1st Mar. Div, Comm. Bn, and the P.C. driver accepted my orders amusingly.

"Used to be this area was safe and sound. Now, the mother fuckin' gooks are everywhere. You got a weapon?"

I told him I just landed from special leave and that I wished I had one. He laughed again. I loaded up in the back of the truck.

"Hol' on tight!"

Fires were burning and I heard deranged gunfire racking on the other side of the barbed wire and fencing that protected the airstrip. It was more frightening without a weapon.

The truck turned up an incline and stopped shortly thereafter, with the corporal telling me that I was home. He pointed to a large, office looking billet. "You can check in over there."

I reached the door with my uniform spotted with the sweat of the night. Inside, another Marine who just checked in followed an office worker dressed in full battle array to his area.

A cold, but usual Marine welcome asked me my name. I told him, and handed him my orders. He was a Gunnery Sergeant, wearing a helmet and a convulsive worry on his face.

"Just got off special leave, huh? You should have stayed back home!" He told me where my area was and to get into my utilities to await further notice. I dragged my gear and bod to my assigned area, finding it as acceptable as the area I lived in before going home a month earlier, and empty. There were 12 living areas in the building, me and the other new standby being the only two milling around. I heard explosions, a close mile away.

Clothes changed, I felt naked without a gun. "Just get in?" I yelled to the other end of my new apartment building.

"'Yah! How about you? It sounds like hell around here! What's happening?"

"A newspaper a few days ago said that the country is getting overrun!"

With that, the Robert Redford look alike dropped his cargo on the floor, and walked over to me. His face was grim, as he told me that he was going to stay home with his wife and kids awhile longer, but she convinced him to leave or face brig time.

He went back to his area quietly, brushing his full, red moustache with his fingers.

The noises outside ebbed.

After settling in we B.S'ed and read the Company Orders the Gunny quickly handed to me in his office.

"Ski! We gotta get haircuts tomorrow! And the new C.O says "No mustaches?"

Robert's mustache was fully formed, like out of an ad for mustache wax, but mine was sparse and ignorant looking, so the new orders didn't bother me in the least but the cracklings in the distance did.

"Robert, do you have a weapon?"

"Nope. Where the hell is everybody at?"

"Maybe they're on 100% alert! That leaves just you and me!"

Loud tramping of jungle boots against wooden boards came to our attention. We stood up abruptly.

A closer crash sounded outside, Gunny ordering "C'mon with us! Let's Go! Move it!"

We followed to a 6 by near the office. I was near full of heartburn after seeing the truck and its compliment of combatants.

Introduced to the crudiform, we were loaded on for who knows what, to who knows where, without any combat gear in any way, shape or form. The truck took off helter-skelter into the darkness with a cartload of crushers sliding haphazardly on the worn-smooth steel floor, as rifle butts bruised the knees of the seated.

Choppers did a dragonfly dance and their spotlights showed traces of fog mincing with dustings of insects. I guessed our conveyance was to an airport.

It was; a sky harbor with big transport's blades cutting the air apprehensively, almost beckoning, "Come hither."

A sergeant or who ever, was yelling and pushing us out of the truck to the LZ.

Pitch black awaited us in the flying contraption, packed in like peas in a pod with noise level reaching a deafening tone as the motor only idled. I wondered how any communication could be realized from a commander to his troops.

The excruciating noise had me plugging up my ears with my fingers during the flight. We landed on an LZ *somewhere,* and disembarked with the rest of the troops, still without common knowledge of our future. It was in a large out- post, encircled by more jungle and hills, looking like 22 but much bigger, aided with 4 towers spotlighting the perimeter.

The rest of the Grunts jogged off in different locations, splitting off to the towers and bunkers adjacent. Robert and I were left standing alone in the middle of the 'sand pit', looking for somewhere to turn. Finally, we hustled passed a tent with "Psycho" light that invited us in.

It was a makeshift office, with a lieutenant who looked not much older than Robert or me. He watched us approach his desk where his 45 sat, cocked and loaded.

"You just got off the chopper? Where are your weapons? And helmets? No 782 gear?"

Robert got the call. "Yes, sir. We were pushed on the helicopter without any weapons."

"What kind of weapons have you been using?" He looked at me.

"Sir, we just got back in country from special leave and got shipped here. No weapons or flack gear."

"Those a hole office pougs in DaNang would fuck up a wet dream! Look, tomorrow we're all going to Hue City. You heard of the place?"

We both looked stupid, without an answer.

"It WAS the old capital of this goddamned country, but the NVA took it over." The swinging light bulb added horror to our future. "Reinforcements are needed, and we're part of the shipment tomorrow morning so get rifles at first light. The armory is two tents to the left. As for now, find an empty supply tent for some rest. Use the ground."

End of mystery.

"This is NUTS!" remarked Robert. I agreed, but we crashed in the sand in a near vacant supply tent, nonetheless. If it were my turn to go, it wouldn't matter if I slept in a supply tent or at North Avenue Beach on Lake Shore Drive.

The moon shone through a flap, aiding me to slid sand aside like a turtle preparing to deposit eggs. It provided a minimum of cover but I took any precaution to get back to Bonnie, alive.

"Ski, you said Hue City was in the paper?"   "'YAH!'" I cranked out to him. I was tired and pissed off and frightened, heartburn unrelenting. Three days ago my life was content and smooth, now *this* without a paddle.

We laid in the sand foot to foot, staring out the front and rear of the tent. Robert looked at what could have been the front gate; concertina with a vengeance. A roofed tower about 15 feet high stood opposing with 2 Marines at a machine gun. The bunkers were also at the ready.

My view showed sleeping helicopters with blades sagging in boredom, waiting for the rising sun to awaken them to another day of fire deportment. There were at least 10 of them sitting on paved and painted surface, assuring me that we were at a well used out port, and that the enemy knew about it well.

"Robert, I think that we'll get some incoming tonight. Those choppers must be tempting targets for the VC."

"I hope you're wrong, Ski." He lighted a cigarette. "You got sand fleas by you?"

"I got all kinds of fleas here. Wanna trade places?"

"Nope! G'night."

He snored as I wondered where the beach was to go to with this sand and where the hell we were, while trying to get to used to not having a Sealy under me, or a weapon.

Shortly after dozing off, a popping hand flare awoke me. The night was quiet enough to force the flare's sizzle into my half aware right ear, as it swung down under its parachute for longer illumination.

An explosion, and I was defenseless! Jesus in Heaven help me I prayed, and dug deeper into my gritty chaise lounge for refuge, like the proverbial ostrich turned chicken.

More flares were flattered with small arms fire and frag grenade concussions, so close that I didn't need to imagine what was starting up ½ block away. How in God's name could the Corps do this to 2 of their most

194

patriotic enlistees? We extended our tour for this rat's nest and they put us up for grabs with nothing more than our fists and brains.

"Ski! This SUCKS! It really, REALLY SUCKS! How the fuck could we end up like this? GOD, I hate the Marine Corps! Buncha STUPID BASTARDS! God!"

Robert was losing it, and the shelling continued. Laying flat on the ground gave a body the full impact of concussions, and it felt to my stomach that an ulcer was being cut loose and spun around with each violent intrusion that cast our fate to the wind.

A siren sounded from our perimeter. It sounded like a police car chase breaking the silence on a hot night on Chicago's south side during the Roaring 20's. Bootleggers fired machine guns from big, black sedans, trying to save their truck's shipment of whiskey from the prohibiting F.B.I. The firing stopped but the siren whirred on for another minute or so until it was choked out.

"Honest to GOD, Robert, I cannot believe this!"

I lit up 2 cigarettes, and warned him that I was sending one over.

"Camel's? That all you got?"

"Yah! People don't bum Camels too often." Camels were filter- less back then.

After a few puffs, I slept with one eye open, sleeping and observing at the same time. Pure bonkers.

Then a much heavier barrage began. We were far enough from the small arms fire to hear rounds thudding into and through the parked chopper's hulls and glass, or whatever the zapping metals could find.

I turned to see what was happening on Robert's side of the story. The gate looked to be around 15' wide and crocheted with barbed wire, that after the concertina. We could see muzzle flashes from enemy guns, and I was waiting for one of us to get shot for sure. Their tracer rounds ran aimlessly though, some at 20 degree angles over our heads to example either bad marksmanship or too much donkey-piss beer.

Regardless of where we were, it was hell not being able to fight back. Just lay in the sand, shivering and worthless to the cause.

Then, mortar rounds thudded on the airstrip. I saw no direct hits on the aircraft, but they had to have taken a beating to the shred with hot metal's chaotic projection.

"Robert, you okay?"

"'Yah, Ski. Screw this place!" His hands covered his head.

Most of the heavy firing ceased, but the pinging of small arms by the gate 200 feet from us sniped on, like a firing range at carnivals in the streets. Patrons plinking at a red starred sheet of paper with a .22 cal. Rifle, shot to eliminate the star for a color T.V. or a Rolex wristwatch. Both prizes were dust covered in a showcase. A 'ping' every 15 or 20 seconds for fifty cents.

Another salvo of mortar rounds landed on the airstrip, causing mass confusion to parable pilots who were trying to get into the choppers for out of range purpose and give the enemy a 'what for'. It was a terrible position, seeing fellow Marines scramble for cover not knowing where the next round would hit, not helping. Some of them made it away unscathed. Some rolled in agony.

Personnel Carriers ambulanced with gears gnashing and drivers cursing as I returned my attention to my sand bed, resembling a dog digging for treasured bones in grasping for more cover in a deepened sand wedge, or reaching L.A.

The far side of the outpost, maybe 1/4 mile away, erupted into another skirmish, and our havoc re-hummed, completing a stereo blood sport that Romans would have been proud to compete in.

Machine guns from our bunkers seemed to hold the tide, and grenades added to the 'rebelry' of the Grunt's howling in anger, again asking for more competition from the foul lines on the other side of the wire. I was cringing in the sand when I heard jagged clumps of metal thumping on the foreground.

I turned once again to see the enemy trying fruitlessly to gain forced admittance to our camp through the closed entrance. The guns from the bunkers were tearing the NVA to shreds, as were helicopters behind them. I turned away finally, as all noises of explosions subsided and voices of the injured, ejaculated.

I went into a dazed doze, my mind filled with the enemy aiming their weapons at Robert and me, like they had just done in real life, only they weren't shooting. They just grinned, and turned to walk away.

I came out of my disturbing half comatose, soaked from stress sweat, as pilots and their crew were readying their birds for take-off. I rolled out of my body box of sand, and tapped Robert with my boot for reveille, then felt rheumatically impaired as I made an attempt to push up on one knee.

In the struggle to balance, I thought about the purgatory we were sanctified with. All the madness of the grim-visage onslaught we just saw took only about 5 to 10 minutes, but who was counting? It was just another Armageddon Robert and I beheld from our sand lot seating.

"Let's GO! GOOOO! MOVE IT!" emanated from a squad leader running in front of us, circling his unarmed arm at his fire team, towards the whirling dervishes on the LZs.

The last officer I spoke to came with his 45 in hand at our tent. "What's his problem?" he screamed, above the helicopter's strict commotion. He was pointing at Robert's quiescent leftovers.

His utility cover was darkened with his own blood, and he lay face down in the sand with his arms stretched outward and fists clenched. It's one of my worst recollections of the war, Robert dying in the sands, not of Iwo Jima.

Lieutenant 'Louie' cried for a corpsman, and yelled for me to go to the armory for my weapon.

The Armor was squatting in the tent when I barged in.

"14 or 16?"

"14!" Like shopping at a shoe store.

I signed for it, and ran back to Louie with bandoliers slapping me on the chest and arms, stopping to see what happened with Robert. Two stretch marks in the sand showed evidence of his body being dragged away, with his feet leaving the impressions.

GOD, I thought. He bought it for me! I asked him if he wanted to trade places because of the bugs, but he refused. Robert's gone, and I remain. I was so close again to becoming a statistic. But then again, that's what war is all about, a game of inches.

More mix-master's hummed in harmony, though some were quiet and unfashionable, mutilated like aluminum foil from a hot fire at a barbeque.

Louie screamed and waved convulsively at me from the chopper. He hung by one arm with one foot on the ground and one on the running board. "C'mon Herstowski, MOVE IT!"

I jumped passed him. It wasn't a big transport, but it's motor still kept that metallic beat with its two accessories to compete with the roar of the crowd praising a Ron Santo home run.

We were airborne for a minute when Louie began to yell out a synopsis of Hue City and how it was overrun and how we were going to kick the gooks to hell. I was loading my magazine when he said that I fumbled cartridges neatly. The jerk didn't bother me, but my guts were lied up in knots like a pretzel and just as hard.

He was cold about Robert getting killed, but maybe be had his reasons. Leaders in combat have no room to let compassion complicate their scheme for complete victories.

And maybe I took it too hard and personal, but before his death, we talked and joked. His children will never know him.

First light magnified the vision of the crumbled cement and brick that used to make Hue a city. Waves of gun smoke mixed with dust engulfed a corner of the old capitol: a mile of pollution, not unlike big cities of the world.

Our pilot saw danger or had a premonition when he slapped a 'Launch' gear, to dart us out of small arm range. Red tracers in the dark hue of the morning must have made him reach for the top speed.

We advanced, and banking maneuver gave us glances out of windowless side ports: disruption incarnate by the fighting forces of the twentieth century. Bombs, napalm, grenades and other war paraphernalia removed the ancient city from tradition and antiquity it once explained, to a massive jigsaw rubble-puzzle.

We circled the brickyard a few times to reconnoiter for a landing area to be had without resistance. Muzzle flashes came from buildings and the jungle frame that rebuffed the on- slaught of our explosives, but we were unable to tell if they were shooting at us or trying to repel ground troops, or even whose side they were on.

Louie tapped on the pilot's shoulder and pointed to what looked like an area to be a safe drop-off point, and with a nod, the pilot dropped the chopper in a swift dive like a first hill thrill.

We crowded out a few hundred feet from muscled down walls, with tall grass abiding us for immediate cover. The chopper expelled itself straight up the instant the last of us touched terra firma, drawing small arms fire from a tree line close by. I fell to the ground for cover but I couldn't see where the hell I could fire or any of my teammates.

When Louie started yelling and the team began firing, I regained my bearings and fired towards the puffs of smoke from the concealed snipers. When firing ceased, I saw arm signals waving the line of us towards the rubble. Still crouching in our fighting through the elephant grass, some buildings could be seen upright with vacant doorways and windows resembling faces that laughed at their crushed cousin's storefront remains, dispersed at random where there used to be walkways.

We reached the fitful route of cement and brick opposition, finding no even stride to keep, no way to balance to retaliate resistance from hidden enemy. I had no flack gear or helmet for protection, but the misery I felt for the entire arena we were put to play in made me bitter and ready to unload my magazines on the spot.

My research found that near the end of January 1968, almost 70,000 Communist soldiers launched their surprise offensive of startling scope during Tet, the lunar New Year. Over one hundred cities suffered who were never before even meddled with, but Hue's twenty-five day siege boasted the fiercest nettles and atrocities that our enemy could coordinate. In violating the truce that they themselves had pledged to honor, the communists showed their true colors, if there is a color for war. 'All's fair...' goes the saying, so the color of red should be obvious.

Joining with another fire team, we totaled 40 to 50 in line, tripping into the wrecked municipality. Chunks of buildings that must have been parts of castles or temples looked like ancient pottery that fell off a shelf, turning to dust. Centuries old, they were lost forever.

Sniper rounds ricocheted off of walls, demonstrating an invisible hammer and chisel that saved a piece of cement for my unprotected neck, leaving a large red bruise. Leatherneck?

Hand signals gave the order to shelter, as the front of our pack went to burn out snipers.

Heavy mortar fire or rockets became our next plight. Worse yet, was the impact of the rounds throwing not only metal, but already broken building blocks, adding killing potential.

I was on one knee when the first shell hit, not too close to the rear of our teams. But the second hit knocked us all face down, with me reciting the Our Father and aiming my M-14 at the sky. I saw some men scurrying to a house still erect, for shelter from the storm. Some were trying to hide behind misshapen building materials, but I decided on the dwelling, over flotsam and jetsam. I must've stumbled over the corrugated masonry ½ dozen times before I rolled through the doorway that introduced me to dust and Marines in an otherwise empty room.

Two more Marines rolled in after me, then one more, completing a compliment of 9, all ready to go home.

The most accurate foe in Hue City so far, turned out to be the concrete that nicked my neck. Concrete that skinned up my knuckles when I slid into 'home-base' tore me up worse; grasping my rifle on contact with the floor made them bleed liberally. I treated my cuts with iodine, oblivious to quibbling small arms fire out in the countryside. It silenced our roomful.

Then a crash mutilated something about a block away. I was a nervous wreck, quacking in a corner of the room, waiting for a bomb to drop to end our sorrows. The Grunts saw it in a different light. Angry, they looked ready to kick ass without taking names, fondling their weapons impatiently, with the look of the vengeance in their eyes. They waited to kill.

"Let's go out there. The snipers still at it!"

KABOOM, and plaster fell from the ceiling. It brought a squad leader to the door. "C'mon, we gotta move!"

We popped out of the doorway, separately. Some looked both ways to make sure the coast was clear, as if a sniper would stand out in the open. Others ran out like hell.

We moved at a quicker gait this time, assembling in a walled-in area that looked like a small jail yard with brushed bricks for décor.

A sergeant gave out orders. "We're stayin' for the night and you'll each get a listening post. Some will be in a building and some will be behind walls. C-rats and ammo will be dropped off soon." He paused and looked down. "The slants have hit every inch of this country. The Citadel up here is lined with VC and NVC, and the first company of Marines is pinned down tryin' to take the fort back. Nobody sleeps tonight! I wouldn't be surprised if the gooks ran wave at us, either. They're tearing up the rest of this F---'in place, so I'd expect 'em to use everything they got." He finished his speech in a quiet tone, waiting for the worst. He looked like he was in his early thirties and that he'd seen his share of carnage.

We all sat quietly for 4 or 5 hours with incoming for a few seconds, then morbid silence. We wondered what they were thinking. They would drop rounds in the city, and never hit a vital position. Ignorant bastards, I thought. They might be persistent, they might be sneaky and two faced, but they lacked enough brain and body coordination to win the war if the Pentagon ever cut us loose with our full hatred of commie-dom prevalent.

A case of C-rations was thrown in, and my luck fed me a can of beans and franks, cold, with a can of peaches. I wouldn't miss it for the world. It was pig heaven, second only to a large Home Rum Inn pizza with extra sausage and mushrooms.

My mind went back to Bonnie and the grand leave of absence we spent together before I left her for this hole on earth. Our New Year's Eve Duo Party forced me to stay in position, instead of running at the VC on full automatic.

The night's clouds reflected the fires burning around us in a warm and humid spell. Insects teamed. The strange and fierce looking wasps or the Satan mandible red ants were still always in ample supply. Ants left welts on arms and legs, quickly. I can believe scientist's claim of world supremacy for insects in the event of nuclear war. Their present swarms would give them a good head start for many a millennium.

We sat on, bitching. It was a common pastime for Marines, complaining about everything, because we were always sent into the worst situations under the worst conditions at the worst times.

The incoming had stopped earlier so we bided our time again, quietly. There were no jokes to be told, no referrals to jobs waiting upon completion of service, no talk of the girls next door keeping the faith. That subject was kept inside the heart of most of us. Sometimes it would become the topic of conversation, but not *there*. Talking about your girl back home while in a horrific situation was almost like putting her on the spot too.

For a while, a Grunt's portion of ham and lima beans produced the only disturbing noise. His first 3 were humorous, after that, he was threatened with eviction from the area.

"Moose, you eat another can o' ham an' limas, and you DIE!" committed a friend of his.

We all had friends while on tour. We hated each other like Rams butting heads for the privilege of the heated female, but comradeship couldn't be lanced between men who fought in the severity of war.

In the early morning we began to take in fire from the jungle passed the city's eliminated protective wall. I was dozing as 2 or 3 stood guard by the doorway, cupping Luckie Strikes and watching the stars flicker in the dark blue.

I was near the back semi-wall as a Grunt fired from the hip, another fired prone. The night gave no disclosure of hits, but firing at them kept them from firing at us, so the volley continued sporadically, with echoes off walls deafeningly violent.

Flares became popular with the Grunts outside, with their screams of war added to the automatic fire as four of the enemy died before their pith helmets hit the ground.

Grenades were tossed jungle ways, choppers started to settle in, and the ground started to shake with mortars turning more concrete to dust. Behind us, explosions seemed to repeat a hundred fold. I wondered if the squad leaders were all dead or wounded.

A Grunt yelled "Let's MOOOVE!" so we rambled out to the racket of hell that created the breeze of death. Not hot or cold, but incensed with gunpowder smoke and hot metal decimation.

I lay in the white rubble, hearing the stupid order of "KEEP FIRING!" The whole thing was insane to me. Why did they put all of us in ultimate jeopardy when the B-52's could have ended the strife with the enemy suffering the only casualties? I think our government tried to save the city from permanent damage due to respect for cultural value the antiquated city held.

My shoulder was black and blue from 14's recoil, and I began to take ill from the bloodletting I saw, but I matched the Grunt's intensity of fire and gritted my teeth in anger. 'B' and 'F' and 'M' words flowed until the fire fight broke off, leaving only the chords of the mangled on both sides to syncopate for a melody of the misbegotten with helicopter drone.

Medevacs landed to our front where the enemy lay dead or wounded, and I could almost hear their bones cracking under the weight of the whirly birds.

Firing now was infrequent, almost stopping in mercy for the choppers to finish their job of pulling out the now useless fighters. But as they disembarked with their load, the killing resumed almost jokingly, as though the choppers raised the curtain in the theater for act 666, scene 1968.

I lay there still bursting 7.62 mm rounds, waiting for my turn to go, but the wickedness encompassing us at these bizarre moments kept the spark of life alive. With Scratch at the trigger, we would survive.

More were wounded to the left of me, to the right of me, continuing to fire if they could squeeze a trigger. The sanctuary we had an hour earlier went to hell with the blast of some explosive, and looking around me, signal flares from gun ships silhouetted Grunts standing and firing from the hip. Then I did one of the stupidest things in my 19-month tour. I stood up and joined them, feeling glorious and hell bound. I stared angrily as they must have, and tossed a grenade, responding to the sense that nothing was going to stop me from getting home alive. I have heard that patriotism is often the refuge of scoundrels that express dissent, rebellion and all-around hell rousing, which are true traits of patriots.

It was one satisfaction of war, eliminating those who stood in the way of one's peaceful endeavors. I mean, one could faithfully cut loose all frustrations and anxieties, with the willingness to pay the Piper if Lady Luck took a break from your shoulder for but a moment.

When I stood up with the Grunts, I felt as true as I could, to myself, to my country, to my folks, and to Bonnie. Mislead or not, I was going to kill every misbegotten commie I could before they stepped on my turf with their insane policy of 'State first, family somewhere in the background'.

I lay back down and reloaded, setting my head on concrete pillows, thinking about the stupid thing I did without second thought. And I asked myself, where the hell is an Ontos?

Choppers fluttered overhead with their bright beams on the smoked out jungle, occasionally lifting out some trees and bodies with a well-placed rocket, and then gashed the same area with machine gun blasts.

I lay in cover, as the last of the wounded and dead took their final flight out of a combat zone, making me bitter and extremely remorseful as Americans were being flown away. I embraced us as innocent bystanders, non-aggressors, walking and talking until fired upon. On Hill 22, we sat and talked, and were fired upon. We patrolled and operated in the jungle, and were fired upon. With all of this in consideration, ANY area in the country should have been a free fire zone. Move friendlies to refugee camps until the war was over. Amen.

At first light, birds came back chirping to signal a temporary cease fire and we moved back to a barrier for tally. It became follow the leader again, and we left the clumpy cesspool to first view the enemy bodies paled and lifeless, than to a village that expressed business as usual. Our leader left a few Grunts to 'guard' the VC's remains.

"Don't mess with the bodies!" he warned. "May be booby-trapped!"

I showed fatigue with the weight of my 14, but it was a necessary evil that could've fooled watchers of our follies. I saw the villagers, including some very beautiful women, selling their goods, appearing not at all capable of death and destruction. Unfortunately, some of them were.

Another act from war was being consummated in a grass hut, one placed behind the others on the roadside. Groans and moans not freeing from the dead, corrupted quietly from the shack, as a P.F.C. asked, "Who's next gettin' some leg? After ME, that is!"

Being engaged, I laughed and stepped aside. "Take all of the sloppy seconds you want. I'll stand guard, thanks."

If a woman promised her warrior that she'd be faithful to him until the end, I found no reason for him to break his word to her. The price of love meant more to me than a $2.00 carton of Salem cigarettes.

We left the vil as rain fell through it's own mist again. Times like that had me wishing for a helmet. My cover just sopped the rain as a rag, and in the cool of the morning, it acted like a soaked dishcloth that was tossed in the sink heavy with water and food particles, not drying on contact, eventually stinking to high heaven.

The formless city was still being rearranged with Air Force tact and tyranny as we marched towards it on both sides of the thoroughfare, and from our distance I pictured the hands of God piercing through the clouds in apocalypse resolve, to crush the city and run His fingers through the rubble like a child's hand through sand at the beach.

Being in the bamboozled shambles found us in and out of grudge matches, deciphering small corners and least likely walls for cover in turns for the worst. It became a game of cat and mouse, not knowing what hole the enemy might find hiding in, not having a brick of cheese in which to coax the rodent with.

Deafening, desolating days later, more Grunts were led into the action to replace the first fold that mimicked Zombies. Without a mirror or clean water for reflection, I guessed my appearance to be the same, just like we looked during field ops. Despondent, dirty, dilapidated young men who looked like heroes should, after giving their all.

We mounted 6 by's for a scenic return trip that took us through a dozen vils, including one of Montagnard tribes that drew chorus's of whistles and promises on sight of their topless women.

Further down the road, kids frolicked as kids do. Urchiningly defiant, I could think of nothing they wouldn't accept, except for the unnecessary exhibition of cruelty expressed by a Grunt.

"Hey, watch this." A lighted, blue heat tab that looked like candy was tossed into a crowd of Vietnamese and snatched up for a terrible burn. Some Grunts laughed, pissing me off but what could I say? The hammer of this conflict put us all over the edge. But those acts of betrayal, multiplied by others in the country, proved to cause the natives to never side with us absolutely. Moreover, social adherence we'd tacked together would become unglued.

And the usual water 'Boo' waved their horns at the diesel engine's smoke and growl, with 10 year old girl's patting, calming malice.

Villages seemed to bunch up and become larger, with more hawkers, signaling 'Big City' on the horizon. I wouldn't become familiar with city merchants as I did with those of the Hill 22 territory. These appeared more in the 'Rat Race' syndrome with their sales taking more precedence than friendship. Where money is, money goes, and the dealers learned that quickly.

So I was dropped off a half mile from my billet without any fanfare, never crossing paths again with those I fought together with for life and killed people a few, long hours ago. We'd never remember faces or names, never share a beer, never shake hands. I watched the truck drive away with the murderous mob, the winners, the losers, over the bumpy, uneven stretch, wondering how many would return home alive. Me, I wanted to see the sun blotted out from the sky. They were all nuts, anyhow.

We were ALL nuts…

Meandered with blank mind and ringing ears, I finally reached my cabin. To my surprise, a Marine bunked in my cubicle. I thought that I flipped out from the fighting or was lost, so I walked down the wood walk and found it familiar enough, then found Sutton clicking away at the typewriter in the office. He stopped when he saw me in the brown/green jungle utes.

"Ski! Where 'ya been? You missed it!"

His mouth remained partially open when I finished, and after a 10 second intermission, "'Member that sergeant you met when you first got here? Him and 4 other guys got killed a few days ago. The bunkers you and I sat in got overrun!" He stopped to squeeze his nose. "JESUS, Ski. You'd better get those clothes off and bury them! You said you were in Hue City?"

"Yah. Now, where's my cube supposed to be? Somebody new moved in."

"We'll find you a new one."

I led us through the door while he told me more about their faulty guard assumptions.

"Somebody must've fallen asleep, 'cause the gooks crawled through the wire and cut some throats. THEN, they got all the way up here and cut more throats and then they threw satchel charges in two of our billets! Honest to god, Ski, they didn't even shoot a bullet but they killed 5 Marines and got away untouched!"

He looked shaken, getting more broken up as he talked.

"Take it easy. I told you to stay awake on guard. Now where is my area?" I needed rest and I didn't want to hear about office problems. My *own* mind was condemned.

"Go inside and find a place to lay." He walked away.

After settling in anew, I showered then crashed, with some comm. expert playing AFRVN boldly.

Rumblings of thunder woke me up sometime later, along with newfound pain of bleeding knuckles, torn knees and elbows. I slept devoid of mosquito netting, so bugs added insult to injury. And they now bled from my unconscious scratching, and worse yet, I ball park figured 240 days left in country! And finding out that this area was insecure played more on my mental being.

Then, "Where's Herstowski?" He saw my arm wave. "Go see Gunny."

I dressed quickly. You never want to keep a gunnery sergeant waiting.

"I hear Hue was a tough nut to crack, Ski.
They're still fightin' up there, but we had some problems here, too…"

I didn't let on that I heard the story already.

"…personnel inspection every morning. Hair cut high and tight, no mustaches or beards, polished boots, clean utilities but they don't have to be starched. We're on 100% alert 'til further notice. Any questions?"

None. I was brain dead.

"You'll be assigned radio watch in a few days. Dismissed."

I went back to my cube for more Bonnie on my mind. I didn't get enough of her during that all too short leave and it drove me nuts. We were a half a world apart, not even able to talk to her, but I felt better when I wrote. It was difficult finding things to tell her, except of love and the future.

Then things got worse again. I remained depressed from the circumjacent insertions that war presented me. Waiting to be with Bonnie made days seem like weeks. I finally wrote to apologize for sparse letter attendance, but it was hard to explain. I guessed that my mind was just plain warped.

I talked to myself as dreariness took its toll. I reasoned that if we had nothing to do here, then send us home. Half the battle of any war is keeping the sanity.

One commonly hot day, I reached for my towel for a quick wipe without looking at it closely, and proceeded to infest my face with red ant horror, getting bit to dozen times in the process. They found their way to every nook and cranny in the god forsaken country, their route to my towel being up two by fours from their stomping grounds 5 feet below; piss ant city.

I practically cried with my remorse of placing myself in this pit of terror just by signing my name for enlistment bondage, as I swatted the ants off of my face, stomping and cursing the wood we walked on. They fell on my chest and down my pants. Biting and holding wherever they could, I did a barn dance to rid them from my privates which the rest of the men found as amusing as a Bob Hope show, sans girls.

"Be easy on them, Ski! They gotta eat, too!"

The cheerless comment came from J. McAllister. We became good friends, and helped each other through the rituals of worry and tedium that non-field technicians struggled against to return home safe and sane. We both missed our mid-west originalities, his in Ohio, about 400 miles from my hometown. Even Jay couldn't refrain his sorrow for the Cub fan's perpetual vigil in waiting for a National League Champion to emerge from Wrigley Field.

He called me recently, telling me that he found my name in a phone book, with my last name being an easy one to trace. He's a man of great intelligence, one who could remember the spelling of my Polish label. When we first talked, I became truly elated. With the many associates I rubbed ammo with, I remembered him well, and enjoyed hearing his voice again after 30 years of silence.

Some of his tidings were not happy, finalizing our phone talk with some sobs of resentment from the tragedy we contained within, through three decades. He told me the names of some of our friends that had their names scribed on 'The Wall' in Washington, D.C. Getting a little choked up, I promised to call him back in a few weeks.

So I sat at our kitchen table with a paper towel to wipe my eyes as I did with my 'duty towel', and my wife put her arm on my shoulder to console me, not saying a word. She usually cries along with me, with my repeated tantrums. I told her who it was while we were still on the phone, so she easily guessed what my refueled troubles were.

Outpost assignments were always looked forward to. If nothing else, we escaped the contemptible 'didn't shave? Didn't shine the boots?' surveillance practiced by the Gunny back in our non-combat, combat zone.

We loaded up in a large transport chopper one day in August 1968. Large enough for two jeeps and then some, it was able to move bridges and maybe a tank or two. Issued four days worth of C-rats for four men, we knew the stay would be in-country R&R.

We were dropped off on a mountaintop having a few hundred square feet of flat ground. 15 or 20 Grunts had already made themselves at home, with food containers littering most of the area.

The space was bare of vegetation, and the dirt was carroty tinted with dust. The life of the previously rich and famous was exhibited with two partial walls that must have been built by the French as a tourist attraction 20 years earlier. The ceiling was on the floor of the 1/1000 scale model of Hue City, so no shelter was provided, and we'd throw a few frags in it before we left, leaving another mark of our valor.

Our mission was to set up 292 antennas to re-transmit communications from headquarters in DaNang to the commander of an operation being conducted down in Happy Valley.

The radio mounted in the jeep had stronger capabilities because the battery was always charging with the engine running, so after the hookups were made we became bored again, ready to throw rocks and lob grenades down the 45 degree slopes that led to our posit.

Jay and I walked through the doorway of the razed French hotel to collect praise on our homecoming, being patrons of the French Riviera of the 'Nam': something to remember.

Some Grunts came to walk with us by our jeep. They liked the wilds, too. Even Daniel Boones had to face Marine Corps inspections when not in the bush.

"They dropped this orange crap all over the place, and it looks like it's killing the trees and weeds. You'd best be careful you don't get any of it on yourself!"

A word to the wise is sufficient, but no one would have guessed that combatants would begin dying from Agent Orange years after they left the war, to become combat casualties.

Barbed wire-less, our outpost put us in a calamitous condition. We guarded all night, watching for would be trespassers while the Grunts had fun throwing tear gas grenades. The hilltop was small enough to allow easy comm. with each other with yells, so when the Grunts lobbed frags down the hill, Jay would question, "What the fuck's goin' on?"   "Not a fuckin' thing!"

The Grunts would start their own firefight with a palm tree, and we probably had incoming fire but with their ecological abandon, we couldn't really tell, so we fired with them.

Hue City was still in my blood, so I wasn't enjoying the noise making sprees they continued with for the next three days. If we pissed off an NVA platoon, we'd have surely been run over. But being with Grunts before, I knew that most lived for ass kickin' times.

One day, Jay told me more about the attack they had on the Tet offensive. Some of the enemies laid across the wire to let their family of fighters walk over them to get to the sleeping Marines.

I reflected my fate again. If I missed the truck to the LZ that night, I would have been in DaNang when the roof caved in and MY throat may have grinned all the way to the morgue. Funny, how things work out.

Finally, the chopper dropped in to remove us from the firing range. Grunts still fired for effect, knowing that sometime or another, Victor Charlie would answer their call of the wild. They lived for enemy contact, and died with enemy contact.

I didn't know it then, but it was the last of my days in a free fire zone, the last time I would fire any automatic weapon and my last night under the stars and in the elements.

Gimmie shelter.

I love, I love, I love my calendar girl.

Short-timers (fighters with a few days left on their tour of duty) whether tenting in the field or in a rear billet, usually displayed an outline of a woman covered with 395 numbered sectors to be filled in for each day of service in Vietnam. On his final day, the naked body was finally colored in and fully exhibited, and it was back to 'the World' for another lucky soul. Myself, I spent a total of 579 days there, and the girl's hair I colored red, had a face that bears a striking resemblance to the wonderful girl I married in 1971.

About a week before my orders were due, I packed my sea bags with 20 pounds of mail that Bonnie perfumed; cultivated paper, teasingly enhancing me to desire her even more.

After a 50 cent haircut, "HERSTOWSKI! 'Yer orders are in!"

I remember the staff sergeant congratulating me, but more poignantly, I remember tearing down my area and throwing all non-debris into my sea bags. Comic books came home with me, Playboys stayed.

Checked out at the armory and all other Marine related obstacles, I wrinkled into my stagnant uniform to look as military as need be.
Getting out of miserable green jungle utilities forever was transformation extraordinaire. "Never again" I thought, civvies incessant. I looked around the vacant playpens of those on radio watch to mutter a goodbye to no one and everyone, good luck to the walls and the floors.

Sitting outside the gate of the compound gave me more time to think of what I had seen and done for 19 months for the Corps, the Vietnamese people, for America. It was worth it but not ultimately, until Bonnie came into my life. Anything I had to do for her was worth the struggle, anything at all.

Firefights, sniper rounds, patrols, Hue City, grave sites, early August '67, heat, rain, desolation and terrors incarnate all became clear now. It was for flag and country, but mostly, for her. Live it. Love it. Cherish it. Bonnie is all that matters.

Needing a shower, I finally reached the cool comfort of the jet, not noticing the beauty of the mini-skirted stewardesses offering 'coffee, tea or me.' Wondering how Sgts Jame and Hayne, the Butlers, Tex's and Lukes fared in skirmishes or in peace, I also wondered how much I had changed during my tours and that if Bonnie would truly love the new Ski.

I was in a stupor as the plane tugged off from DaNang, with eyes shut to hold back tears of disappointment from a job left undone. Others let out cries of joy and hugged each other while flinging profanities window-wise for the future of Southeast Asia.

I let out a feeble 'Yay', really too choked up to do much else. I was going home.

You belong to your own country as you belong to your own mother.
Edward Everett Hale

213

Country roads, take me home, to the place I belong…I hear her voice in the morning as she calls me; radio reminds me of my home far away. Riding down the road I get a feeling that I should have been home yesterday, yesterday.

"Ladies and gentlemen, shortly we will be landing at Chicago's O'Hare International Airport. Please fasten…" was my greeting back to my home town by a girl's sultry voice. I fantasized a marching band for background music to pin back my deafened ears.

And shivering down the aisle, bumping for a 10-yard gain, I saw my wonderful Aphrodite with Mom and Dad wide eyed, displaying Cheshire cat smiles as cheers for reserved victory recognition from the land of the free.

My Dad's education in the South Pacific during the early '40's assumed me as part of his status with an open arms agreement, but he waited until the girls gave me the more traditional reception. I don't know how they were before I reached them, but upon arrival, they jumped for me like teenyboppers for Elvis.

In the tear swabbed, crushing embraces, my mind went blank with the celebration. A visualization returned me to the sand to see Robert, smiling with a gathering of angels.

I can't imagine the anxieties my family experienced while I was gone, as the 5 O'clock newsreels produced frowns of anticipation for a government courier with the worst of communications. They had their own hell to deal with, while I had mine. God bless them.

Bonnie and I hugged until my Mom cried out "Hey! You're not married yet. Save some for me!"

I had little to say, but smiled from those divine encroachments. Booming jets made me cringe and shake, but Bonnie said she'd comfort me whenever I needed to be.

"It's all over, Bill. You don't ever have to go back there again." My smile grew a little more after that. Accentuating the positive: God, it was great to be home! Fantastic. Indescribable.

It's not so hard in your own back yard, to be set for peace or war.

I've looked at life from both sides now…
I really don't know life at all.

The 30-day leave kept Bonnie and I together until mid October, not nearly enough time for me to decide whether we'd be a successful husband and wife team or better off as stragglers in the league of life. My decision wasn't easily reached.

On September 30th, 1968, "Let's go to the swinging bridge", she almost commanded. Did she wish to be engaged at this romantic setting and how did she know about the ring? "Have you ever been there?"

Upheld by chains, the 120 foot long relic over the Desplaines River in Riverside swayed with wind and walk. We held each other, stepping lazily and cautiously over it to reach the opposite bank.

"Hon, I hope this thing doesn't cave in. I've had my fill of leaches, thanks." We used hot cigarettes in 'Nam to remove the bloodsuckers. Salt, if at hand, would work too.

Off the bridge I turned us right, towards a boulder I picked worthy for engagement elevation.

"Let's go sit down on that rock, Hon. I'm worn out."

"Hey, I thought you were a MARINE!" she quipped.

"Always. And I love you."

"I love you too, Bill."

After kissing and relaxing and kissing and relaxing on the rock, we kissed then watched the river flow. It took me back to you know where. The water looked dark and dirty, like over there.

Completing a battle sequence, a person is never really completely well adjusted.

Bird's melody of chirps encouraged me to cheer Bonnie's life with the halo boxed, but it sat in one back pocket, sticking into my rump.

I squirmed for position without pain for an hour.

"Are you okay, Hon? Do you want go back to the car?"

"Yah. I don't feel so hot" was my fib. I was as nervous as when I reached MCRD. The Corps got me for 4 years, but this would be *forever*.

As previously, our day was passed together, bowling then visiting Playland Amusement Park for their fab Tilt-A–Whirl. The place is now a trailer camp. Finishing at one of our favorite resting places, the Bel-Air Drive In, we paid to see half of the flicks while leaving buttered popcorn residue on the upholstery and streaked windows from body steam.

Back in the front seat, "Bonnie, could I have my ring back?" I didn't tell her why, but I saw that I had better do this in a hurry to dike the waterworks.

As high school girls do, Bonnie had the ring entwined with blue angora yarn for better fit. She added a teardrop to it as she placed it in my hand. "Don't you want to be with me anymore?"

I could scarcely understand her minced words with her waterfall.

"I love you, Bill. What did I do wrong?"

Fumbling the box of ring to get her to stop the waterworks, "Bonnie, will you marry me?" It was to no avail. Her eyes and nose ran impatiently as she dried them on my shoulder with, "Oh YES, Puppy Dog Eyes!"

I was getting perturbed with her third crying match, her confessing to be sooooo happy!

I guessed this not to be the best of places to propose marriage, but getting so unnerved at the riverbank left me grasping for any locale to finally make clear my complete love for Bonnie. And most importantly, she was elated beyond all of my expectations. The thought of her forsaking my hand in marriage never came to mind until I had the ring ready to slip on her finger. God, if I had thought of that possibility sooner, I might still have that pointed as hell box sticking me in the ass TODAY!

All of our parents knew the day would come when their babies would leave their homes, and my Mom did the most crying.

"It won't be for a few more years, Mom!"

"But Billy, you're both so young."

Boohoo. I was in a war for 19 months, and God help me if I were to get married at age 23!

"Yah" said Art. "Get to know each other better so 'yer sure."

And with that, everyone held up a can of Hamm's beer for a toast of good luck and health.

Sentenced to Camp Lejeune, N.C., I phoned home every Sunday afternoon, until an early December leave ran me back to Bonnie to tell her I had orders for Guantanamo Bay, Cuba.

"Billy, after Vietnam, this shouldn't bother you. They're not shooting there, are they?"

"Not that I know of, Hon. But DAMN! I just got back to the states! To YOU! What the hell 'ya gotta do?"

With war service and just a few months stateside, spending Christmas on a desert island really set to piss me off. I met guys at Lejeune who never left country in 2 or 3 years, so why *me* again? Go figure.

Marines on Gitmo were banished from decent liberty and surroundings, and the only transportation to and from our posit was via ferryboat. I don't recall if we were on the windward or leeward side of the bay, but the opposite bay held the Navy with a more civilized appearance. It's always that way. Our zenith was an E-club with a nickel pinball machine and snorkeling in Mother Nature's fish bowl for tropical fish off an uncharted beachhead. It was more an Eden; crystal clear salt water buoying bodies with arms hanging limply, and views of rainbow hued fish darting through the gulf's fauna to escape predatory teeth. We never competed with a shark, but barracuda found us interesting enough to circle our team once. Splashing water and yelling gave them reason to search different quarry.

Once, a giant, voracious looking eel undulated not far enough away to suit me in the free fall aquarium. I floated loosely so as not to attract his attention, and he rippling off.

Spending much time in the brine, I still needed to keep tuned into my job as platoon radioman. I was blessed with a 10x10 cement bunker from which I radioed to Battalion, if nothing else, that the Cubans aimed their guns at us through the barbed wire and we were zeroed in on them. We were all armed and a mortar platoon shone our best weaponry. Not a shot was fired.

Tarantulas were poisonous protruders, and one visited me nightly outside my bunker near my Cuban toilet. I'd stand with a flashlight beaming at its long legs as at a starting line from a hole in which he called home. At first sight, I tossed a rock near its lair, expecting it to crawl meticulously, but it surprised me to goose bumps as it hopped out and scrambled towards me, without abandon. I jumped back to the bunker and its sinister glare, expecting the arachnid's mother to be waiting to even the score, finding nothing but the sound of the Navy D.J. echoing from my pocket Toshiba.

Guessing artist's names and songs, with the next request being the jackpot payoff was a contest won by yours truly throughout his stay in the Caribbean.

"Ski, with the Marines on the far side of the bay, correctly identified...rewarding him with The Beach Boy's, Sloop John B!" It was revitalizing, being able to use a phone while sitting in the desolation of non-leaved tree branches and sand based scorpions.

10 months of my 4-year "hitch" remained as I returned with one last 20 day leave in the May of 1969, to the Midwest. My life was ever so slowly repairing itself with Bonnie prescribed in heavy doses, but thoughts of Donna still reoccurred, with reflections of the war ever present.

Staying on base at Camp Lejeune on weekends didn't help at all. There wasn't much to do there except lay in a rack and think, or visit Jacksonville for a beer or 9. Weekend "Swoops" helped eliminate boredom installed by Air-Naval Gunfire repetitions across radio waves. 3 to 5 of us pooled our resources with the owner of a '65 Lemans for a ride home on any given Friday, leaving camp at 5 PM, arriving Lyons 10 AM, departing for N.C. 10 AM Sunday morning.

Everyone called us 'Nuts' to travel such a tight schedule but I argued that it was well worth it, once in a while anyhow. The biggest gamble was being out of bounds. 600 miles was the limit for weekend leave and we almost doubled that count. Oops.

"Dad, I've been away from home for 2 ½ years and I'm tired of it. What are they going to do to me? Cut off my hair and send me to 'Nam'?"

"NO! They'll throw you in the BRIG!"

Time spent in a military jail was tacked onto enlistment duty, so it became imperative for me to stay straight for freedom's sake. October contained my last "Swoop."

But finally in mid December 1969, my request for an early, education release came about. Inconceivable it was, that I would not have to report to anyone, anymore. I wouldn't be inspected daily or wear a uniform. I'd be free forever, clearing my brain from the bad, magnifying the tradition and glory of the USMC.

The '57 Chevy I bought a few weeks earlier for $600 was cherry, and it took me to the gate with my honorable discharge papers. The guard at the front gate looked envious. "Lucky, huh?"

"Yep. Never again, buddy. Never again."   He waved me on and I drove off slowly, then I pulled to the shoulder to look through the rear view mirror at the sign explicating the world's finest fighting force, the United States Marine Corps.

I was there for but a moment, but my Marine career flashed before my mind and through my heart, from the March of '66 to the present. There was no Robert to see me off. No Hayne, no Butler, no Luke or Jame to shake hands with while listening to the Star Spangled Banner or Stars and Stripes Forever. But all of it was in my mind, as I found it almost tough to say goodbye forever to the Marine Corps and its terrible peripherals. My pride would embellish every time I'd see our flag raised and at each National Anthem.

If nothing else, my pride is boasted for guys like Robert.

...through the perilous fight.

***...hiring man said, "Son, if it was up to me...went down to see my
V.A. man, he said "Son, don't you understand?"***

The semester was a few weeks away, and Burl Ive's "Holly Jolly Christmas" filled the airwaves for my most relaxing Christmas season to date, so I lay back with more contemplation. I had a crazy scheme, that we could help the Vietnamese by bringing them here for training, while bringing our troops home. Crazy.

But with the season upon me, I shook off the bad for the good. Being with Bonnie and relatives, old and new, was a joy to behold without a palm tree obstructing the view. Uncle Henry became a favorite of mine, he and his brother arguing about the slightest of instances with no one deemed victor. Just listening to the ways of his world became an adventure with each visit.

"Henry Kissinger should drop dead!" he'd dispatch. "I was in the army, and I never saw so much crap as in these peace talks!"

I'd leave them when 'Nam' as the subject, with my future father-in-law intimidating his brother even more.

"You weren't in the war, Mike, so what the hell do you know about it?"

Bonnie confronted the two battlers. "Dad, you two are both cracked in the head!" with beers and a bowl of Yo-Ho potato chips.

The dream police arrested my Dad in the Laz-E-Boy as the other two cursed Henry Kissinger to hell while the Blackhawks crunched the Red Wings on channel 9. It was all too comfortable, being with the one girl and a house full of relatives, and no more Marine Corps.

Journalism class didn't hold my interest, so after a few weeks I just quit going, much to my parent's disappointment. And I didn't want to leach off of them, so I went back to Wire Cloth Products, the factory my Dad worked at. They needed me as a lathe hand for a few months, and then I got the pink slip. I found companies inhospitable to war veterans with blue collars. No bed of roses. No pleasure cruise.

Western Electric kept my inspection services for a year and a half. Bonnie also worked there, but 6 months after our marriage, we were both on unemployment insurance. The giant in the telephone racket eventually closed its doors to a onetime staff of 10,000 workers.

Danly Machine, also in Cicero, gave good pay and benefits to the Steelworkers of America. In contrast, I experienced 3 disabling injuries, a 3-month strike and a 9-month strike during my 27 years a attendance before the plant closed forever in December 1998.

Three or four new owners in 15 years milked the factory as clean as a whistle. The original Danly brothers would be rolling over in their graves or wheel chairs if they saw the "CLOSED" sign nailed on their baby's front door.

Severance pay? There was none. Just as Western Electric was razed for a shopping mall, Danly Machine's 4 square blocks was rejuvenated with a junior high school, complete with gymnasium.

Both Danly and Hawthorne Works built parts that helped us win World War II. Decidedly, machining took a second seat to my job ventures, so I undertook a career of Quality Control at an air filter supplier, also spotted in Cicero. As it turned out, the job title isn't inspector or quality control but that of complete, adulterated, compulsive slavery. We've been advised to "use the door" if we don't like our job, which may be anywhere from running punch presses, shearing steel, assembling filters and sometimes, even inspecting parts.

I never knew how important Union status was until I fell into the QC. Not so much for pay increases and benefits, although as of this writing, 27 months have passed since my last pay increase, but more so for human and working-man's rights. Workers need some kind of protection from unethical employers.

In June 2002, bankruptcy was filed and 25 to 30 of us were out of work until the plant reopened a month later, all minus 2 weeks pay we haven't retrieved in one year; $40,000 S.U.V.'s can been seen outside the front door of the plant. Where is the justice for the American working class in Illinois, in 2003?

And justice was surely ignored, as some chose to accept the apologies of a female Jane called Fonda, the misguided entertainer who sided with the North Vietnamese while our boys died in the war. It nauseates me to see her videos on display, wanting me to ban calisthenics. She should always be ashamed of the way she denounced our troops. She could have backed us up while protesting our political decisions. Benedict Arnold, are you listening? But time marches on, as it surely must. 35 years have passed since *the* reunion at the airport and I couldn't have expected much more from my family circle. Ups and downs, ins and outs of 5 decades worth of American Dreams, family fulfillment, partnered prudence and hopeless happenstance resolved me to decree; I paid for my country's freedom and that I should live the life I choose to live.

I disliked leaving a job undone and still do, and I had a prayer that the mêlée would end soon, with the Peace Talks overriding the gunshots so that all Americans could return to their free world at peace with themselves and a victory under their belt. My evaluation of Vietnam: we didn't lose the war, we just gave up on it.

500,000 Vietnamese were left homeless in 1968 while 50,000 were killed, tallying until April 30, 1975 when we were humiliated by what some determine to be the first defeat America had ever experienced, darkening my Easter Sundays forever.

It didn't look that way to me. Perplexing with speeches of quicksilver, our leaders dropped out or professed that they'd never lose. We heard General Westmoreland's "We have reached and important point when the end begins to come into view", unknowingly confessing that none of the leaders knew what the hell they needed to do for victory and that they surely under calculated the strength and determination of the enemy.

Being enlightened by returning home with honor wasn't congratulatory enough for the families of the 58,000 who lost their lives or the paralyzed still being hand fed at V.A. hospitals. War veterans should be allowed some kind of monetary compensation if needed. After all, even $1000 a month wouldn't return youth that all participants lost from war, and we offered ourselves as sacrificial lambs so why shouldn't we get something in return? Many people receive "Something for nothing" while never even giving a thought to our social climate. Not many would disagree, except those who never wore a steel helmet.

Maybe if a vet worked as hard as he could all through his life in a stinking factory under dangerous conditions, got laid off 4 or 5 times, spent over a year and a half recuperating from job related injuries, spent over a year out of work without unemployment compensation due to labor disputes, tried a "Mom and Pop" birthday restaurant that failed because a millionaire duplicated their theme a block away that the town saw fit due to the free enterprise system, never hearing of zoning ordinances that helped keep existing entrepreneur's heads above water, the government could help out that hard luck guy whose American Dream never fully cycled to, with a loan of ultra low interest pursuance.

Waste not, want not, I won't throw out a half of a burger and I like to pump up the volume. I love ice cold drinks under the hot summer sun, which never gets too hot for me now. I still love the Cubs and the Bears and can't get enough of my chicken, barbecued. I appreciate everything I have, and knowing that life is intangible, I take nothing for granted.

Maybe the sight of the last helicopter crashing into the South China Sea influenced me a hardnosed attitude towards losing any clash, big or small. (Being a Cubs fan brings me misery on most summer days.) Bonnie called me into the living room that day, with ABC broadcasting our exodus, big as life. I wasn't up to date with the finality, so it quite surprised me.

Young Vietnamese men forced their way aboard our planes in DaNang to escape the tightening communist grip reclaiming the country. They abandoned olden parents, wives and children.

A planeload of orphans crashed, killing all aboard. Misery was synonymous with Vietnam.

Bonnie noticed my few tears, most of them released when I evacuated to our attic bedroom, for the guys who didn't make it back, their families, for John Wayne's spirit, for no parade, for jobs that veterans won't get, against hundreds of thousands who had more excuses than Carter had liver pills, for

"Yankee Doodle Dandies" that Cagney couldn't coax out of "The Home of the Brave", against dividing America and for God, who left me with a happy ending that started in 1967. And yes, Bonnie and I have strolled the bridge with our boy and girl, and we've strolled the bridge discussing their spouses. We've slipped in the mud on the opposite bank, finding the bodacious boulder immersed murkily from the river's enveloping edge with my protest, "We can't get to the rock!"

   "Not today, Bill. Maybe tomorrow."

After all, it's a great country, but you can't live in it for nothing.
                                          Will Rogers

Bonnie & Author

Best Friends
Lois & Bill

TỬ-THẦN LUÔN SÁT BÊN ANH, ANH THEO CỘNG-SẢN SỚM THÀNH MA THÔI. CHẾT ĐI ANH THIỆT MỘT ĐỜI, GIA-ĐÌNH TANG TÓC AI NGƯỜI ĐOÁI THƯƠNG?

Flyers dropped
from choppers

Hill 22/Ontos Copyright William Hiles

Printed in the United States
By Bookmasters